Carole an...
Naugahyde ...
where the girls waited, while Carole ordered
up at the counter adjacent to the bar: hamburgers for Juli and Silvina, and a veggie
burger for the weight-conscious Mrs. Sund.
She had recently tipped the scales at 145,
and found herself in an escalating battle
with extra pounds with each passing year.
No sense in adding more, even if she and
the girls were on a holiday.

Juli and Silvina wolfed down their food,
but Carole nibbled at hers, ultimately asking
to have it wrapped to take back to her room.

At 7:35 P.M., the trio paid their $21.13
bill and retired for the evening. Carole's
half-eaten veggie burger remained on the
counter, neatly wrapped and ready to go
back to her room, but she had forgotten to
take it with her. The burger remained on
the counter until closing time. Carole never
returned to pick it up.

In fact, the waitress who had served
Carole Sund and the two teens never saw
them again.

Neither did anyone else.

By Dennis McDougal:

ANGEL OF DARKNESS
FATAL SUBTRACTION: How Hollywood Really Does
   Business (with Pierce O'Donnell)
IN THE BEST OF FAMILIES
THE LAST MOGUL: Lew Wasserman, MCA, and the
   Hidden History of Hollywood
MOTHER'S DAY*
THE YOSEMITE MURDERS*

*Published by Ballantine Books

THE YOSEMITE MURDERS

Dennis McDougal

BALLANTINE BOOKS • NEW YORK

A Ballantine Book
Published by The Ballantine Publishing Group
Copyright © 2000 by Dennis McDougal

www.randomhouse.com/BB/

Library of Congress Catalog Card Number: 99-091638

ISBN 0-345-43834-5

Manufactured in the United States of America

First Edition: January 2000

10   9   8   7   6   5   4   3

In memory of Steven Stayner,
an authentic American hero
who did the right thing . . .

. . . and to Fitz,
who teaches me every day
that all it takes is an
act of will
and a little help from your friends
to kick the Devil's ass.

Introduction

During the last week of June 1999, I set out from Los Angeles in my trusty old Ford Explorer to retrace the last known movements of a Eureka, California, woman and two teens during their fateful, final visit to Yosemite National Park.

Just three months earlier, the bodies of 42-year-old Carole Sund, her 15-year-old daughter Juli, and family friend Silvina Pelosso, a 16-year-old Argentine exchange student, had all been found some ninety miles north of Yosemite. The three tourists had last been seen alive in the pastoral setting of Yosemite Valley in mid-February, apparently vanishing into the thin mountain air after they had checked in at the Cedar Lodge motel in El Portal, just beyond the northwestern boundaries of the National Park.

What began as a routine missing persons report turned into a frantic family search that, within days, had escalated into a massive FBI-supervised canvassing of the entire Yosemite Valley and its surrounding area. Before it was finished, the air and land search encompassed more than five hundred square miles. Satellite trucks and mobile news vans materialized in El Portal like a swarm of hungry ants. But after a week of false trails and crossed fingers, the ants began to disperse. There would be no happy ending. Only the family and a few loyal friends stayed on to maintain the desperate vigil.

When the bodies of the three women were found a month later, the TV trucks and news reporters returned en masse, asking a new set of questions and introducing a whole new layer of media—this time, with a Spanish accent. Televisa and Univision both joined the array of U.S. networks and newspapers that broadcast the unfolding tragedy. Silvina Pelosso, whose charred remains turned up in the trunk of an immolated rental car along with those of Carole Sund, was from a prominent Argentine family, and now Latin American voices were joining the chorus of angry and bewildered U.S. citizens who demanded to know: How could this have happened in Yosemite—perhaps the only public gathering place in America that can still pass for Hallowed Ground?

If you grow up in California, Yosemite is holy. It is Mecca to outdoorsmen and indoorsmen alike. Every desk-bound, urban-dwelling, child-rearing hack or harridan who has ever experienced the spiritual hunger to return to nature, even if just for a weekend, will invoke the image of Yosemite's natural beauty in their mind's eye. Yosemite renews. It is the *true* magic kingdom. Along with the Ansel Adams vistas of Half Dome, El Capitan, Glacier Point, and all of the other sights, smells, and sounds that make this valley one of the seven wonders of world tourism, the waters themselves that trickle from permanent ice packs high in the Sierra Nevadas and pour into the Merced River seem somehow sacred. And while Yosemite, Vernal, Bridalveil, and Nevada Falls should never be mistaken for the mystical spring at Lourdes, they are just as brimming with the stuff of life— majestic reminders of the ethereal and eternal wonder of Nature.

To defile Yosemite is surely as great a sin as spitting on the Shroud of Turin, despoiling the Islamic shrine at Medina, or shouting anti-Semitic curses at Jerusalem's Wailing Wall. To spill blood into the waters of the Merced is as foul an act as defecating in a baptismal font.

Murder at Yosemite is no less a desecration than murder in Eden.

While I am an author and journalist by profession, I took personal umbrage at the blasphemy in Yosemite. I wanted to know from the very first report of the Yosemite murders what kind of monster could wantonly destroy innocence in the persons of Juli Sund and Silvina Pelosso, silence the sweet strength and maternal presence of Carole Sund, and do it all within the cathedral canyons of Yosemite. Careless hikers and foolish high-country campers die here every year by way of trail accidents or exposure to the extremes of heat and cold, but almost never at the hand of another human being. Yosemite's last reported homicide prior to the Sund-Pelosso murders happened nearly twelve years earlier, when Navy veteran Stevie Allen Gray pushed his wife over a precipice in December 1987, in order to collect a $500,000 insurance policy he'd bought shortly before her death. Even that mercenary horror made more sense than the killing of three innocents on a pilgrimage to Yosemite.

The deaths of Carole and Juli Sund and Silvina Pelosso were utterly without reason. I had to understand. I got in my truck and I drove.

The last week of June was hot—exceptionally hot. The San Joaquin Valley topped out above the 100-degree mark every day. Even higher up in the mountains, at the El Portal entrance to Yosemite, the temperature still sizzled in the 90s.

I stopped first in Fresno to visit Charley Waters, an old friend who edits the *Fresno Bee*, and to make two new friends: Kimi Yoshino and Matt Kreamer, reporters who had been covering the Sund-Pelosso case for the newspaper. There were lots of leads and a host of ex-cons who had been jailed as possible suspects, but no solid answers yet on how or why the three women had died. Still, Kimi told me that the prevailing feeling was that it was only a matter of time before the grand jury that met each Thursday morning in Fresno's federal courthouse would begin issuing indictments.

Fifty miles to the northeast, in the hamlet of El Portal (pop. 635), that sense of cautious optimism also hung in the air. I checked in at the Cedar Lodge, where the three women had last been seen alive, and I strolled past Room 509, where they had supposedly spent their last night on earth. I tried to imagine how they could have fallen prey to predators, but nothing clicked. The room was directly in the center of the downstairs tier of a two-tier dormitory-style building, and even though it had been wintertime, with far fewer guests than normal, the building where they were apparently abducted did not seem so far off the beaten track that anything as heinous as the slaughter of three women could have gone undetected.

I spoke to a couple of chatty waitresses at the Cedar Lodge Restaurant, one of whom was a mother just about the same age and build as Carole Sund. She had spent decades in El Portal raising a whole new generation of Yosemite dwellers and had nothing but praise for the community's wholesome atmosphere. The other waitress was a younger snow-bunny type who only worked at dinnertime because during the day she loved hiking in the summer and cross-country skiing in the winter. She, too, could not comprehend the murders. Up until then, she described the most dangerous thing in El Portal as getting safely across Highway 140 without becoming part of a truck's grillwork. Neither the older waitress nor her younger counterpart could fathom how or why such an inexplicable tragedy could happen here.

I talked to desk clerks and maids and a bartender. I

spoke to several among the horde of summertime motel guests who had already begun to descend upon the valley. I spent some time with Hugh Carter, the manager of the El Portal Food Market, which comes as close to being a civic nerve center as the tiny town has, and I stopped in at Jon Bevington's Chevron for gas and a schmooze about the hideous crimes that had been committed just down the road, apparently under the noses of the hundreds of people who either live or pass through El Portal every day, even in the dead of winter.

About thirty miles west on Highway 140, Managing Editor Jill Ballinger of the *Mariposa Gazette* told me that folks around the county seat of Mariposa were as bewildered by the Sund-Pelosso riddle as the citizens of El Portal. The prevailing wisdom was that a gang of ex-cons high on methamphetamine had committed the sacrilege. There was some comfort in the belief—fueled by the law enforcement leaks to the press—that the FBI had rounded up at least a half dozen felons as suspects and socked them away in jail for various parole violations.

Regardless of the beliefs and the rumors and the suppositions, however, everywhere the general reaction was the same. People were shocked, then appalled, saddened, and finally outraged at the killings, but no one had any clear answers to the two nagging questions, How and Why.

I found not even a hint of an answer where the women had last been seen alive. Perhaps there were clues to be had where they were first discovered dead. I headed north, up Highway 49, to the places on my map where Jill Ballinger told me their bodies had been dumped.

The turnoff for Mocassin Vista Point at Lake Don Pedro is not marked well on Highway 49, and easy to pass up. I drove past it twice before recognizing the lakefront parking area on the southwest side of the reservoir as the place where Jill Ballinger told me the nearly decapitated body of Juli Sund had been found.

The location itself is beautiful, especially in the morning, when the sunlight burns the mist off the calm, blue water while the scrub brush dotting the yellow hills and shading the lake's many coves is as green as it will ever get during a hot, dusty Gold Country day. There was a small makeshift shrine at one corner of the lot, beneath a sign reading $1,000 FINE FOR LITTERING. The shrine contained vases of artificial tulips and plastic daisies, a dead wildflower in an empty Lipton Iced Tea bottle, a white satin pillow, and scribbled notes of condolence left by those who, like me, have stopped to pay their respects and to seek answers.

It was high on a hillside overlooking the vista's parking area that investigators located Juli's body in a clump of manzanita. As of late June when I visited, no one outside of law enforcement had any idea as to why the FBI had finally decided to look there in that relatively public location in the third week of March, after scouring the surrounding countryside for weeks beforehand. The guessing game among the media at that time was that the investigators must have been tipped off, just as they had been when they discovered the red Pontiac Grand Prix in which Carole Sund and Silvina Pelosso had been incinerated. A week before the discovery of Juli's body, a 40-year-old local carpenter named Jim Powers had blundered on the ruined automobile higher up in the mountains, when he happened through that way after returning some rented videos at a nearby store. He stopped in the woods for some target practice with his .22 and found the wrecked automobile by chance. Most media types I spoke with surmised that chance must have intervened again a week later on March 25, with some Samaritan calling in the tip to the FBI after stumbling across Juli's remains.

Three months later, when I began my own search for the murder and body dump sites, finding where the Grand Prix had been ditched turned out to be far easier than finding where Juli's body had been discarded. It was merely a matter of turning right off Highway 49 and onto Highway 108, the main road over the Sonora Pass—one of only about half a dozen thoroughfares that motorists can use to cross the formidable High Sierras into the Nevada desert. I was told to keep my eyes peeled for the Wheeler Road intersection, near a school bus stop just past the mountain hamlet of Mi-wuk Village, elevation five thousand feet. There I would see a logging road on the left side of the highway, and it was down that single-lane dirt road that Carole and Silvina had apparently taken their final ride.

As it turned out, the entrance to the logging road was clearly marked by an ABC-TV camera crew. The camera and sound men were just finishing up their shoot when I arrived. They were there to capture footage for a *20/20* segment about the same kind of roadside shrine that had decorated the place where Juli's body had been found some thirty miles back down Highway 108, at Lake Don Pedro.

Shaded by towering lodgepole pines, this highway memorial was several times larger than the one at Don Pedro. Pilgrims and passersby emptied their closets of symbolic kitsch at the same time that they emptied their hearts of genuine anguish. There was a pink plush bunny, a leopard Beanie Baby, a Smokey Bear pin, stuffed bears and a lion, plastic calla lilies, wooden crosses, pinecones, poems, entire letters two and three pages in length, articles of clothing, necklaces, piles of flowers—many still fresh—and even coins, as if tossing them into the jumble might evoke a wish or a prayer in the same manner as Rome's fabled Trevi Fountain.

Staked to the ground with a two-foot length of plastic pipe was the top of a shoebox, bearing an inscription about the "monsters" who took the lives of three women, and an admonition about a Biblical "eye for an eye."

The ABC producer told me that the place where the burnt-out car had actually been discovered was farther down the dirt logging road, perhaps another hundred yards or so. The scar in the landscape where it had been torched back in February during an apparent lull in the winter snows was still easily visible. I thanked them. The ABC crew then drove off down Highway 108 toward Modesto. It grew eerily quiet. Except for the occasional car whizzing by, it was windless and hot and still. I was alone in the forest.

It would have been just as easy and far more practical to walk down the road to the place where the Pontiac had been set ablaze, but being a native of Los Angeles, I opted instead to drive. Inside my air-conditioned four-wheel-drive cocoon, I could listen to Bob Dylan wailing from my stereo and take comfort in my personal security as I inched down the single-lane dirt road.

When one's automobile is just another in an endless string of RVs, SUVs, and plain old garden-variety automobiles zipping by at sixty miles per hour, the depth and occasionally creepy calm of the forest goes undetected. It isn't easy to tell from the main highway, but the woods this high in the Sierras really *are* as dark and deep as those that Robert Frost described in his famous poem about stopping by for a few moments on a snowy New England afternoon. Inside my Explorer, I heard myself muttering, ". . . and miles to go before I sleep, and miles to go before I sleep."

Just seconds away from the hum of trucks and traffic, the trees themselves bestow a kind of grand, seductive silence that is at once intoxicating and a little forbidding. Even in the hot afternoon sun, it is easy to imagine how dense the darkness could be on a moonless night, enshrouded by these thousands and thousands of trees, and muffled by miles of rocks and dust and underbrush.

Along with chipmunks, squirrels, and sparrows, there are rattlesnakes, bears and an occasional mountain lion ranging through these woods. It is not always the safest place for city fools to tread. The higher one travels into the mountains, the thinner the veneer that separates civilization from the sheer horror of Darwinian natural selection.

I put my Explorer into low gear and headed farther down the road. The place where the Pontiac had been jettisoned was obvious: a swath of red, raw earth that plummeted at a 45-degree angle off the logging road and into a thicket, where visitors like myself had erected yet another makeshift shrine of plastic flowers, stuffed animals, and doleful notes. A poem written by someone who called herself Sabine was nailed to a nearby tree. It was a eulogy to the fallen mother and her daughter, and their friend from Argentina.

The destruction of the Pontiac must have been quite a conflagration. Trees and bushes thirty feet away were charred, and the dirt was still peppered with ash. I lost track of time puttering around the thicket beyond the shrine, snapping photos, sitting on a log, making notes. Silence combined with the hot weather to transform the clearing in the forest. It began to feel more claustrophobic than expansive.

As the sun sank toward the horizon somewhere beyond the wall of trees, I felt the forest close in on me. It was time to leave. When I climbed back in the Explorer and fired up the engine, it was almost a relief.

But the truck would not budge.

I rolled down my window and looked to the rear, where I saw a tire stuck and spinning in the loose soil and pine needles on the forest floor. I gunned the engine again and moved a little bit up the hillside, only to lose traction and slide back down farther than before. This time, I punched into four-wheel drive and gave the engine another jigger of gasoline. Again, I was up a yard or two and then slid back down the slope, as though some invisible magnet was fighting the engine and drawing the Explorer down into the forest. I panicked and jammed the gas pedal to the floorboard. Sweat rolled from my hairline to my neck, chest, and arms, puddling in the seat between my legs. The engine roared and the wheels spun furiously, but the truck wouldn't even make a token move up the hill now. I smelled the smoke at the same time that I saw the fire.

"Holy shit!"

All I had in the cab was a two-liter container of Pepsi—which does not go far when both the oil pan and a right front tire are blazing. The flames crackled in the dust, and had I not shifted into an adrenaline automatic pilot, I could easily have been spooked. Loose soil to toss on the flames did not seem so loose when dug up with fingernails far too used to computer keyboards. In my frantic imagination, every handful of dirt seemed only to fuel the fire. I saw the futility within a minute or two, and bolted up the hillside, sprinting as quickly as my sedentary legs would take me to the main highway.

I flagged down a driver, who sent his brother back to the volunteer fire department in Mi-wuk Village for help, while the driver himself leaped from his truck and returned with me to my now flaming Ford. Grubbing like cats in a litter box, we were able to put out most of the blaze by the time the fire trucks arrived, but they doused it anyway to make certain the fire was out. My beloved Explorer, however, was declared a total loss.

As I clambered aboard the tow truck that hauled me and my SUV out of the forest an hour later, the tow truck driver observed that he had been to this same place before, not three months earlier. The call had come from the FBI via the California Highway Patrol, he said. The vehicle he pulled up the hill that time was Carole Sund's burnt-out Pontiac Grand Prix—cherry red when she rented it back in February, before it had been fried to a crisp in that black spot in the forest.

"The funny thing is, your truck was on the exact same spot, even the same position, as the car where they found the two murdered women," the tow truck driver told me.

I am not a superstitious person, or at least, I try not to be. Friday the 13th is just another day to me. In third grade, I gave up avoiding stepping on sidewalk

cracks for fear of breaking my mother's back. I read
my horoscope each morning, but if it tells me that
my day is going to be less than stellar, I simply buy
another newspaper and read a different interpreta-
tion of the Zodiac.

Despite my enlightened pragmatism, however, I
still cross my fingers at the finish line. I still invoke
the supernatural aid of "somebody up there" when
things aren't quite going right down here on Mother
Earth. And I believe, now, that there is darkness
as well as light in the forest—even in as sacred a
meadow as that of the Valley of the Yosemite.

The day following the fiery destruction of my
truck, I spent some time at a Sonora bookstore while
I waited for a rental car to be prepared so that I could
drive back home to Los Angeles. There, in the bookstore, I found a shelf devoted to the lore of the California Indians, including the Miwok tribe, which
populated the Sierras from Yosemite to Tahoe during
the two millennia prior to the arrival of the Spanish
in California.

"The myths are related by the old people," began
one of the books, "after the first rains of the winter
season, usually in the ceremonial roundhouse and always at night by the dim light of a small flickering
fire. . . ."

In uncanny ways, Miwok tales reflect Judeo-
Christian stories of creation, the discovery of fire,
and even a global flood that closely resembles the
Old Testament saga of Noah and his ark. But woven
amid these myths is a different kind of lore too.

Generation after generation, shamans of the Miwok related cautionary accounts of heart-spirits that follow the pathway of the wind, hiding in stumps and dust devils. These fables have the substance and style of ghost stories, which tell how the heart-spirit remains with the body several days after death, and how it shies away from the mournful shriek of the owl and the meadowlark. The dead cry out for justice, according to Miwok lore. Those who have died a violent, untimely death at the hands of another cry out loudest of all.

The Miwok elders also told tales of the Rock Giants—bogeymen who emerge from nowhere to prey on humanity. These early day versions of Sasquatch or Bigfoot, as the primordial ape-man of the Northern California forests came to be called, were human in form only. They might resemble men, but in fact, they were demons.

"*Che-ha-lum'-che* comes out only at night and wanders about seeking people to eat," wrote historian C. Hart Merriam in *Dawn of the World: Myths & Tales of the Miwok Indians of California*. In his 1910 retelling of the Miwok fables, Merriam said that a Rock Giant "prefers women. Of these he catches and carries off all he can find. Sometimes he makes a crying noise, *hoo-oo'-oo* like a baby, to lure them. If they come, he seizes them and tosses them into his big pack basket and carries them to his cave, where he eats them. . . ."

At the time I first read those lines, I felt a little chill run up my backbone, but soon enough I replaced the book on the shelf and bought a daily newspaper instead. The front page told me that there was nothing new in the Sund-Pelosso murder case, so I turned to my horoscope. I saw that it was a good day to travel, and thus I began my six-hour trek back to L.A. in the rental car.

I would not give another thought to Miwok heart-spirits, Rock Giants, or the murderous ways of Bigfoot until many weeks later, when I again picked up a daily newspaper. This time, my eyes remained glued to the hideous revelations on the front page. I never even bothered leafing to the back pages to read my horoscope.

I

On February 12, 1999, 42-year-old Carole Sund left the northern California logging town of Eureka with two teenagers in tow for a whirlwind winter holiday in the High Sierra wonderland of Yosemite. Four days later, all three vanished into thin air and theirs became a story of chance encounters of the worst kind.

This is how it happened.

Carole was a five-foot-two human dynamo, marshaling her four children like a field commander and calling in the tall, somber presence of her husband of twenty-one years, Jens Sund, only when she needed a tough-love backup. She was also a stickler for detail—downright anal when it came to scheduling. During the week prior to their departure, she even mapped the trip out online, using her Rand McNally software to figure travel times and distances. The meticulously scripted plan was printed out and clipped to the family refrigerator. This trip was going to be precisely five days in length and cover approximately eight hundred miles, by air and automobile.

Carole promised Jens she would fly to San Francisco, rent a car, amaze the girls with the sights at Yosemite, return her rental car to Modesto, then fly back just in time to rendezvous with her husband in San Francisco on the evening of February 16.

A good plan, Carole believed. The whole trek would go like clockwork. It was to be a farewell gift for 16-year-old Silvina Pelosso, the daughter of Carole's lifelong Argentine friend Raquel Pelosso. Silvina would be returning to her own family in her home town of Cordoba on March 3 after a three-month visit in the United States, and Carole intended to send her back with a lasting "Ooooh! Ahhhh!" impression of the startling majesty of Yosemite Valley. During the days leading up to the trip, Carole bubbled over with excitement about the waterfalls and canyons they'd be seeing, while her 15-year-old daughter Juliana, a popular sophomore at Eureka High, registered less enthusiasm. If she'd had her choice, she'd have been on her way to the mountains to ski over the three-day President's Day holiday with her friends.

But the outgoing Juli and the Sunds' shy Argentine houseguest had become much closer friends during Silvina's stay, so Juli kept her grumbling to a minimum and soon took up her mother's mantra about fabled Yosemite. Mother and daughter were tailor-made tour guides. Carole was a native—a fourth-generation Californian, to be more precise, and that made Juli Sund fifth generation. Californians knew Yosemite. It was part of their birthright. Back in the disco '70s, when Jens's hair was very nearly as long as Carole's, the newlywed Sunds even honeymooned there, spending their first night in the baronial Ahwahnee Hotel before camping outdoors the rest of the trip.

The one detour Carole planned for Silvina's inaugural Yosemite trip was a stopover in Stockton, where Juli was to participate in the American Spirit Association cheerleading competition at the University of the Pacific—a school Juli had her eye on, once she graduated from Eureka High. Carole and the two girls flew in to San Francisco from Eureka's McKinleyville airport, picked up a bright red Pontiac Grand Prix from Avis, and made the easy drive to the Central Valley city of Stockton in a couple of hours. They spent the night at a Days Inn motel.

During the competition the following day, Carole huddled with one of her Eureka neighbors, who had also come down from Northern California to sit up in the bleachers and watch. Like Juli, the neighbor's son, who was also competing, thought he might want to attend the University of the Pacific following graduation. The two moms decided to make a date to meet up again at the end of the Sunds' Yosemite trip and tour the campus with their teenagers.

This new wrinkle in Carole's precision planning would make keeping to a timetable during the trip a little more challenging, but she had no qualms. Carole would make it work. She always did. She made a commitment to meet her neighbor back on campus at precisely 2 P.M. on Tuesday, February 16. Allowing two hours for the campus tour and another two hours to race back to San Francisco Airport from Stockton, Carole figured she could just squeeze in all of the activities she had planned and still be able to meet Jens on time to make their flight.

In San Francisco, Carole, Juli, and Silvina were to join Jens before he and Silvina caught a plane for Phoenix, accompanied by the Sunds' three younger children, Jonah, Gina, and Jimmy. Carole's master plan called for her and Juli to fly back to Eureka so that Juli could get back to school after the long President's Day weekend while Silvina, Jens, and the younger kids visited Jens's sister and brother-in-law in Arizona. From Phoenix, they'd take Silvina to visit the other great national park of the American Southwest, the Grand Canyon. By the time she headed home to her family in Cordoba, the young Argentinian would have seen the very best that the western United States had to offer, and Carole could take some pride in having orchestrated it all.

Following the cheerleading competition, which ended late Saturday afternoon, Carole and the two girls drove south to the Central Valley farm community of Merced and checked in at a Ramada Inn just off the freeway.

Named for the river that flows out of Yosemite Valley, Merced is one of the chief entry points into the National Park. Though the river itself actually flows several miles to the north, Merced has long taken civic pride in its Yosemite connection, and everywhere there are references to the park and its lore, from Yosemite Auto Body & Towing to Yosemite Sam's Saw & Stove. The city itself is sleepy, small and undistinguished—the Bedford Falls of California's San Joaquin Valley. Fast food drive-thrus and shopping centers have invaded on the fringes, just as they have everywhere else in America, but the core of the town remains a time capsule, as if the century that were about to turn were the 19th, not the 20th. Beneath the rococo dome of the century-old Merced County Courthouse at sundown, a bell still tolls the hour. It's easy to imagine Clarence the angel sitting on its front steps, whispering to Jimmy Stewart: "Every time you hear a bell ring, it means that some angel's just got his wings!"

Carole Sund and her girls weren't in Merced to re-make *It's a Wonderful Life*. The place was strictly a stopover, as it is to most tourists. They stuck to the more modern fringes of Merced, like Costco Wholesale, a brand new hippodrome-sized discount store, where Carole stopped late Saturday to purchase some camping equipment. On Sunday morning, Carole made one more visit to Costco to withdraw $200 from an ATM and stock up on snack food. Then the three women were off, driving the final leg of their journey up winding state Highway 140, past the Gold Rush town of Mariposa, and high into the canyon of the Merced River itself, to the tiny settlement of El Portal.

Spanish for "the entrance," El Portal had been the

front door to Yosemite Valley for centuries before Mexican and, later, American settlers discovered it. Originally an old mining town, El Portal sits at an elevation of 1,919 feet, just outside the western boundary of the National Park and several miles from the park's western, or Arch Rock, entrance. The National Park Service uses a portion of the town as an administrative site for Yosemite, and many park employees live in El Portal, which relies heavily on tourism.

The hamlet's modern history began in 1870 when a farmer named James Hennessy staked out forty acres on the south side of the Merced River. Over the next forty years, the rudiments of a community began to take shape: a general store, a blacksmith's shop, a lumber mill, a volunteer fire department . . .

By 1907, the Yosemite Valley Railroad came through, bringing with it the first throngs of city adventurers anxious to catch a glimpse of the fabled valley first made famous by the 19th-century naturalist John Muir. The rambling four-story Hotel Del Portal opened for business the same year that the railroad arrived, and began serving thousands of tourists each year until 1917, when the grand Hotel Del Portal burned to the ground. After its destruction, overnight accommodations came and went roughly every ten years or so: the El Portal Inn, the El Portal Motor Inn, the Hotel El Portal, and the Portal Motor Court, among others. In each case, fire eventually claimed the Hotel Del Portal's successors, just as it had the Hotel Del Portal.

More than Yosemite itself, El Portal was at the absolute mercy of nature. When it rained, the river could easily rise above its banks, and when it didn't, the valley could dry to a tinderbox in a few weeks beneath the hot summer sun. Besides fire and flood, El Portal was subject to the same volcanic forces that created Yosemite's striking geology and, occasionally, it experienced a tremor. On either side of the narrow canyon, rock walls ascended nearly one thousand feet, blocking out light for much of the day.

People who lived here had to *want* to live here, because the elements argued against it. Thanks to the popularity of the national park, however, the economics of living in El Portal made up for the erratic weather and geography. During the summer months, the daily population of Yosemite could swell as high as 50,000, and even in the winter, thousands still flocked to the Valley each week for a glimpse of snow-covered Yosemite, and they all had money to spend. Carole Sund and her two teenagers were venturing into El Portal at the slowest time of the year, but they had cash with them, and they were definitely not alone. Slow or not, Yosemite National Park logged in 107,999 visitors during February.

The women arrived at Cedar Lodge, the latest incarnation of the Hotel Del Portal, some time after noon on Valentine's Day. Though it has 210 rooms, Cedar Lodge is not laid out at all like most hotels. A half dozen two-story dormitories are scattered over twenty-seven acres and are linked by parking lots to accommodate the daily swarm of automobiles.

There's a swimming pool and Jacuzzi adjacent to the restaurant and bar complex on the northeast side of the property, but the dorm where Carole, Juli, and Silvina were assigned was in the southwest corner, half a football field away from the lodge's nerve center.

There was snow on the ground and no neighbors on either side of the Sunds' suite—in fact, there was no other guest in the entire building—but it was a spacious nonsmoking room and it was located on the ground floor, so there was no lugging heavy bags up a flight of stairs. What was more, the room had cable and a VCR, and there were plenty of videos for rent at the gift shop next to the Cedar Lodge registration desk. While the trio were a little isolated, set off in a dorm building all by themselves, they also had the calming consolation of being warm, toasty, and entertained in a dry, comfortable room.

The one vexing issue they had to deal with was the daily closure of Highway 140. For close to two years, the California Department of Transportation had been making major repairs on the only road in and out of the western entrance to Yosemite National Park, and since the beginning of 1999, Highway 140 was closed down to all traffic through most of the daylight hours. Anyone who wanted to drive into Yosemite Valley from the western side of the park had to do so before 8 A.M. or wait until after 4:30 P.M. Tourists who arrived midday, as the Sunds had done, just had to bide their time. Carole did manage to sneak into the park at sunset that first day, so that Juli and Silvina could get a peek, but their big day at Yosemite would have to wait until Monday, the 15th of February.

They were up early, bundled against the freezing weather in blue jeans, sneakers, sweatshirts, and windbreakers. And it did turn out to be a great day. The skies were clear, the sun was out, and the roads were navigable. They left in plenty of time to have breakfast and still circle the entire valley if they wanted.

Carole had custody of the camera, but deigned to pose for one shot with Silvina. Juli snapped her mother clowning it up a bit with her hand on her hip, the Merced River and a sheer granite wall so typical of Yosemite at her back. Juli and Silvina also posed for snapshots. Friends since infancy, the girls could have easily been mistaken for sisters. They both stood just a couple of inches taller than Carole and weighed around 125 pounds, with the same olive complexion and brown eyes. Only on closer inspection did Silvina's darker brunette hair and eyes and halting English give her away. Hugging and mugging, the two teens grinned for the camera with Yosemite Falls in the background. Juli and Silvina also tried out their ice-skating skills at the Curry Village skating rink. Both managed to stay upright long enough for Carole to get a couple more photographs. The rest of the day was devoted to snowball fights, food, and souvenir shopping. By the time the trio headed back to Cedar Lodge late in the afternoon, they had clearly played themselves out for the day.

Back in their room, Carole phoned her husband, quickly spelling out her pique at CalTrans for shutting down Highway 140 at the most inopportune hours. She continued with a promise that she and the girls would head out the following day to keep Juli's campus tour appointment at the University of the Pacific and make it back to the airport in time, but Carole did add that she wanted to venture back into Yosemite one last time the next morning before they had to leave, even if it was only for a couple of hours. The entire conversation lasted less than four minutes.

Later on, the girls rented a video from the front desk and all three women went to the pizza parlor at the Cedar Lodge Restaurant for dinner. At the entrance was the parody poster of artist Edward Hopper's famous *Nighthawks*, featuring James Dean, Marilyn Monroe, Humphrey Bogart, and Elvis seated at an all-night lunch counter, with a legend beneath that reads "Boulevard of Broken Dreams." Decorated like a *Happy Days* diner, the restaurant had a jukebox, portraits of Annette Funicello and Elvis, and a signed and laminated 45 by Jan & Dean on one wall.

There was a bar on the north side of the diner, adjacent to the restrooms, which usually drew an eclectic crowd of tourists and locals alike regardless of the day of the week or the time of year. The cocktail hour at Cedar Lodge was El Portal's great equalizer, because it had one of the few bars near Yosemite where alcohol was poured, so bikers and bimbos showed up just as regularly as off-duty park rangers, lodge employees, or biologists who worked at the upscale Yosemite Institute. From parolees to professionals, the Cedar Lodge lounge served all comers.

Beyond the bar was another more formal restaurant which featured menus, wine, linen napkins, piped-in classical music that made no distinction between Mozart and Mantovani, and a much tonier—and expensive—selection of entrees than burgers and pizza.

But Carole had no interest in booze or mingling with the locals, and apparently saw no sense in getting fancy with food. She and the girls took a Formica and Naugahyde booth near the front door, where the girls waited while Carole ordered up at the counter adjacent to the bar: hamburgers for Juli and Silvina, and a veggie burger for the weight-conscious Mrs. Sund. She had recently tipped the scales at 145, and found herself in an escalating battle with extra pounds with each passing year. No sense in adding more, even if she and the girls were on a holiday.

Juli and Silvina wolfed down their food, but Carole nibbled at hers, ultimately asking to have it wrapped to take back to her room.

At 7:35 P.M., the trio paid their $21.13 bill and retired for the evening. Carole's half-eaten veggie burger remained on the counter, neatly wrapped and ready to go back to her room, but she had forgotten to take it with her. The burger remained on the counter until closing time. Carole never returned to pick it up.

In fact, the waitress who had served Carole Sund and the two teens never saw them again.

Neither did anyone else.

II

Jens Sund checked his watch. It was 10:40 P.M. on Tuesday the 16th of February, and he had only ten more minutes to board the last plane to Phoenix.

Stormy weather had delayed him and the three youngest members of the Sund clan by five hours, which Jens knew would throw Carole's carefully crafted schedule way out of kilter. By the time he and the kids had finally arrived at San Francisco International, he guessed that his wife had simply grown weary of waiting, taken an earlier flight back home to Eureka, and sent Silvina on ahead to Phoenix. Or perhaps he'd misunderstood where they were supposed to rendezvous. After all, it was Jens who was the forgetful, somewhat disorganized and shy half of the Sund combination—the polar opposite of Carole. If there had been some logistical mistake, it had to be his, not hers. When it came to coordinating things, Carole never missed a step.

29

"Carole is a doer; from the first time we met in high school at the age of seventeen, I realized this," Jens observed later on. "Carole would rather change something, or at least try to make a difference herself, than stand back and complain."

Of course, he assumed that Carole, Juli, and Silvina might just as easily have gone off to the air terminal restroom, or lost track of time getting a bite to eat. So Jens waited, had his wife paged over the airport speaker system, and waited a little longer. Still no response.

Finally, he and the three younger Sund children could wait no longer. They boarded a commuter jetliner and continued on to Arizona. But when they arrived at Phoenix's Sky Harbor Airport shortly after midnight, he could not find Silvina waiting anywhere for them. He called home, but Carole didn't answer.

Jens didn't panic. He knew Carole and that was enough to know that everything was under control. It was possible that Carole had run into delays and bad weather just as he had. It was possible she simply had a last-minute change of plans and hadn't been able to get in touch to let him know.

"I really didn't think anything was wrong," Jens recalled. "We had never had anything bad happen to us."

Just before the three set out for Yosemite, Jens gave Carole a carved wooden box for Valentine's Day. For having the presence of mind to give that token of affection to her ahead of time, he would say later, he would be forever grateful.

Earlier in the morning that same Tuesday, the dispatcher for Sonora's Courtesy Cab Co. had received a call from a man who was stranded up on Highway 108 and needed a ride back to Yosemite.

About an hour after receiving the call, Jenny Paul, the 30-year-old wife of the cab company's owner as well as its chief driver, made the trek to the mountain settlement of Sierra Village, some fifteen miles east of Sonora, where a tall, trim, athletic-looking fellow stood patiently waiting next to the pay phone at Sierra Village Market. He looked to be in his mid-30s, wore a ball cap and casual clothing, carried a backpack, and had the slightly stubbled, ruddy complexion of a man who spent a lot of time outdoors.

"He was really tired, worn out, he hadn't shaved in a couple of days," she remembered.

Though Jenny demanded no explanation, the fellow volunteered that some of his so-called friends had left him stranded there, miles from his job. He was doing some rewiring work inside the National Park and was already late for work. Jenny forewarned him that the trip wouldn't be cheap. It was eighty-five miles to Yosemite—a two-hour drive over narrow, winding roads, and if it rained or they hit snow, it would take even longer. He was unfazed, paying $125 cash in advance.

She checked her watch. It was 10 A.M. Jenny told him to hop in the backseat of her 1994 Chevrolet

Caprice while she radioed dispatch to let them know where she was going and when she'd be back. It was a comfort to her, especially on long trips like this one, that her husband—who also doubled as dispatcher much of the time—was only a quick radio call away.

The drive itself was uneventful. Her exhausted passenger had collapsed in the backseat, and nodded off most of the way, almost as if he'd been up all night long. When he did rouse himself, he didn't say much—just small talk. She remembered mentioning to him that she wished she had a four-wheel-drive vehicle and the fellow mentioned that he had one: an International Scout. Mostly, he just glanced around for his bearings and went back to sleep.

By the time they arrived at the park ranger's checkpoint just beyond El Portal, he was fully awake. Jenny rolled down the window and the ranger demanded a $35 commercial entry fee because she was driving a cab. Her passenger piped up that he shouldn't have to pay because he worked in the park.

When the ranger asked for his boss's name and the address of where he worked, the man had no answer.

"He said he didn't know," recalled Paul. "He worked all over. Then he just paid it."

His behavior struck her as a little odd, but no more so than that of many of her other fares. She got all kinds of crazies up the Sonora Pass. It wasn't even the first time that she'd been asked to drive all the way to Yosemite.

As the taxi entered Yosemite Valley, however, her

passenger genuinely creeped her out. He pointed out a cabin off the right side of the road. Several years earlier, he said, he'd spotted Bigfoot there. Since then, he'd seen the elusive half-man, half-ape Sasquatch of Indian lore, that supposedly still ranged through the wilderness of Northern California on several other occasions. He wanted to know: Did she believe in the legend of Bigfoot?

No, she answered, she didn't.

"Well, you should, because it's real," her passenger warned in a chilly voice.

She fell silent until she dropped him off a few minutes later at Yosemite Lodge. She used the restroom there before heading back to Sonora. Her passenger was still staring at signs and pictures on the walls of the lodge when she came out of the bathroom.

Jenny Paul climbed in her cab, dropped it into gear, and didn't look back. She drove out of the valley as quickly as possible.

Moments later, the man with the knapsack caught a bus out of the park heading toward Cedar Lodge.

That same Wednesday morning, about six hundred miles to the southeast, Jens Sund called home from Phoenix, Arizona. The phone rang and rang, but no one answered. Something of a stoic, who does not easily display his emotions, Jens ranged between irritation and worry at Carole's absence, but still refused to show any panic. Instead, he set out from his sister's place to play a round of golf. He didn't get back until early in the afternoon, and Carole still hadn't called. He remained outwardly calm. Only after he'd phoned his in-laws, Francis and Carole Carrington, and learned that his wife had not called her parents either did fear begin to set in.

He started phoning everywhere, retracing the three women's route from Eureka to Yosemite, beginning with a call to the Cedar Lodge. A front desk clerk reportedly found a bag containing T-shirts, receipts, and souvenirs that might have been left behind in their room, but nothing else.

Gary Cole and his wife Delores, who operated the lodge, said later that they didn't see the trio check out Tuesday morning, but that wasn't unusual. Visitors routinely awakened early and were gone long before the front desk opened. From the look of Room 509, the three women appeared to have showered, left their room key behind, loaded their baggage into their car, and left. Carole told her husband Monday night that they might try to get in another few hours at the park Tuesday morning before heading out. According to park rangers, there had been no accidents befalling anyone who fit the description of the three women. Could they have been victims of an accident that had gone unreported?

Carole Carrington, who had joined her son-in-law by this time in his increasingly frantic phone search, also shared his growing dread. She remembered that her daughter never checked out of a hotel without leaving her key at the front desk. After a few more calls, Jens and his mother-in-law learned that Juli had also missed her appointment to tour the University of the Pacific campus on Tuesday afternoon. If Carole stuck to her trip plan—and she always did—that narrowed their last known whereabouts to Yosemite. By nightfall Wednesday, high anxiety had crossed over into the worst kind of fear. Just after 7:30 P.M., a now shaken Jens Sund called the California Highway Patrol and the Mariposa County Sheriff and officially reported his wife, daughter, and Silvina Pelosso missing.

A search began the following day, with TV and radio broadcasts and flyers posted in and around the El Portal entrance to the park. Jens left the three younger children with his sister and flew back to San Francisco, where he met Ron Caton, his brother-in-law, who had agreed to accompany him on the drive from San Francisco to El Portal. While Sund and Caton were crossing the Central Valley on their way in to Yosemite, another vehicle was on its way out.

Driven by a tall, husky male who routinely wore a ball cap, the 1979 powder-blue and white International Scout pulled out of the parking lot next to the restaurant at Cedar Lodge and headed west on Highway 140. The driver turned north at Mariposa, weaving up Highway 49 toward the Tuolumne County seat of Sonora, over an hour away, but when he got there, he bypassed Sonora itself. Instead, he dropped the Scout into a lower gear and begin the climb up the steep Highway 108 grade, toward the Sonora Pass.

A little over a mile past the mountain community

of Sierra Village, the driver turned off the road at a dense, dark spot in the forest, where a logging road snaked down into the pines. He climbed out of his Scout and made his way down the logging road, well out of sight and hearing of the main highway. He stopped at a clearing where, a few yards off to the northeast, a bright red Pontiac Grand Prix rested in a snowy ravine, next to a fallen log.

The driver carefully stepped down the steep embankment to the automobile and popped open the trunk, rummaging around inside. He came up with a black leather billfold, then shut the trunk and stepped back, surveying both the wallet and the Pontiac. Then he lit the metallic corpse on fire.

A few moments later, back on Highway 140, the driver glanced in his rearview mirror as he drove back south on Highway 108, toward Sonora. A plume of smoke that nobody else but he was apparently able to see that day rose out of the forest, and the bright red Pontiac crackled to charcoal gray in a blaze so hot that it melted the snow and singed the surrounding trees. . . .

And cremated everything inside the automobile.

"It's a complete mystery," puzzled Deborah Downs, a family friend who worked with Jens Sund. "We don't know if they've driven off the road. We just don't know what to think. It's every parent's nightmare."

The Mariposa County Sheriff's Department told Jens and his brother-in-law they had already begun searching around Yosemite and along the Merced River by the time the two men arrived in El Portal. What deputies did not say was that the Merced is deceptively shallow to the untrained eye, and that the river actually has a number of very deep icy-cold pools in which a car could be totally submerged and missed during a cursory search from the highway. A car that plunged into such a pool, especially during bad weather, would likely have no survivors.

When investigators got their first break in the case, however, it was nowhere near the Merced River, or even Yosemite. On Friday the 19th, 86 miles to the northeast of Yosemite National Park, a Modesto High School student found the credit card insert of Carole Sund's wallet at a busy residential intersection in the Central Valley city of Modesto.

Perhaps best known as the boyhood home of *Star Wars* creator George Lucas, who based his classic coming-of-age comedy *American Graffiti* on growing up in Modesto, the city is a larger and slightly more cosmopolitan version of the farm town of Merced, where Carole, Juli, and Silvina had spent the previous Saturday night. The Modesto Airport was also where the trio was supposed to have dropped off the rental car before flying back to San Francisco, leading investigators to speculate that they might have left El Portal and gotten as far as Modesto before they disappeared.

While the neighborhood immediately adjacent to the airport is notorious for its poverty, methamphetamine traffic, and high crime rate, and might not have been the best place for three women in a sporty red late-model car to get lost, it was not that section of Modesto where the insert from Carole's wallet had been found. With credit cards, health cards, and her driver's license still in it, the billfold appeared to have been tossed onto a paved median strip at the corner of Tully and Briggsmore in a middle class neighborhood several miles to the northwest, on the "good" side of town.

What was more, none of Carole's credit cards appeared to be missing. A check of the receipts at Cedar Lodge showed that the last time one of them had been used was Valentine's Day. But a canvass of the area within a half mile of the Briggsmore-Tully intersection, completed by a dozen detectives and two search dogs, turned up nothing. How the missing woman's wallet wound up on a Modesto street corner 86 miles away from Yosemite remained a mystery.

Friday night, Jens Sund phoned Argentina and broke the news to Raquel Pelosso that her younger daughter was missing.

"I had to call up this girl's mother and tell her that her dream had become a nightmare," he said, adding that it was "the hardest phone call I ever had to make."

Saturday morning, five days after the women disappeared, Jens joined his in-laws in announcing the offer of a $250,000 reward for information leading to the trio's safe return. By that time, hope was fading that they might have had an auto accident and simply run off the road. Investigators eventually located nine abandoned vehicles in their search—two of which had been stolen—but none of them were fire-engine red or a Pontiac Grand Prix. Carole and Francis Carrington, who had earned millions from their Santa Rosa real estate firm, put up another $50,000 for information about the whereabouts of the missing automobile.

At a press conference in the cheerfully decorated Sunrise Suite at the Modesto Holiday Inn, Jens told reporters he had hired private investigators and chartered private planes to assist with the air search. When asked about the generous size of the reward, Jens pointed out that $250,000 was about the price of a California middle-class home.

"Who wouldn't exchange a house for their wife and daughter?" he asked.

With so much reward money at stake and a prominent upper middle-class California family involved, the media's normally lukewarm interest in missing persons cases transformed literally overnight. Carole, Juli, and Silvina were no longer faces destined to appear on post office bulletin boards or the sides of milk cartons. Their disappearance from one of the best-known natural shrines in the country suddenly became national news. Sunday morning, one week after Valentine's Day, their photographs appeared in newspapers and led the evening newscasts from coast to coast. Soon, a forest of satellite dishes and TV transmitters sprouted from the cramped parking lot outside Cedar Lodge and from the Modesto Holiday Inn headquarters of the Sunds, Carringtons, and Raquel and Jose Pelosso, who had made the 24-hour flight from Cordoba to participate in the vigil.

"This was Silvina's dream, to come here," Mrs. Pelosso told reporters upon her arrival Sunday afternoon. "You never imagine that such a thing could happen."

As she was putting Silvina on the plane to California three months earlier, Raquel Pelosso remembered telling her daughter, as worried mothers everywhere tend to do the first time their children leave home, "It may be the last time I see you." The sting of that irony brought tears welling up into her eyes.

On Sunday, too, the Modesto police and the Mariposa County sheriff's office admitted that the investigation had them baffled and had strained their local resources to the breaking point. They deferred to the big guns.

The Federal Bureau of Investigation announced that it was entering the case.

"We are working it as a kidnapping or possible carjacking," said FBI spokesman Nick Rossi. "If it was just an adult, we would not be bringing as many resources to bear. But because minors were involved, it creates for us almost a presumption that a kidnapping may have occurred."

In all, over 50 FBI agents would eventually join the search, from the bureau's offices in Fresno, Modesto, Sacramento, and San Francisco. Mariposa

County Sheriff Pelk Richards gratefully posted a sign on the front door of his office reading: business office only. MEDIA CALL FBI COMMAND CENTER AT 557-9900.

The FBI-led task force set up temporary headquarters at the Modesto Doubletree Hotel and created a hotline for news updates to feed the quickly escalating media frenzy and to gather tips from the public—more than 2,000 of them were logged in all before the investigation was over. Almost immediately, the hotline was flooded with reports of sightings. Most could not be accurate, unless the women were in two or three dozen places at once. They all had to be checked out though, and led agents on routine wild-goose chases.

There were two separate reports that Carole, Juli, and Silvina had been seen in Buck Meadows, about 20 miles northwest of Yosemite on Highway 120 on Tuesday the 16th.

"The two girls came in and asked for a room rate, Tuesday night, eight-thirty, nine o'clock," said Joe Zarate, manager of the Yosemite West Gate Motel, about twelve miles from the park. When Zarate told them the price was $79, they left. The cook at the Buck Meadows Café next door said she too had seen the three women that night.

But shopkeeper Penny Mann told the FBI that the three women had also visited her gift store that same day, in the mountain town of Twain Harte some 63 miles from Yosemite.

"I've gone over this so many times," Mann said. "I'm sure it was them."

Louise Guthmiller, a 71-year-old gas station owner near the Sonora Pass community of Sierra Village, tried reporting her own sighting to the FBI hotline that day, but claimed that it was so busy that she could never get through. Guthmiller told the *Stockton Record* that after she sold three women a small amount of gas around the time of the disappearance, Guthmiller asked if they were on their way home. One of the women answered, "No, I'm from Argentina."

Greeley Hill resident Larry Razzano said he saw the women's red Grand Prix a day or two after the disappearance. It was being driven by a man near Briceburg, about 17 miles southwest of El Portal.

"I followed him for 23 miles," Razzano told the *Fresno Bee*. "This was too suspicious to overlook."

He reported the sighting to the FBI, including a partial matching license plate number, adding that the driver had two passengers with him and kept turning back and taking side roads that switchbacked up the mountainside.

In Modesto, there were even more sightings: the Pontiac was spotted at the Holiday Inn on Sisk Road; it was seen next to a fruit stand near the suburb of Escalon; it was parked just outside the lobby of a motel in nearby Oakdale. One woman reported seeing the missing Grand Prix sitting at the side of the eastbound lanes of Briggsmore, just west of Tully, on Thursday, February 18th. Its emergency lights were flashing, but she didn't see anyone in the car.

None of the sightings led anywhere.

Over the next few days, while Modesto police continued to pore over the area around the Briggsmore and Tully intersection, the FBI began searching the Tuolumne Grove area north of Yosemite Valley. On the basis of the nearby Bucks Meadow sightings, that the FBI regarded as "credible," agents concentrated their efforts on the stand of giant sequoia trees in the northwest corner of the park. In all, three different witnesses recalled the three missing women asking directions to the grove on the morning of Tuesday the 16th. Fueling this new hope were additional reports that a red Pontiac Grand Prix matching the description of Carole Sund's rental was spotted in the Tuolumne Grove parking lot between noon and 2 P.M. that day. But two days of searching turned up nothing. From there, agents moved farther north to Calaveras Big Trees State Park, but again they came up empty.

Following these snafus, Sacramento's Special Agent in Charge James Maddock, who headed the FBI investigation, wouldn't comment anymore on any of the sightings.

"There is not much more information, frankly, that we can or will release," he told reporters.

Traditionally, the FBI has had a one-way policy in dealing with the media, and the Sund-Pelosso case was no different. Agents take information from the press, carefully cataloguing reams of newspaper and magazine articles to be salted away in the bureau's celebrated central filing system in Washington, D.C., but they rarely give anything in return.

Despite the paucity of information that Maddock was willing to share, he began calling regular press conferences at the Doubletree, chiefly to announce that no new progress had been made and to entreat the media to keep repeating the hotline number in their reports. Even though the Bureau played its cards close to its vest, Maddock tried to give TV correspondents and metropolitan dailies alike the illusion that they were in on the investigation. He even gave the case what he perceived to be a catchy title—an operational label that sounded almost military: TourNap.

But "TourNap" never really caught on with the press. As the days dragged on and TourNap mushroomed into the biggest missing persons case in Yosemite's history, the investigation routinely became known in newspapers and over network TV alike as either the Sund-Pelosso case or simply the Yosemite murders.

James M. Maddock, a 47-year-old triathlete and martial arts expert from Alexandria, Virginia, personified the clean-cut hubris that has been an FBI hallmark since the J. Edgar Hoover era. In a crew-cut sort of way, he even resembled Efrem Zimbalist Jr. as Inspector Lewis Erskine during the actor's ten years on ABC-TV's *The F.B.I.* Among Sacramento and Central Valley law enforcement officials, however, Maddock was privately and somewhat derogatorily known as "Mr. Personality."

Maddock first joined the bureau in 1980, a year after earning his law degree from the University of Virginia, and he rose quickly through the ranks: first, in the Washington field office, from which he was dispatched to New York for investigation of terrorism and violent crime; next, he was promoted to supervisor in Detroit, and then San Juan, Puerto Rico; and, finally, he was rewarded in 1983 with a twelve-year stint at FBI Headquarters in downtown Washington, D.C. There, he supervised the FBI Undercover Program, among other duties, until he was briefly named Assistant Special Agent in Charge of the field office in Jackson, Mississippi.

He didn't stay long in the South. In 1995, Maddock was asked to return to Washington as one of four deputy special counsels who supervise the Office of General Counsel. The OOGC is the FBI's legal advisory branch, maintaining a small army of about 70 lawyers whose job it is to keep the Bureau out of legal and Congressional hot water.

Maddock showed up just in time to dip his toe in the Bureau's hottest water since Watergate. He immediately locked horns with Frederick Whitehurst, a longtime employee of the FBI's highly touted forensics laboratory, after Whitehurst blew the whistle on sloppy, incomplete, and inadequate lab work that had been passed off in the courts as unquestioned scientific evidence. Because several of the FBI's best-known cases—the World Trade Center bombing, the destruction of the Oklahoma City federal building, and the blood, hair, and fiber evidence from the O. J. Simpson murder trial—rested heavily on results from its lab, Whitehurst's charges sent the FBI brass scurrying for cover.

All except Maddock, who seemed to believe the credo of the University of Virginia's football team: the best defense is a good offense.

In his role as OOGC deputy special counsel, Maddock investigated and attempted to transfer Whitehurst out of the FBI's forensics lab, especially after a *Playboy* magazine exposé detailed the kinds of abuses and incompetence at the lab that Whitehurst had been revealing to Congress and the independent Office of the Inspector General. In an unusual show of defiance, even for a lifelong agent like Maddock, he even fought the Senate Judiciary Committee over its right to interview lab employees.

And even though both Congress and the Inspector General found serious problems at the lab, and Whitehurst himself won a $1.5 million judgment against the FBI for releasing false and derogatory information about him without his permission, James Maddock apparently wasn't chastised or sanctioned at all by his supervisors. As a matter of fact, he was rewarded with a promotion—this time, to Special Agent in Charge of the Sacramento FBI office.

As the FBI's top man in California's state capital at the same time that former professor Theodore Kaczynski had been exposed as the so-called Unabomber, Maddock's public profile grew daily, eventually be-

coming second only to that of FBI Director Louis
Freeh himself. Even Maddock's wife, Leesa Brown,
rose to the media occasion, when she became the
U.S. Department of Justice's official spokeswoman
during prosecution of the Unabomber case.

But Maddock's approach/avoidance conflict with
the media didn't end upon his arrival in Sacramento.
Almost immediately, Maddock announced that his
top priority would be investigating official corrup-
tion in the state's capital. He began publicizing a
toll-free tip line soliciting whistle-blowers to turn in
corrupt government officials; if he saw any hypoc-
risy in asking others to come forward the way that the
much-persecuted Frederick Whitehurst had in Washington, D.C., Maddock did not mention it in his press
conferences.

With the fast-developing revelations in Yosemite,
Maddock seized the opportunity to raise his profile
once again and burnish the Bureau's tarnished reputation in the offing. While relishing its public percep-
tion as the nation's most elite police force, the FBI
had gained a certain notoriety in the 1990s for bran-
dishing the full power and resources of the federal
government in selected cases, but with frequently
modest—or even disastrous—results. Congress, the
courts, and even Attorney General Janet Reno herself had been critical of the FBI's role in the killing
of militia member Randy Weaver's 14-year-old son
Samuel and wife Vicki during a shootout at Ruby
Ridge, Idaho, in 1992, as well as the 1993 incineration of the Branch Davidian compound near Waco,

Texas, which cost the lives of more than 80 men, women, and children. If Maddock's FBI team could crack the high-profile Sund-Pelosso mystery, the Bureau might harvest a little good publicity for a change.

As soon as it became clear that the missing women were probably not victims of any accident, investigators looked to Jens Sund and other family members as their first possible suspects. After all, while Sund held a good job as vice president of the Eureka branch of Carrington Co., it was Carole who was the fourth-generation member of the founding Carrington family, which started its lucrative real estate business in Santa Rosa in 1882. It would not be the first time that a greedy son-in-law tried hurrying up his inheritance by doing in his wife.

But Jens did not fit the pattern. A check of his background, credit, habits, and the family's insurance policies turned up nothing untoward, and when law enforcement asked him to submit to a lie detector test, he readily agreed, passing with flying colors. Three other family members took the polygraph and passed as well.

Francis and Carole Carrington, who lived on a 2,000-acre cattle ranch in Butler Valley, near Eureka, flat-out dismissed the idea that their daughter's husband could be involved in a kidnapping or murder-for-hire plot.

"Jens is part of the family," Carrington said.

Even the FBI's Maddock praised the family and

Jens Sund in particular for their forbearance and cooperation.

With the clock ticking and clues scarce, however, Maddock could no longer perpetuate false hope.

"I've told the families that you have to consider that the longer it goes on, there's a likelihood they're dead," Maddock announced during a February 26 press conference, 11 days after the women vanished. In his most candid public statement to date, even Maddock lowered his "can-do" facade enough to display a very human befuddlement.

"It is very strange. Something has happened," he said.

But what? reporters demanded.

"Your guess is as good as mine," Maddock answered. Nothing could be ruled out, and nothing could be ruled in.

With much fanfare, a pair of elite FBI profilers were flown in to begin compiling a psychological blueprint of suspects. After weighing all the available evidence, they came up with the astonishing theory that the three women must have died in a car accident. Maddock's troops thanked them for their efforts and dispatched them back to Washington.

The disappearance was now nearly two weeks old. With more than 110 full-time searchers coming up empty in and around Yosemite, the investigation shifted once more back to its starting point. Agents and local detectives interviewed everyone in El Portal who might have seen or heard something, concentrating on employees at Cedar Lodge.

They spoke to everyone on staff, from managers Gary and Delores Cole on down to the most humble minimum wage worker. They were particularly interested in those employees who lived at the lodge in rented rooms above the lobby and over the restaurant complex. Those questioned included a six foot one, 200-pound handyman named Cary Stayner who lived in a room above the restaurant where he ate regularly, often twice a day, for lunch and dinner. He took care of squeaky doors, plumbing problems, and faulty electrical wiring at the lodge, and carried a radio so that the front desk could contact him if guests needed towels, an extra cot, or a toilet plumbed.

But after interviewing him, investigators dismissed the bland but affable Stayner as a suspect. He had a girlfriend. He'd worked there since August 1997 without causing any problems, and had been recently laid off, but expected to start back up with the lodge when the tourist season picked up. He looked like an all-American guy with a Brad Pitt grin and a Gary Cooper shuffle. Outside of a two-year-old marijuana bust in the Atwater suburb of his hometown of Merced, for which charges were ultimately dropped, Stayner's record was stainless.

He seemed so benign that agents even asked his help in gathering up blankets from Room 509, where the missing women had spent their last night. The blankets would be tagged and catalogued as potential evidence that might yield fibers to match to the victims or suspects, should the "TourNap" team ever find any of them.

Instead of Stayner, agents zeroed in on the 39-year-old night janitor at the Cedar Lodge Restaurant with the unfortunate name of Billy Joe Strange. Not only was his girlfriend a desk clerk supervisor at the lodge on the day that the three women disappeared, but his roommate was a convicted sex offender. Billy Joe also had a prison record and a checkered, alcoholic past. What was more, he was still on parole.

Billy Joe Strange made a far more convincing suspect than Cary Anthony Stayner.

III

For quite some time, Billy Joe Strange had lived
with Becky Buttermore in a tiny shrub-enshrouded
cabin at 5020 Abbie Road, within a stone's throw of
the constant hypnotizing rush of the Merced River.
While it might sound rustic, even a bit romantic, the
reality was a cramped hovel in an unpaved trailer
park area just off Highway 140, about halfway between Cedar Lodge and the center of El Portal.

Unlike the vacation homes up the slopes of the
canyon, where well-off retirees barbequed in the
summer and went cross-country skiing in the winter,
or the relatively posh hotel accommodations at
Cedar Lodge or its sister motel, the Yosemite View
Lodge another five miles east on Highway 140, the
pocket-sized home that Billy and Becky shared was
one step above poverty. Along with dozens of others
who eked out a living at the lower levels of the
Yosemite tourism trade, the couple drove used cars,

could rarely afford new clothes, and generally scraped by on their combined meager salaries.

In November of 1998, they shoehorned in a third roommate who also worked part-time as a janitor at Cedar Lodge. At 55, Darrell Gray Stephens was nearly a generation older than his new roomies, but he shared a secret history with Strange that made him both welcome and comfortable around the younger couple. Like Billy Joe, Darrell was a felon with a violent past who had done his time, paid his dues, and was now trying to stay clean enough to make it on the outside.

But, as Becky Buttermore lamented often and angrily to the reporters who would come to hound her in the coming weeks, it did not seem to matter that both men were attempting to live a better life or that their record of living in harmony with everyone in El Portal had been spotless. What really mattered when the FBI needed scapegoats was that Darrell and Billy Joe were in the wrong place at the wrong time, and that they were both ex-cons.

"The only reason they got him as a suspect is because he was working there that night and he was the only one working. It was just his bad luck," said Darrell Stephens.

Off-season during the winter months, Strange worked the 11 P.M. graveyard shift on Mondays and Tuesdays, cleaning up at the Cedar Lodge Restaurant. Billy Joe was an El Portal regular. For nearly four years he'd been employed at the restaurant, and was known throughout the small community as the quirky guy with the Chihuahuas.

"He used to float down the river on his back with one of his little dogs dancing on his chest, barking like crazy," recalled a waitress at the Cedar Lodge Restaurant, adding with a laugh and a wave of her hand, "Billy Joe was harmless."

He'd recently lost one of the tiny dogs, but still had the remaining Chihuahua with him wherever he went, including the night of February 15, when he was cleaning up the restaurant— the same night that Carole Sund left her half-eaten veggie burger sitting on the take-out counter and never returned. A little over a week later, the FBI and then the media had transformed Billy Joe's bucolic life along the beautiful Merced River into a living hell. Residents who still retained a sense of humor about the FBI/media glut even talked about changing the town's name to Hell Portal.

On Thursday, the 4th of March, Billy Joe and his Chihuahua stopped in at Jon Bevington's Chevron station, where Strange complained bitterly about the FBI following him around everywhere he went, asking questions.

"I think it's ridiculous," Billy Joe told Bevington. Strange didn't appear nervous at all when talking about the FBI, but he was genuinely peeved that they were shadowing him.

"He didn't have anything to hide," said Bevington, who had hired Strange as a mechanic in 1992 and used him at the service station off and on for more than five years. Bevington had come to appreciate him as one of El Portal's more colorful local characters. For a time, the FBI showed an interest in James Randack, another of Bevington's former employees, but that interest faded.

"We all talked about our theories. We said the car could have gone up over the edge of a cliff. It could be in a river. Time will tell, I guess," Bevington said at the time.

Miles Menetrey, manager of the Indian Flat RV Park, located about a half mile from Strange's cabin, also scoffed at the notion that Billy Joe would be capable of killing three people and concealing the crime. Before moving in with Buttermore, Strange had lived in the RV park, during which time Menetrey got to know him well. Menetrey felt investigators were picking on the wrong guy. What was more, Menetrey had his own bone to pick with the FBI.

"The FBI and the searchers, about 24 of them, just showed up Tuesday morning and started walking shoulder to shoulder through my RV park," Menetrey said. "It was really irritating. They didn't say a thing. They just started walking."

Menetrey, Bevington, and virtually every other local who knew Billy Joe Strange described him as both innocuous and hardworking. As for the FBI, its agents quickly built up the same kind of resentment any civilian population eventually develops against an occupying army.

On Friday the 5th of March, nearly three weeks after the disappearance of Carole, Juli, and Silvina, the FBI stopped following around after Billy Joe Strange and arrested him instead. He was hauled off to the Mariposa County jail for allegedly violating terms of his parole. The charge: drinking alcohol. While technically a parole violation, no one in El Portal believed for a moment that it was really Billy's drinking habits that had landed him in jail this time, even though booze seemed to be the catalyst that had repeatedly gotten him in trouble in the past.

In 1992 and again in 1996, Strange had been convicted of violent crimes—the first time, for spousal abuse, and the second, for assault causing a serious injury. He received a three-year prison sentence on the second conviction, but was released on parole after serving 18 months. According to court records, Strange had waged a ten-year campaign of harassment against his sister-in-law, with eight prior misdemeanor convictions and two drunken driving convictions.

Kathi Strange told the FBI her former brother-in-law grew up in Southern California, joined the Army after high school, and came to Mariposa after he was discharged, where he moved in with his brother David, and Kathi. The agents were more interested in Billy Joe's current friends than his past, and asked Kathi if he had any particular "hiding places" in and around Mariposa.

She could not, and did not, help them.

Billy Joe's alcohol rages did not seem to extend to the people he worked with in El Portal. Employers like Bevington and James E. Houtz, who ran the

Cedar Lodge Restaurant, gave him glowing character references. Houtz said Billy Joe had been coming to his bar for years and had always gotten along well with customers and coworkers.

"Bill has been a regular customer for about three years," Houtz said in a letter to Mariposa County Superior Court Judge Richard L. McMechan prior to Strange's sentencing on the 1996 assault conviction. "He is well-liked by others and has never caused any trouble . . . if Bill needed work tomorrow, I would hire him."

But Judge McMechan was not persuaded. He told Billy Joe at his sentencing "your problem seems to be the way you deal with confrontations through violence . . . as soon as you go out and get a snoot-full, then we have the same old Billy Strange that has been in court for a long time."

With his latest arrest, the booze seemed merely a transparent pretext for getting him back behind bars. Mariposa County Sheriff's Lieutenant Bruce Pickard told the media they'd get no interviews while Strange was in sheriff's custody. As for the FBI, James Maddock refused to discuss Strange or "any potential suspects or evidence. There are no suspects in jail charged in this case."

Despite Maddock's denials that Billy Joe might be a suspect, the FBI showed up in force at Strange's cabin during the next few days, cutting two squares from rugs in the kitchen, carting off several articles of clothing and a knife, and picking through his personal papers and dresser drawers.

"They went through everything," said his room-mate Darrell Stephens. "The FBI has been harassing us for two weeks now. They've harassed all of El Portal."

At Cedar Lodge, the FBI seized Strange's time cards and payroll record. One of Billy Joe's acquaintances told investigators that in 1998 Billy Joe had talked about "jacking" someone, killing and raping women and hiding their bodies. A search of the shed where he kept his cleaning supplies turned up a waterlogged laundry bag with a stain that looked like blood. They also impounded his van, which had been previously owned and was still registered in the name of an Arizona man who had died the previous July at nearby Bass Lake. A search of his van yielded a bloodstained piece of carpet. Becky's Chevrolet Citation was also impounded. It was returned within a few days, after agents had vacuumed it and removed some of its contents.

Her voice breaking and barely under control, Becky Buttermore defended Billy Joe when the police came for him. Wearing large-lens horn-rimmed glasses and a ponytail, she was normally effusive and as well liked in the community as Billy Joe. But when fighting off reporters through a crack in her front door, she was angry, befuddled, and near tears, all at once.

"All I know is that me and Billy didn't have nothing to do with the disappearance of that family!" she hollered before retreating inside.

By the first week of March, the media had become

as pesty as the police. Becky and Darrell Stephens even went so far as to post signs on the front porch and on a bicycle that simply said NO MEDIA. Besides parading to her front door, the growing army of reporters began accosting Becky where she worked, at the front desk of Cedar Lodge.

"Becky nearly suffered a nervous breakdown," said Hugh Carter, manager of the El Portal Food Market. "I got down on the news media after the initial flush, just as did everyone else."

Carter described the TV crews as "especially obnoxious" and, after the 11th or 12th interview, even he began refusing to talk. By March, the normally friendly and open folk of El Portal began removing the welcome mats from the porch and refusing to answer their doorbells.

On Sunday the 7th of March, Billy Joe Strange called his boss at Cedar Lodge from jail. He would not be coming in to work Monday, he said.

Spring was approaching. And with each passing day, hope of ever finding the three tourists alive melted as swiftly as the snow. The cloud cover over the Sierra Nevada mountains had lifted, the sun had come out, and the white winter playground where Carole, Juli, and Silvina had once clowned and capered on Yosemite Valley's floor had begun to dissolve into trickles of tears, flowing down into the Merced.

Five days after Billy Joe's arrest, Jens Sund

appeared broken and without hope before the gathered media.

"I'm devastated," he said. "My worst possible fears have come true."

Upon instructions from the FBI, he would not elaborate about what evidence might have made his fears so real. He had just come from a briefing and would say only that "they've made some discoveries, but I'm not supposed to comment on it." Within 24 hours, he was back before the press, apologizing for his outburst, but giving no further clue as to what discoveries the FBI had made that had so unnerved him. It was merely that he had been on an emotional roller coaster, he tried to explain.

As for the FBI, the working theory had clearly shifted from accident to violent crime, probably committed on the night of February 15 or early in the morning on February 16, and probably at or near Cedar Lodge. Teams were going over ground they had covered before, in the area above and around the lodge. James Maddock maintained that his agents had "indicators where the victims and their car might be," adding that "it is a vast, vast area with a number of hiding places."

By mid-March the search had covered thousands of square miles in Mariposa, San Joaquin, and Stanislaus counties with special attention given to anything that resembled a shallow grave. Searchers were also instructed to examine the hundreds of tunnels and mine shafts that riddled this part of California, where the Gold Rush first lured thousands of fortune seekers to drill, dig, and scar the earth 150 years ago. After the Yosemite Valley Railroad linked the San Joaquin Valley city of Merced to El Portal early in the 20th century, the area around the entrance to Yosemite was also identified by miners as a central source of tungsten and barium, a mineral essential to drilling oil wells, and thus, even more mine shafts were sunk into and around El Portal. While the last mines closed in the 1940s, the abandoned shafts were frequently left wide open, some as deep as 2,000 feet, and filled with water during winter storms. Their entrances were still visible from Highway 140 and frequently made convenient hiding places for stolen goods, drugs, or other evidence of criminal enterprise. Using high-tech sonar equipment, investigators began probing lakes and river pools in addition to flooded mine shafts.

As some TourNap task force members continued to comb the countryside looking for places to hide a red Pontiac, others were running El Portal residents through lie detector sessions. Several of Billy Joe Strange's friends had been asked to take polygraph tests, including his roommate Darrell Stephens.

"I don't see how they can make anything stick. There's nothing there," he said.

Stephens told the *San Francisco Chronicle* he submitted to the polygraph test and had been questioned repeatedly by the FBI about whether he was involved in the disappearance and whether he knew the location of the bodies. While Stephens passed his interrogation, Strange flunked twice. He answered questions like "Did you cause the disappearance of those three people?" and "Were you involved in any way with the disappearance of those three people?" in a manner that suggested he was lying.

"Strange and I didn't do anything," Stephens continued to protest. "They're just fishing."

Nevertheless, the same Mariposa County sheriff's deputies that Stephens and Becky Buttermore had been calling upon for nearly a week to keep the media from harassing them, appeared at the front door of Billy Joe's cabin on Sunday, the 14th of March. This time, they came for Stephens. They had reason to assume that Stephens, who was one of the employees charged with making keys for Cedar Lodge guest rooms, may have made the key for Carole Sund to get in to Room 509. And now they had an arrest warrant with them.

The charge? Failure to register as a convicted sex offender. Some 20 years earlier, Stephens had been convicted in Van Nuys Superior Court in Southern California of entering the home of a Los Angeles woman—clad only in a T-shirt—and raping her. He was also convicted of unlawful oral copulation with a minor, robbery, and attempted burglary. Prior to that, he did prison time in Texas during the 1960s and 1970s for burglary and armed robbery. Because of his sex crimes, he was required to notify local law enforcement within five days of any move, and the last address Mariposa County had for him was in the Yaqui Gulch neighborhood of Mariposa, not Abbie Road in El Portal.

Stephens moved to Mariposa after his parole in 1983, had fathered three children, but began drifting from address to address. While he hadn't been in any serious trouble since migrating to Mariposa, in 1995 he did plead guilty to a similar charge of failure to register as a sex offender. He was released with a slap on the wrist that time, but with the FBI now anxious to keep him behind bars, Stephens was ordered held in the county jail on $125,000 bail.

The same day as Stephens's arrest, the citizens of Modesto demonstrated with a "Vigil of Hope" rally just how deeply the Sund-Pelosso case had touched them and, by extension, the rest of the nation. One month after the disappearance of Carole, Juli, and Silvina, over 1,000 supporters of a stronger, more rigorous missing persons movement marched through downtown Modesto. Some wore T-shirts bearing silk-screened snapshots of their own missing loved ones. Others carried posters with descriptions and dates when the missing were last seen. Still others hefted banners that read BRING THEM HOME, and WANTED: HEALERS NOT DESTROYERS.

At an amphitheater in Modesto's Graceada Park where the march ended and the rally was staged, Jens Sund's brother Ken introduced nearly 20 speakers, including Silvina's mother, Raquel Pelosso, who extolled the crowd in both Spanish and English:

"Lots of people are praying in Argentina for the return of our families. We are two countries united in pain."

Several who followed Raquel to the podium spoke

of their faith that the three women, as well as their own loved ones, would eventually be found.

"I know what these families are going through, but I have never given up . . . and I will do whatever I can to make sure that other people don't have to go through this," said Kim Swartz, whose six-year-old daughter Amber disappeared from the front yard of her suburban San Francisco Bay area home eleven years earlier.

Modesto resident Frances Sandoval held out a tiny picture of her nephew Alexander Martinez Jr., who had been missing for 15 years, and said:

"Alex Jr., if you're out there, I'm still praying. . . . Just contact us. That's all we want."

But others, like Cindy Sandlin of Chowchilla, spoke with equal emotion about her despair. She held up a poster of her son Anthony Robert, formerly a resident of the Merced suburb of Atwater. The dark-haired, dark-eyed 18-year-old had left home on a fishing trip in September of 1995 and never returned. For three years, Cindy and other family members tacked up fliers, pressed local law enforcement to redouble their search efforts, and followed their own leads, all to no avail.

"Someone's got to know something," said Sandlin. "Someone's got to do something. He was getting ready to go to college and everything. There's a hole in your heart. You're just waiting for him to come home."

Several other speakers oozed acrimony about a system that responds to publicity more often than it does to personal pain. A handful of high-profile cases got the attention of authorities. Most did not.

"If we got the publicity of President Clinton and Monica Lewinsky, we'd have all these missing children found in no time," complained Beverly Smith of Winton, another Merced suburb, where Smith's 11-year-old daughter Vanessa disappeared in 1996.

As each bereaved parent stepped to the microphone, it seemed as though the area around Merced represented a disproportionate number of missing persons cases. The outcry against the paucity of publicity in many of those cases lent considerable irony to the fact that Merced was home to perhaps the highest-profile missing person case in modern American history, prior to the sensational 1995 abduction of Petaluma's Polly Klaas.

In the case of Steven Stayner, however, most of the publicity came *after* the missing child returned to his hometown and family years later, as a young man.

Just before Christmas of 1972, a seven-year-old Merced youngster named Steven Gregory Stayner vanished on his way home from school one day. In the Stayner case, the parents posted fliers, followed leads, and begged for help from the authorities and the media alike. While local and regional newspapers and TV carried the story for a while, it did not catch on much beyond the San Joaquin Valley. Statewide and national media paid scant attention, and the saga of Steven Stayner died out altogether after a few weeks, when law enforcement concluded that the boy had either been kidnapped and killed or died in an accident far off the beaten track. It wasn't until the Stayners' missing son walked into a police station 200 miles away and more than seven years later that law enforcement, television, and newspapers began to pay attention on an exaggerated scale.

At the age of 14, Steven Stayner reappeared as Dennis Parnell, accompanied by a five-year-old named Timothy White who had been missing for over two weeks. At first, he would say nothing about his abduction seven years earlier, but over the next three weeks, little by little, Dennis Parnell became Steven Stayner once more and related a harrowing story of a convicted child molester named Kenneth Parnell, who had become his "father," and how Steven did not want the same thing happening to Timmy White. Steven said he decided to turn Timmy in to the police because Steven, too, had been abducted by Parnell—more than seven years earlier.

The remarkable story of Steven Stayner's seven-year odyssey as Parnell's captive "son" exploded across the nation as an example of hope rewarded. He returned to his family, testified in court against his former captor, and eventually became the subject of a top-rated NBC miniseries, *I Know My First Name Is Steven,* in 1989. He did not enjoy his celebrity status long, however. Five months after the premiere of the miniseries, Steven Stayner died in a Merced motorcycle accident at age 24.

"It was the biggest thing that ever happened around here for a long time," said Mike De La Cruz, the veteran police reporter for the *Merced Sun Star*. He recalled platoons of reporters from such exotic periodicals as *People* and *Newsweek* descending on Merced like killer bees. For years after Steven's return, camera crews and journalists still wandered into the front office of the *Sun Star*, asking for directions to the Stayners' home.

After Steven Stayner's death, things settled down. The city returned to its sleepy Central Valley routine, with agricultural news or stories about the nearby Castle Air Force Base generally taking precedence over crime on the front pages of the *Sun Star*, the Modesto and Fresno *Bee*s, and other valley newspapers. Occasionally, someone would disappear, like 18-year-old Anthony Robert Ardery or 11-year-old Vanessa Smith. But after a handful of articles, their names disappeared from the news columns. As far as the news media was concerned, the Sund-Pelosso case was easily the biggest missing persons incident since Steven Stayner.

If the Vigil of Hope raised any expectations, however, they were dashed by week's end.

On March 18, a carpenter who lived in a cabin near the Sierra ski settlement of Long Barn called the California Highway Patrol at their Sonora office, some fifty miles east of Modesto, with news that he'd come across an abandoned vehicle off an old logging road on a ridge near the top of the Sonora Pass. Jim Powers told the CHP it was a burnt-out car, located off of Highway 108 near Mi-wuk Village, roughly 90 miles north of El Portal. The fire had apparently burned so hot that it melted the front plastic license plate holder off of the car, so Powers took the plate back home with him to read off the numbers to the police.

By Powers's guess, it looked to be a red late-model car before it had been torched. Less than an hour later, the CHP confirmed his guess. It was the car Carole Sund had rented from Avis two days before Valentine's Day.

IV

Jimmy Powers drove a scarlet Jeep, so he knew the color red when he saw it, even after it had been through an inferno. As he wandered down a dirt logging road about a quarter mile from his cabin on a late winter afternoon in March, he noticed something different in the patchy snow. After a few moments of studying the dark mound at the bottom of the hill, Powers descended for a closer look. He recognized the ruined metallic heap by the few remaining patches of red paint that hadn't charred and bubbled to black.

Wedged against two tree stumps in a ravine about a hundred yards off of state Highway 108, in a heavily forested stand of pines and cedars, it looked like the remains of a car—a new bright red car—that had been soaked in gasoline and turned to charcoal. The area was known by the locals as an illegal dumping ground for everything from used Pampers to eviscerated refrigerators. But this was no abandoned Amana. Surrounding trees and the earth itself were scorched from a fierce fire that had apparently been lit on purpose, and not too long ago. The conflagration had been so intense that it would surely have spread had it not been set in the dead of winter, with plenty of snow to dampen the flames. Powers, 40, a self-employed carpenter, guessed that the metallic corpse he'd found in the forest was probably the missing Pontiac Grand Prix that had been popping up so regularly in the news. Just the previous evening, he'd been talking to his girlfriend about helping authorities with the search. Now he made the call to the California Highway Patrol.

"Stay where you are!" said the excited dispatcher. "Don't move!"

Once the CHP showed up and began its inspection, the FBI soon followed. Powers underwent three hours of questioning at the hands of agents and passed a voluntary lie detector test while—back at the scene of the ruined automobile—other investigators began running several hundred yards of yellow crime-scene tape around a perimeter in the forest that would eventually encompass more than a square mile, with the Grand Prix at its center.

The discovery of the car came just in time for the 11 o'clock news. For several hours following the first bulletins, there was false hope that only the car had been torched. But by Friday morning, some 18 hours after Powers first reported his find to the CHP, the

FBI announced that they had also discovered two charred bodies in the trunk of the Grand Prix.

"I was standing right next to it," a nervous Powers told *Fresno Bee* reporter Kimi Yoshino. "It was even creepier when I realized there were two bodies inside."

The FBI collected evidence from the car and surrounding area throughout the day Friday, then joined other law-enforcement agencies, some who used cadaver dogs, in an inch-by-inch search of a one-mile radius around the car. They were looking for a third body. They found none. By nightfall, they were no nearer an answer as to who might have perpetrated such a horror or how the car and only two of three bodies had gotten there.

The one item of general interest that they did find near the Grand Prix was a roll of undeveloped film that had somehow escaped damage, either from the weather or the fire. Any doubt that the investigators had located the women's ill-fated rental car evaporated when the film turned out to be holiday snapshots of Carole, Silvina, and Juli, posing and playing in the Yosemite Valley, probably taken on the very day that they disappeared. The FBI quickly turned the prints over to the Carringtons, who released them to the media, so that the world might get a glimpse of their three girls at their innocent and wholesome best.

A four-inch blanket of snow fell overnight, shutting down plans to search further on Saturday for a third body. By Saturday afternoon, leaders of the TourNap team concluded that they had done about all that they could do with the damaged car. It was time to move it. They called on tow truck operator Norm Morrison to help them lever the auto's tarp-covered remains out of the forest and onto a flatbed truck. Morrison knew the spot well enough. Several months earlier, he'd pulled a van that had been stolen in Stockton from exactly the same spot. When he mentioned the coincidence to investigators, there was a flurry of discussion, with notepads and pencils poised to take down the details, and FBI demands that Morrison produce his paperwork so agents could follow up on this latest lead.

Morrison drove the flatbed bearing the ruined Grand Prix west down Highway 108, about 15 miles, to a hangar at nearby Columbia Airport, just outside of Sonora. There, arson experts from the Bureau of Alcohol, Tobacco, and Firearms began their search for telltale chemical residues in the vehicle's burnt-out shell.

Throughout the anxious first 48 hours following Powers's discovery, the Carringtons and the Pelossos remained at the Holiday Inn in Modesto, awaiting any word on the identities of the two dead.

"We'd like to stay out of their way," Francis Carrington told reporters. "They're doing their job. They've kept us informed all the way along."

Jens Sund, who had returned to his home in Eureka, kept his three remaining children out of school on Friday. In a handwritten statement faxed to the *Bee* newspapers on Saturday night, Sund poured out his soul in a bitter lamentation about the apparent murders of his wife, daughter, and young family friend.

"The senseless waste of these precious lives is so incomprehensible I can't even begin to understand why it happened," he wrote. "They were victims of a devious, calculating criminal who most likely is still in the Yosemite area."

One puzzle that bothered immediate residents of the area where the car was found was how the Grand Prix could have been driven off the road, set afire, and never even noticed for what appeared to have been close to a month. While the logging road and the clearing where the car found its final resting place were slightly off the beaten track, Highway 108 was a busy thoroughfare, even in the winter months. Restaurants, motels, and convenience stores line much of the road, and directly across the highway from the logging road is the Odd Fellows Sierra Park, with 300 seasonal second homes, at least 50 of which are occupied year-round.

"Looked to me like whoever did it probably torched it twice," said Sonny Hernandez, an assistant chief with the Mi-Wuk/Sugar Pine Fire Department and one of the local officials the FBI called upon to help pull the Pontiac out of the ravine. "I'd guess they probably dumped it, set it on fire, and came back some time later—a few days, maybe a week or two— and set it on fire again."

Whoever the arsonist was cared as much about destroying the telltale odor of decomposing bodies as he did about destroying evidence, Hernandez conjectured. If day hikers and ski buffs who passed regularly through the area caught nothing in the wind but the scent of pine needles, there was a fair chance that no one would find it anytime soon. If Jimmy Powers hadn't obeyed an impulse to try a little target practice in the woods, the wrecked car might have remained there for months undetected.

"It makes me sick to my stomach to talk about this," Powers said a few days after his discovery. "I just want to blend in to the woods and go about my business."

On Sunday morning, the Carringtons, Pelossos, and other family members made the painful pilgrimage from Modesto to Sonora, and then up the foothills to Sierra Village. At the perimeter of the crime scene, the crowds of journalists made way for the mourners, and kept the usual barrage of daft queries about how the survivors might be feeling to a respectful minimum. Agents assigned to sentinel duty were equally gracious, guiding the family to the spot by the side of Highway 108 where the logging road descends into the woods. A spontaneous roadside shrine had already sprung up there, with flowers and cards from anonymous well-wishers assembled in a hodgepodge display beneath a mountain juniper bush.

In their own solemn ceremony, the Sund-Pelosso group trekked down to the spot where the still unidentified bodies had been found. There, they prayed.

Then they laid three vases filled with mountain wild-flowers on the scorched earth.

Later in the day, after the tape came down, media crews—including one from TV's *America's Most Wanted*—joined the curious and the compassionate in making their way down the steep, muddy path to the site where the Carringtons and the Pelossos had left their memorial. Cameras whirred. Local residents and shop owners delivered shocked, disturbed, and astonished sound bites. Networks and newspapers prepared for extended coverage.

The national appetite for the story of three innocents sacrificed to senseless savagery in the primeval setting of Yosemite seemed insatiable. *People* ran a cover story about the missing women and released it just one day too early to include the news of Powers's grisly discovery. On the Internet, a newly developed website detailing every available morsel about the Sund-Pelosso case was getting thousands of hits each week. Sunday evening's network newscasts led with the sorrowful story.

The news the following day that dental records had identified Carole Sund as one of the two bodies found in the trunk came as anticlimactic. By mid-week, the second body had been identified also, as that of 16-year-old Silvina Pelosso. All that remained to complete this phase of the mystery was the discovery of the whereabouts of Juli Sund. Francis and Carole Carrington still held on to the slender shred of hope that their beloved granddaughter might be held captive by her abductors: hurt, injured, abused, tortured . . . but alive.

Knowing that it would mean the key break in the case, for better or worse, the Carringtons had posted a $50,000 reward back in early March for anyone who found the missing car. Jim Powers took no pleasure in claiming the money. When he finally mustered the courage to call the grieving couple to identify himself as the man who found the Grand Prix, he got their answering machine and he could barely keep his own voice from cracking as he left his message.

Three weeks later, Powers collected his $50,000 reward—money that he said he would use to fund his children's college educations.

Try as they might, the FBI could tie neither Billy Joe Strange nor Darrell Stephens to the torched Grand Prix or its two unfortunate occupants. Stephens had a solid alibi for his whereabouts on the night and day after the disappearance, and lab analysis of the items taken from Billy Joe's cabin and van, including the bloodstained carpet, yielded no evidence of any crime.

The El Portal roommates did not fit the bill. But several weeks earlier, before the car had been discovered, the FBI had already begun hauling in other felons who probably could.

Most of the new round of potential suspects were united by a history of petty crime that inevitably escalated to bigger and badder things; an itinerant lifestyle that seemed to hover around the seedier parts of Modesto; and a taste for the cheap, addictive high delivered by methamphetamine, aka speed, "poor man's cocaine," or crank—the nickname Hell's Angels gave the drug a generation ago when it was smuggled as contraband in the crankcases of their motorcycles.

The first crankster to step into the TourNap dragnet was Eugene Earl Dykes, arrested March 5 near Hatch and Carpenter roads in southwest Modesto. A desperate Dykes had a gun and a girl with him, was still high, and knew what would happen if he opened the door when his parole officer came looking for him. After a two-and-a-half-hour standoff with Stanislaus County sheriff's deputies and state parole officials, Dykes finally surrendered peacefully. He was charged with violating his parole by possessing a gun and a non-narcotic controlled substance. Then he was hauled off to the county jail.

Also known as "Rufus," the 32-year-old Dykes looked the part of a typical white supremacist hothead: hooded eyelids, jutting chin, short prison haircut, a permanent sneer, and a Mephistophelian goatee. With a string of felonies dating back more than 15 years, Dykes had been in and out of state prison since he turned 18, and spent the next four years in San Quentin for statutory rape. In 1986, he was sent up again for five years after being convicted on forgery and false imprisonment charges. In 1992, a parole agent called him a "danger to the community." By the time he stood off police the first week of March 1999, Rufus Dykes had spent most of his adult life behind bars, bouncing right back into jail mere months, sometimes weeks, after being discharged.

While nobody had been injured in the March 5 incident, FBI agents quickly showed a keen interest in Rufus Dykes. For starters, he'd only recently been released from his latest stint in state prison, and his history was that of an ex-con who just could not stay out of trouble for more than a few days. On January 26, he left Deuel Vocational Institute in Tracy, less than an hour's drive from Modesto. By the FBI's reasoning, three weeks was more than enough time for Dykes to find his way up Highway 140 to El Portal and get himself in the biggest jam of his life the day after Valentine's Day.

"If they only listened to me from the beginning," Dykes later told the Associated Press. "I told them I didn't do it."

Dykes began his many interviews with the FBI by flatly denying any knowledge of the Sund-Pelosso disappearances. When the questioning persisted, he tried bargaining with his captors, offering up information on unrelated crimes he'd heard about, either on the street or in the joint. Uppermost in Dykes's mind was the specter of California's new "three strikes" law, which could theoretically send some chronic misfit like himself away for life. He had already established himself in the eyes of the law as a career criminal. Winning a little favor from the FBI when his parole revocation came up for hearing could prove to be invaluable.

But the FBI wasn't interested in hearing about the petty crimes Dykes wanted to share with them. They were only interested in the Sund-Pelosso case.

Dykes grew weary of their hounding. After a while, he had a change of heart. Maybe he did remember abducting the three tourists after all.

When agents assured him "everything would be a walk" once he came clean, provided he did not actually kill any of the women, Dykes switched his initial story and told agents what they wanted to hear.

But his story kept changing. First he was in one place, then another. He couldn't keep it straight. Nevertheless, his FBI handlers seemed more eager than circumspect about what they were hearing pour out of his mouth. For his part, Dykes knew his confession would eventually appear to be bogus, so he enjoyed the moment, spinning the tale as far as he could take it.

The jail scuttlebutt was that no bullets had been used in the murders, so Dykes deduced that the only other logical way that the three women were likely to have been done in was with a knife, and that's what he told them.

Eventually, Dykes even abandoned their admonition about participating in the actual murders and signed a confession, implicating himself in the slashing of Carole Sund's throat. As icing on the cake, he added that he'd disposed of Carole's body in a remote mountain spot. The confession had enough cachet to win Dykes repeated field trips outside of jail. Agents drove him all over the Sierra foothills, trying to jar his drug-addled memory as to exactly where he'd dumped the body.

"I'd tell them to stop and I'd get out. Then I'd say, 'Nope, this doesn't look familiar,'" he recalled.

After several fruitless trips, the FBI agents got miffed and had Dykes transferred from the Fresno County Jail to Corcoran State Prison, formally charging him with the parole violations that had landed him behind bars again in the first place. He was returned to state prison March 16, just two days before Jim Powers stumbled across the burnt-out chassis of Carole Sund's rented Grand Prix. Within days of that discovery, the agents were back, demanding more answers from Rufus Dykes, and he was more than happy to oblige. It was a game of blindman's bluff that would last through the entire spring and well into the summer.

The same day that the FBI returned Rufus Dykes to prison, his half brother, Michael Roy Larwick, found himself in even more trouble, following his own fourteen-hour standoff with police. Unlike Dykes, Larwick did not give up peacefully. In the wee hours of the morning on March 17, Larwick grudgingly surrendered to Modesto police after shooting an officer in the groin and barricading himself in a house.

Hairy and hippie-looking, Larwick resembled a

wild-eyed mountain man. With beard, mustache, tattoos on both arms, and long, stringy flyaway hair, he had a remote resemblance to Charles Manson in his prime. Larwick, 42, was the visual opposite of his shorn and Aryan-appearing younger half brother. Dykes and Larwick shared the same mother, but each had a different father. Larwick, who was ten years older than Dykes, was born and lived most of his early years in the community of Long Barn, where his father, Leroy Larwick, gained a kind of questionable local celebrity as one of two men who claimed to authorities that they had witnessed the legendary Bigfoot wandering up in the woods around state Highway 108. Long Barn was located about a half mile north of the logging road where Jimmy Powers found Carole Sund's incinerated Grand Prix.

Michael "Mick" Larwick had a criminal record that was even longer than his half brother's, dating back nearly 25 years. It began with a 1976 conviction for stabbing a rival in the back 11 times with a seven-inch knife after discovering that the man had slept with his girlfriend. Following his release on that attempted manslaughter conviction, Larwick was again arrested and sent back to prison—this time for kidnapping his former sister-in-law and raping her in front of her two young children. Since then, his arrests and convictions had run the gamut from receiving stolen goods and possessing narcotics to child molesting and attempting to flee a peace officer. Throughout his long criminal career, Larwick always seemed to have an arsenal of illegal firearms handy, from stolen .44 Magnums to sawed-off shot-guns. In 1989, he was even indicted for possessing a rocket launcher.

But his most recent troubles stemmed from a flurry of traffic citations that might not have mush-roomed into a police shooting incident if he had not routinely ignored them. By December of 1998, his driving without a license, carrying no insurance, and four different failures to appear, coupled with a cita-tion for possession of methamphetamine . . . and his failure to appear on any of the charges, finally got a Tuolumne County municipal court judge good and angry. He issued a $20,000 bench warrant for Lar-wick's arrest.

Still, Larwick eluded the cops.

Three months passed before Modesto police of-ficer Steve Silva pulled up behind a bright yellow Camaro with Michael Larwick behind the wheel on the afternoon of March 16. A quick radio check indi-cated that the Camaro had an expired auto regis-tration, so Silva turned on his flashing red lights. Instead of pulling over, Larwick hit the gas. A few blocks later, the Camaro ran into another car and limped into a convenience store parking lot. Silva pulled up in his squad car, blocking Larwick's exit.

Larwick leaped out of the Camaro, pulled a gun from his belt, and began firing. Thirty spent bullets were later recovered. One round hit Silva in the crotch, but he'd already called for backup and the chase was on. Other officers hollered at Larwick to drop the gun, but he turned and raced off into a residential subdivision instead, finally holing up in a house at 3300 Bridle Path Lane, just a few blocks from the Briggsmore-Tully intersection where Carole Sund's wallet had been discovered.

For the next twelve hours, Larwick barricaded himself in the house, alternately shrieking that he would never go back to prison and that he would do whatever he had to do to stay out. When police tossed him a portable phone to try to get him to talk to a negotiator, Larwick tossed the phone right back at them. At 3 A.M., police ended the standoff by shooting tear gas grenades into the house. Larwick came out the back door, wheezing and weeping. Police wrestled him to the ground and he was back in custody, this time held on $1 million bail.

The following week, as forensics experts under FBI supervision were sifting through the wreckage of Carole Sund's torched Grand Prix in an empty Columbia Airport hangar, other investigators searched Larwick's Modesto residence for evidence that might link him or his half brother to the kidnapping and murder of the three Yosemite tourists. Reporters who asked the Modesto police about the FBI's interest in Dykes and Larwick were directed right back to TourNap headquarters.

While the FBI remained mum, other law enforcement sources leaked a morsel to CBS News that seemed to explain the focus on the half brothers. A mystery woman who allegedly knew both men had attempted to use a number on one of the credit cards that had been found in Carole Sund's discarded bill-fold, the network reported. While neither police nor FBI would elaborate on the woman's identity, or how she and the two half brothers might be linked to the Sund-Pelosso case, it did explain why Dykes and Larwick were targets of nonstop interrogation.

Unlike his obliging younger brother, however, Mick Larwick was adamant that he did not kill Carole Sund, Juli Sund, or Silvina Pelosso.

"I ain't got anything to do with this," he said in a jailhouse interview with a correspondent from CBS affiliate KJEO-TV in Fresno. "I done a lot of things. I'm no angel. But you've got the wrong guy."

Larwick agreed to give samples of saliva, hair, blood . . . whatever the FBI might need to corroborate his story. He did all kinds of horrible things in his life, he said, but he did not kill total strangers.

"I volunteered my DNA, you know," Larwick said. "I don't have no reason not to. I'm sorry about that family and what happened to those people. OK? That's not me."

On March 22, James Maddock held his last daily news conference on what had now become the Sund-Pelosso double homicide case, not simply the Yosemite tourist kidnapping, or TourNap, case. He released seven of the bittersweet holiday photos that had been developed from the film found near the burnt-out Grand Prix, and reconfirmed that dental records had shown one of the two bodies to be that of Carole Sund.

But Maddock would not say whether the two half

brothers that the FBI and local authorities now had in custody on parole violations had anything to do with the crimes.

"No suspects have been identified," he said. "We still don't know where the crime was committed. We still don't know who did it."

Nor did he know who sent an anonymous letter that arrived at the FBI's Modesto office three days later, but it seemed at first that it could have come from Mick Larwick. Although postmarked March 15, three days before Larwick's shootout with police, it didn't arrive until March 24 because of a delivery error. There was no return address; just taunting directions scrawled on a sheet of paper, torn from a spiral notebook. Throughout the letter, the author referred to himself and his cohorts as "we," indicating to FBI agents what they had long surmised: that more than one person abducted Carole Sund and the two girls.

The taunting letter with the line, "We had our way with her," contained a map that told agents exactly where to look to find the raped and ruined body of 15-year-old Juli Sund.

V

Up a steep incline off of Highway 49, over-
looking the southern end of the Don Pedro Reser-
voir, James Maddock and his growing team of
TourNap investigators found the remains of Juli
Sund. It was a sad, overcast morning, the 25th day of
March.

Her limp, bloated body was located just where the
anonymous letter said it would be: under a poison
oak bush, partially hidden by branches on a hill
above the "Vista Point" parking lot. Her ankles had
been bound with duct tape and her arms neatly
folded across her chest. The searchers had been here
before, but had apparently neglected to check that
particular spot on the hill. Perhaps it was that it was
just too public, too out in the open. No killer would
try to hide a body there, practically in plain sight.

There were no signs of struggle. The only truly
horrifying difference between this particular body

and those of occasional drug overdose cases that the medical examiner's office picked up off the side roads and backwaters of Tuolomne County was that this one was nearly separated from its head. Juli's assailant had slashed her throat from ear to ear with such force that only a few inches of flesh kept her from being a victim of decapitation. Whoever killed the hapless young woman was both merciless and mighty in his actions. The killer was most likely a man—or one especially bloodthirsty male from among a group of men. It was probably not a woman who killed Juli Sund, for she had been raped.

Again, the yellow homicide investigation tape went up, barring news media and others from entering the crime scene, and again, investigators brought in dogs—not to search for another body this time, but to sniff for any kind of clue that could give the slippery Sund-Pelosso case a motive, a solid lead, a clearly indictable suspect. Six weeks had passed, and now the FBI had only one sure answer to the many questions that had been raised since the disappearance was first reported, back on February 16: all three women had been savagely murdered and at least one of them had been raped.

But why?

The best piece of evidence that the task force had going for it was the very thing that led them to Juli's body in the first place: an anonymous letter that someone handled and, perhaps, used his or her saliva to seal. There was a possibility of fingerprints, DNA, and a postmark that might lead them to a postal employee who remembered a street postal box where such a letter might have been deposited or, better yet, someone who brought the letter into the post office itself. A physical description of such a person, perhaps. A sign. A clue. A cunning killer's telltale mistake.

All slim possibilities, but possibilities nonetheless. The news media smelled a story in how the FBI had managed to locate the body after weeks of fruitless effort, but James Maddock wasn't talking. Was it Jim Powers again? Did he lead investigators to Juli just as he had led them to the scorched remains of the Pontiac Grand Prix? The FBI quickly batted down such absurd conjecture, but refused any further hint as to how agents suddenly knew that the pretty young cheerleader's body could be found in the underbrush on a hill overlooking the Don Pedro Reservoir.

Whoever sent the letter knew why Juli and her mother and her Argentine friend died. It might have been for sex. It might have been for money. It might have been the grave result of a drug-induced orgy. But someone had motive, someone had means, and someone had opportunity, and Maddock's crew aimed to find out who that someone was.

Spring had come to El Portal, and businesses started gearing up for an influx of fly fishermen, day hikers, and early vacationers. Despite the unwanted notoriety, Cedar Lodge no longer had a forest of satellite dishes parked out in the front lot, and most tourists had not canceled their reservations, despite dire TV predictions that tourism would diminish due to the Sund-Pelosso case. Over four million people visited Yosemite annually. It looked as though 1999 was going to be no different from previous years.

On March 20, Cedar Lodge rehired handyman Cary Stayner, who had been laid off in January, a couple of weeks before all the brouhaha surrounding the disappearance of the three tourists.

"He says hello and does his job and is very courteous and doesn't bother nobody," said Billy Joe Strange's girlfriend, Becky Buttermore, who was now living alone in the trailer park cabin she once shared with Billy Joe and Darrell Stephens.

Like other seasonal help who had grown used to the ups and downs of resort employment, Stayner had not given up his $90-a-month apartment over the lodge restaurant, knowing that his job would return along with a change in the weather and new crowds of Yosemite sightseers. Like many of his coworkers, he kept busy reading, hiking, and exploring the Yosemite wilderness during his off-time.

"Nice guy. No problems. Knew everyone," recalled Jesse Houtz, one of the co-owners of the Cedar Lodge Restaurant. "Would hang out at the bar, keep to himself, drink an occasional rum and Coke."

Stayner didn't even like to drink much, and when he did, got drunk easily. When a boozing tourist bought rounds one evening, Stayner reluctantly accepted the freebie, only to complain to a friend the next day that he felt awful. Occasionally talk at the bar turned to the incredible disappearance and death of the three tourists, but if Stayner had any opinions, he kept them to himself.

He also visited a nudist colony.

"When you're nude, to some degree, you're already communicating a certain openness just by virtue of willing to be nude in front of a lot of strangers," said Patty Sailors, who comanaged the Laguna del Sol clothing-optional resort near Wilton, in the wide-open farm country southeast of Sacramento. Cary Stayner was more than happy to display his openness.

Patty and her husband, Steven, had been operating the resort for six years, and recognized Cary Stayner as a customer from as far back as 1996. While he was not a regular member, Stayner did make the two-hour drive north from Yosemite two or three times a year. He registered in the front office, camped out by the lake next to his International Scout, and kicked back in the buff like most everyone else. To Sailors's knowledge, he never gave in to impulses to grab, touch, or otherwise come on to anyone. He wasn't threatening. He did not try to be aggressively seductive.

In the evenings, he'd occasionally mix and mingle at the clubhouse overlooking the lake, drawing considerable attention from the women, given his rugged good looks and tall, buffed-out body. One of the resort's regulars, Jan Ronne, saw Stayner and made a mental note. He was far younger and better looking than the average male at Laguna del Sol, who tended to be gray, sagging, and way past middle age.

Patty Sailors, who heard in a nanosecond from other patrons—especially the women—if anyone behaved rudely or made unwanted advances, never received a negative comment about Cary Stayner. If anything, he was viewed as an enlightened young man who had discovered the healthy, freeing benefits of doffing one's clothing long before most sun worshipers ever did. The typical Laguna del Sol patrons were couples between the ages of 40 and 60 who were well-educated, middle class, had raised families, and were looking for something new and intriguing to do with the rest of their lives. Cary Stayner, on the other hand, was 37, still single, had only a high school education, and tended to be a loner . . . though he did have a girlfriend who did not choose to join him during his Laguna visits.

Back in El Portal, Cary Stayner made no effort to hide his sunny quest for the perfect all-over tan. In addition to hiking and reading, Stayner also liked to strip and lay on a rock next to the Merced River, near a hairpin turn on Highway 140. Located about two miles west of Cedar Lodge at a spot known to locals as the "Two-Five" because of a yellow caution sign advising motorists to slow to 25 miles per hour, the bend in the river was a favorite spot for local nature lovers to swim au naturel and then dry out in the buff on the rocks. Stayner visited often, caring little if anyone saw him from up on the highway. If he flashed a family coming 'round the bend in their RV, it could even be mildly amusing to consider the shock value they might have in seeing a naked mountain man—like a hairless version of Bigfoot—right out there in the open.

At Cedar Lodge, KGO radio reporter Mary Ellen Geist recalled sharing a soak in the hotel hot tub with Stayner late one evening in March while she was covering the Sund-Pelosso story. He wore a black bikini bathing suit and chatted about his brother, Steven, after introducing himself as Cary Stayner.

Steven Stayner, he explained, was the young boy who gained national attention after he had been kidnapped in 1972 and held captive by a convicted sex offender until his escape in 1980. As Cary retold the story, Geist grew increasingly uncomfortable. She couldn't put her finger on it, but there was something about her hot tub companion that left her cold.

"He seemed to want to elicit some sort of sympathetic response from me and I remember just literally jumping, sort of, out of the hot tub," said Geist. "He hadn't done anything in particular, but I became very nervous." She excused herself and headed quickly to her room.

"I ran up the steps, double-bolted my door, and pushed a table and chairs against it," she said. "I got the creeps."

Daily press briefings had ended, but that didn't mean Maddock and his agents were idle. While there were no public statements, the FBI still hinted broadly that the deaths of Carole, Juli, and Silvina might have been the result of a prison gang on an out-of-control crank holiday. By month's end, local police and agents had hauled in for FBI questioning at least eight more parole violators besides half brothers Michael Larwick and Eugene Dykes.

At 21, Johnny Nolan Jr. was the youngest of the bunch. While the Modesto man's first and only stint in state prison was for a 1996 robbery, Nolan had been released and returned to Deuel Vocational Institute twice—most recently on a February 26, 1999, parole violation. He appeared to have a promising criminal career ahead of him.

Others among the group were veterans. On the morning of March 26, FBI agents and Stanislaus County Sheriff's officials pulled six-foot-five Larry Duane Utley "butt naked" from a home in the Modesto suburb of Keyes. Two neighbors and Utley's former housemate, Mike Bradley, said officers and agents showed up at about 7:30 A.M. at the house where Utley was attempting a trial reconciliation with a girlfriend. Agents handcuffed the nude 41-year-old convicted sex offender and his grown son Brian and ordered them both out of the house, forcing them to lie down on the front lawn. They let the elder Utley go back inside to put some clothes on, but subsequently arrested him for possession and sale of a controlled substance and failure to register as a sex offender.

But law enforcement—especially the FBI—were not nearly so concerned with Utley's drug use or his sex life as with his connections to Michael Larwick.

Utley said he knew Larwick, but that was all. He was even willing to take a lie detector test to show he had nothing to do with the Sund-Pelosso murders—a test he eventually did take and pass.

At Stanislaus County Jail, they went ahead and booked Utley, then released him on $12,000 bail.

But when Utley returned to Bradley's house, he found that the FBI still didn't believe his story. Agents had hauled away his bed. When they returned it several days later, Utley complained he found fingerprint dust smeared all over his mattress and bedsheets.

Another parole violator authorities caught in their March sweep was 32-year-old Jeffrey Wayne Keeney, who led police and FBI agents on a brief chase through a Turlock neighborhood, some 15 miles south of Modesto. Keeney was on his way to visit his young son when he noticed he was being followed. He took off on foot. He'd been ducking his parole officer for several days and he figured he was being dogged once more by his case workers. He was surprised when it turned out that the FBI was coming down on him like a ton of bricks.

As had been the case with Larry Utley, police and agents arrested Keeney on a drug charge before quizzing him incessantly about his acquaintance with Larwick. Although Keeney maintained that he wasn't Larwick's friend, he did admit to meeting him once or twice.

Like Larwick, Keeney had been in and out of prison and the Tuolumne County jail most of his adult life. He kicked off his criminal career at age 19 in 1986 by firing a rifle at a Stanislaus County couple during a robbery. He got four years for that offense and followed it through the years with convictions for grand theft, evading a police officer, causing great bodily injury, and drug possession.

Also like Larwick, Keeney took and passed a lie detector test and voluntarily provided a sample of pubic hair for investigators. No one ever accused him in the Sund-Pelosso slayings, but Keeney said, "they treated me like I was a suspect." He cooperated, he told one newspaper reporter, because he was not involved and wanted to clear himself.

"I had nothing to do with it," Keeney said. "I have no idea why they connected me with that. I've done a lot of things, but I could never do something like that. My morals are good, you know what I mean? I was brought up right."

Despite his morals and his cooperation, Keeney was still held without bail in the Stanislaus County Jail.

The FBI's interest in Larwick, Dykes, and most of the ex-cons they hung around with stemmed in part from their relationship to a 36-year-old Modesto woman whom investigators believed had somehow come into possession of Carole Sund's Wells Fargo checking account ID number.

Twice in the five days after Carole's billfold insert had been discarded on the streets of Modesto, someone had tried to gain access to her bank account.

With Wells Fargo's help, agents began flagging suspicious calls that had been made to the bank's toll-free number on those two days, in an effort to sift out who had made the Sund account inquiries. Unfortunately, the list Wells Fargo gave them to winnow through contained more than 800,000 telephone numbers.

Then, in an unrelated case, investigators thought they might have gotten a break.

Rachel Lou Campbell and her roommate, Ben Alex Paiz, were accomplished forgers who used sophisticated equipment to bilk hundreds of thousands of dollars from individuals and businesses in the San Joaquin Valley, according to the *Sacramento Bee*. From February 1998 to February 1999, the pair allegedly stole checks from the mail, deposited them into bank accounts opened under false names, and wrote their own checks on the accounts, either to themselves or for merchandise. They had a thriving business in stolen credit cards too, according to a 75-count indictment handed down by a federal grand jury in Sacramento. The couple also possessed counterfeit postal service keys, according to the indictment—keys that fit postal lock boxes and drawers in both Stanislaus and San Joaquin counties.

While a task force investigating the mail theft scheme searched Campbell's residence, they were surprised to come across information that they believed had come from Carole Sund's check ID and ATM cards. At the time of the search, Campbell made "incriminating statements" linking herself to

Rufus Dykes and Mick Larwick, though she herself was not a suspect in the slayings, a federal source told the *Bee*.

Modesto attorney Frank Carson denied that his client made any such statements, that she had possession of Sund's account numbers, or that she was involved in the case in any way. While Campbell "might have some peripheral knowledge" of the suspects, she "knows nothing about any murder," he said.

Nevertheless, Campbell was jailed and named a key witness in the ongoing murder investigation, and became one of the first to appear before a federal grand jury convened in Fresno the first week of April to begin taking testimony in the Sund-Pelosso murders.

VI

Nearly 200 people gathered under gray skies on Monday, March 28, at the foot of the steep hillside, overlooking Lake Don Pedro, where the FBI had recovered Juli Sund's body. Some wore shorts and T-shirts, and some brought lunch for the quickly-organized memorial service. One woman burned sage to sweeten the air and clear the place of negative energy. There were several toddlers in the crowd and at least one man brought his dog. Were it not clearly a solemn occasion, punctuated by shaky choruses of "Amazing Grace" and "Swing Low, Sweet Chariot," the gathering might easily have been mistaken for an early Easter Sunday picnic.

The ever-present news cameras lined up behind, in front of, and among the mourners. To get a better view, one reporter trampled a bouquet left at the serendipitous monument that had blossomed at the foot of the hill. Another shouted a rude question

at Francis Carrington as he approached the makeshift shrine: What comment did Juli's grandfather
have about the KMPH-TV report the previous evening quoting a "high-level source" who tied the three
murders to the Chicken Ranch Bingo and Casino
near Jamestown?

Carrington sighed his response, tired and worn out
from a nonstop journalistic barrage that had begun
weeks earlier and showed no signs of slowing. Sure,
he'd heard the latest rumor that the three women had
been last seen at the bingo parlor, but then he'd heard
most of the rumors that had spread unchecked through
the media since the first week following their disappearance. The rumors, he said tersely, and with as
much dignity as he could muster, had been rico-
cheting since day one. Virtually all had proven base-
less and utterly untrue.

The Carringtons had grown quick to listen but
slow to believe all that they heard and read about
their daughter and granddaughter's disappearance
and untimely passing.

Beyond the bingo parlor story, no less a purveyor
of truth than CBS News reported during the last
week of March that the FBI had "three to four suspects in custody." They were "sexual predators"
linked to a woman who attempted to use Carole
Sund's credit card, and were known to stalk hotels
and motels trolling for female victims, according to
the network. While CBS got much of the story right,
there were enough flaws in it for the FBI's Nick Rossi
to quickly deny its accuracy. No woman had been

arrested for using Carole's credit card, he announced to the media, and no arrests had been made in the case. A reluctantly chastened CBS followed up its original report with: "The FBI is saying today that reports about arrests, or dramatic new theories about suspects, are not accurate. However, they have not said which reports are false."

CBS was present for Juli's memorial, as were NBC, ABC, CNN, and more than a hundred representatives of every other major news outlet in the nation. Before the public and the press were invited beyond the police barricades, however, the Carringtons were allowed to join Juli's other relatives, along with Silvina's mother Raquel and father Jose, and her older sister Paula, in a private memorial ceremony. Accompanied by FBI Chaplain Mark O'Sullivan, a handful of agents, and a few volunteers, the Sund and Pelosso families planted tulips, daisies, and an Easter lily in Juli's memory. Then they tearfully embraced each other on the asphalt plateau overlooking Lake Don Pedro. O'Sullivan read a short prayer entreating God to grant justice for the victims and peace to their survivors.

"These things before us are confusing," he said. "Give us peace . . . take the anxiety from us."

After the private service, O'Sullivan extended the families' thanks to the swelling crowd. Then the victims' relatives briefly mingled with well-wishers, accepting hugs and hands, tears, and notes of condolence. The spot where the Carringtons had planted their flowers was soon festooned with flowers, memorabilia, and greeting cards—most addressed in present tense to the late Juli Sund. Total strangers stood side by side with those who had known Juli, weeping, heads bowed, expressing sorrow, shock, and outrage. Even members of the news media maintained a respectful, if brief, hush to their incessant questions. All the mourners, strangers and family alike, found a sad bond in grief.

"We've been following this since the beginning," said Penny Morford of Modesto. "I'm a mother and a grandmother and just can't imagine this. My heart goes out to the family. It's horrible. You just can't believe it."

By midmorning, the news cameras were gone, the crowd had dispersed, and the sun came out, glinting eerily off the still waters of Lake Don Pedro, and illuminating the Mylar balloons, smiling stuffed animals, and gaily wrapped and ribboned flowerpots that decorated one corner of the parking lot.

Juli's father didn't attend the memorial service. Jens Sund had no desire to visit the place where his daughter's body had been discovered. Ironically, he'd stood at the Don Pedro vista parking lot early in the search for the three missing travelers. He didn't climb the grassy knoll then, and he vowed that he would not do so now.

Jens did hold a news conference in his family's hometown that gray Sunday in March. Before making his first public appearance in weeks, he reflected with the *Fresno Bee* 's Mike Kirkorian on how overwhelmed he was with the simplest tasks: rousing his three younger children for breakfast, getting them off to school or soccer practice, shopping for groceries, taking his younger daughter to the orthodontist to have her braces removed. The balance in his life was gone. He would instinctively reach for the phone sometimes, thinking he should call Carole, and half believing that he might get to hear her voice again at the other end of the line.

"Not only is Carole my wife, she is the unequivocal manager and leader of our family. I am heading into uncharted territory," he had written some days earlier in a special article published in the *Bee*.

Despite his grief, Jens showed no ambivalence about administering the death penalty. When they finally caught the killers, he would gladly pull the lever, he told reporters during his press briefing. He had just finished writing the obituaries for his daughter and his wife. No father, he observed, should have to write his own daughter's obituary.

"I'm dealing with emotions that I've been told to expect, yet when they happen to me they are completely unexpected. It is bizarre and unusual," he said before setting out with his media guests on an impromptu tour of the five-bedroom home where Juli grew up.

Juli's room was silent, where it once rang with the twitters and chatter of a nonstop parade of teenage girls. Her father described her as "boisterous, loud, and fun-loving . . . constantly looking forward to something new to challenge her."

Jens stood in the middle of the room, wearing Juli's emerald-green Humboldt All-Stars fleece jacket. His daughter had been a pianist for seven years and played violin for five. She was a member of the city orchestra and had recently taken up guitar.

But there had been no music spilling out of her room for weeks—only the excruciating silence of a life cut short. Juli had just finished applying for a driver's license before the trip to Yosemite. She had become a young woman, but she still collected dolls. Her grandmother had a few that she planned to contribute to Juli's ever-expanding collection, but the sentiment had come too late. The dolls remained in boxes in the Carringtons' closet, prompting Carole Carrington to openly lament that she had not given them to Juli sooner.

The obligatory poster of Leonardo DiCaprio was pinned to one wall of her room, but mostly it was decorated with photos of Juli and her pals. In the margins of the pictures, most of her buds had scribbled "best friends forever." One of her high school chums recalled for Jens how his daughter had written individual notes to every single one of her friends at the close of the previous school year and put them in their lockers, telling each how wonderful they were and how much she loved them.

"You could see Juli coming down the hall at you from a mile away," said her friend. "She was so happy all the time, always smiling."

If there was any of Jens's brooding Danish blood in Juli Sund, no one could recall it ever surfacing.

Jens Sund parsed through her library: *Far From the Madding Crowd*, *Jane Eyre*, a pile of John Grisham mysteries . . .

He didn't even know about "Juliana's Giant Scrapbook" until after she had vanished and he started going through the things in her room. He found newspaper articles in the thick, aptly named scrapbook of souvenirs, photos, and clippings that told of another missing Eureka girl named Karen Mitchell, as well as a story about the student awareness group, Girls Against Violence, that Juli helped launch at Eureka High after two of her own friends had been raped by a knife-wielding stranger not far from the Sunds' home. Deeper inside the scrapbook was a bar of soap she had saved from a 1996 family outing to Yosemite, and five ticket stubs from *Titanic*.

Jens recalled a child who had been irrepressible from day one. At six months, he claimed that Juli tumbled from her crib early one morning and crawled into her parents' bedroom.

"A month later, she started walking and running," he said. "She never stopped."

Juli got her restless energy and stubborn determination from her mother, mused Jens. Even as a sophomore in high school, Juli reminded Jens of Carole, whose own fiery temperament first attracted him when they were both still teenagers back at Montgomery High in Santa Rosa. During the early 1970s, Jens wasn't exactly aimless, but his demeanor was far more pensive than that of his future wife. His mother came from El Salvador while his Danish father was a retired commercial painter, and some of their laid-back laissez-faire disposition rubbed off on Jens, his two brothers, and his sister. Jens wore a long beard, drove a van with Spiderman painted on the side, and made a rueful first impression on his future in-laws. In time, he lost the beard, traded in the van for more conservative wheels, and gained the unconditional respect and support of the Carringtons.

But not before his Carole went through her own rebellious period. The third of five Carrington children, whose family real estate business generated millions, Carole had been born to wealth. Yet she and Jens refused at first to be a part of her parents' business and chose instead to make it on their own. Carole breezed through an undergraduate business course at San Francisco State University before taking her state real estate license at the age of 21. The Sunds were married that same year, in 1978, and spent their honeymoon at Yosemite. Francis and Carole Carrington paid for the first night at the baronial and exclusive Ahwahnee Hotel; the rest of their stay, they were on their own, just the way Carole wanted it.

It was Carole who wanted to carve out her place in the business world. She took a job in real estate outside of her family's business while Jens dropped out of college to drive a beer truck.

"We were maybe a little reckless," Jens recalled to *People* magazine.

Carole was the fireball of the family. She wanted

no children. She planned to beat her father and mother at their own game, and in the rough-and-tumble real estate business, there was no time nor room for babies. Then she got pregnant, and the Sunds' whole world changed.

"They had Juli, and then they just fell in love with being parents," recalled her mother and namesake, Carole Carrington.

Just as vehemently as she had denied maternity before giving birth, Carole Sund totally embraced the whole concept of children, children's rights, and raising the very best possible family after Juli came into their lives.

"As a mother, Carole was passionate, fierce as a tigress," said Valerie Bish, a close family friend who came to know Carole in the late 1980s when the two were first becoming activists on behalf of abused and neglected children.

Bish recalled first meeting Sund at a "mom and kids" potluck lunch at the Sunds' Eureka home. Carole grinned when she saw Valerie at the door, looking her best, with earrings and lipstick, even though she had five kids in tow. Laid-back and unpretentious, Carole instantly recognized a comrade-in-arms. Valerie and Carole both loved kids but still had enough self-respect not to let the rigors of motherhood transform them into faded flowers. Both women eventually became foster mothers and adopted three children each.

Like Carole, Valerie took parenting as seriously as

a stockbroker takes the Dow Jones Industrial Average. The two of them studied the nuances and techniques of being the best possible parent, even though Juli was the only one of the Sund brood to whom Carole had actually given birth. She and Jens adopted their first son, Jonah, less than a year after Carole had Juli, and their second daughter, Regina, a year after that. By the time they adopted Jimmy in 1989, the Sunds had become well-respected movers and shakers in the underappreciated world of adoption and child advocacy.

Carole sat on the board of the Council on Adoptable Children for more than a decade, and eventually became such a champion for abused and abandoned children that she and Valerie joined Eureka's Court Appointed Special Advocate (CASA) program, taking on the task of reviewing child welfare records to uncover abusive parents as well as negligent or incompetent social workers. Carole's will made generous contributions to three child welfare agencies. Jens told those who asked how to remember his wife to contribute to organizations that helped abused and neglected children.

"When I read those tabloid stories about mothers who, in a rush of adrenaline, lift five-ton trucks off their trapped toddlers, I think of her," Bish recalled.

Busy as her schedule was, Carole Sund still spent hours volunteering in each of her children's schools. She kept all of her kids as active as she was, shuttling all four to weekend soccer games, swim meets, and basketball camps. She also served on a safety committee for schoolchildren and was active with Butler Valley Inc., a nonprofit agency that runs two group homes for developmentally disabled adults. When most of Carole's Eureka neighbors opposed the opening of a methadone clinic in town, she supported it.

"Those people need help too," she said.

Ironically, Carole and Juli had both been enrolled in self-defense courses, and Carole got a canister of pepper spray as a gift at Christmas. Despite her nearly maniacal obsession with being prepared for crime or catastrophe, Carole took neither the pepper spray nor her cell phone with her on the Yosemite trip.

She had also taken an evening class for parents of teenagers when Juli passed through puberty, and became so enthused that she took the required training to begin teaching the class herself.

Carole "was the kind of mom who would be late for her own appointment to make sure you got home safe," said Juli's friend and fellow Eureka High sophomore Sarah Johnstone. "She was a very caring mom."

The Sund family's loss wasn't theirs alone. The entire tight-knit community of Eureka suffered. Teams of counselors were imported to the high school to help Juli's classmates cope. The local television station produced a one-hour special to air upon the return of the two Eureka women's bodies for their burial. And two weeks after the discovery of Juli's body, the town turned out for the first of three memorials: one in Eureka, another to be held in Sonora on April 11, and the last communal farewell, scheduled for the following evening in Modesto.

While Sacred Heart Church in Eureka had seating for 850, hundreds more were expected, so large-screen televisions were set up under a tent in the parking lot, with shuttle service offered between the church and the county fairgrounds.

Scores of photos filled the lobby, tracing Carole and Juli's lives from infancy to the final set of snapshots that had been taken in Yosemite Valley on Valentine's Day. Next to a photo of Juli and Silvina, sitting on a bridge over the Merced River, were poems Juli had written.

Unfortunately, in its collective rush for sound bites and visuals, the media phalanx was, once again, less interested in being in everyone's heart than in getting in everyone's face. As people entered the church, two TV cameramen got into a shoving match inside, each trying to get a shot of Francis Carrington. Much to the disgust of those in attendance, other cameramen further distinguished themselves by clogging the church's tiny lobby to such a degree that Carole Carrington couldn't even get inside.

"This is bizarre," she remarked. "It is somewhere between a dream and a nightmare."

When the two-and-a-half-hour "celebration of life" ceremony actually got under way shortly after 2 P.M., more than 1,000 people had crowded into pews, sat on folding chairs, and stood along the stained-glass walls.

Following the invocation, Monsignor Thomas Keys of the Star of the Valley Church in Santa Rosa, who had known the Carringtons for 15 years, set an upbeat theme for the occasion, imagining how Juli and Carole would address their friends and neighbors.

"I think they would say, 'We went to Yosemite to be with God and beauty. We went to revel in the peace and tranquility. We were celebrating with friends and family, and we discovered a little bit of heaven. And though our journey in life came to an abrupt end, do not be sad, for we will meet again.'"

Throughout the service, there was as much laughter as tears—an opportunity to celebrate the lives of the fallen rather than to grieve. More than two dozen people took the microphone to talk, sing, and offer prayers. When 13-year-old Gina Sund stood at the pulpit, she spoke of her mother and sister as the closest people on Earth to her, and how—in her most desperate moment—they were not there to comfort her. They still looked out for her, though.

"So when you see me on the street or in the store, don't be sad," she said. "Think about my mother and sister and smile."

Juli's classmates changed the words to the sentimental 1960s Dion anthem, "Abraham, Martin and John," substituting the names of Carole, Juli, and Silvina, and bringing lumps to the throats of all who listened.

Bruce Hancock, who had known the Sunds for more than a decade, told how Carole had taken a chance on his daughter, who was recovering from a serious addiction problem. Carole gave her a job and once again tapped into her maternal instincts, advising and watching over Hancock's daughter until the girl's untimely death from an illness.

"More than 2,000 years ago, Sophocles wrote 'one must wait until the evening to see how splendid the day has been,'" Hancock said. He looked upward for a moment and added: "Carole, your life has been a splendid day."

Juli's best friend Emily Oehler offered a bittersweet story of how the two bonded when they were both fourth-grade misfits, not among the playground's social elite. It began with a fashion statement.

"I was in the bathroom before school started, and this girl came in wearing multicolored pants, a velvet turtleneck, a leather jacket, and black cowboy boots, and it was absolutely the best thing that ever happened to me," she said, half laughing, half crying.

And the eulogists kept coming to the front of the church, one after another, quoting Robert Frost, Mother Teresa, and Shakespeare. They read from the Bible and Henry Wadsworth Longfellow. They recalled moments. They wept. They chuckled. The same theme Jens delivered to those who asked him personally how to remember his wife and child resonated throughout the service: If there was a lesson to be learned from their lives, it was to give unto others—especially children.

"I know that Carole would want everyone to go out and do something good, something nice for somebody, especially a child," said Carole Carrington. "This whole experience is going to make me a better person."

Monsignor Keys again took the podium for the benediction, after more than two hours of emotional ups and downs.

"Tonight," he said, "as you look above at the sky that is over Eureka, Yosemite, and Argentina, say a special prayer for Carole, Juli, and Silvina. Perhaps they are not the stars in the sky, but the openings in the heavens that pour through the sky into our hearts."

In a private service the day before, on Saturday morning, the 10th of April, the Sunds and the Carringtons made a small ceremony of laying a headstone at a grave site where Carole and Juli would both be laid to rest. But only Juli had been turned over to the family. The FBI continued conducting forensic tests on the remains of Carole and Silvina, which meant that burial would have to wait. Likewise, Silvina's remains could not be returned to Cordoba until later in the month, so her parents flew back to Argentina to prepare for that sad occasion.

But the memorial tributes continued in California. Another service for the women was scheduled for 7 P.M. on Monday in Modesto. Titled "Forever in Our Hearts: A Celebration of the Lives of Juli Sund, Carole Sund, and Silvina Pelosso," it drew an even larger crowd than the Eureka tribute. Reverend Bet Hannon of the College Avenue Congregational Church began two hours of recollections, song, and prayer with:

"You have made us wish Carole and Juli and Silvina were our next-door neighbors, and indeed in a sense they have become our neighbors."

A poem 13-year-old Gina Sund wrote for her mother which had first been read at the previous month's "Vigil of Hope," was reprinted in the full-color eight-page "Forever in Our Hearts" program, distributed at the door by volunteers who wore T-shirts bearing snapshot portraits of each of the three victims. Local junior high student Marie Hafeman recited the poem for the crowd of 1,500:

Late at night I await your return
But deep in my heart I know something my mind
   doesn't want to learn
What is this thought?
Even I do not know
Soon the running river will become solid snow.

I shiver at the thought of what I might have to
   see
Whether or not my mother will be.

At a time when I need my mother's touch most,
All I see of her are pictures nailed to a post.

When it is time for bed, I rock myself to sleep
With memories of you held tight in my heart
Memories, that I will always keep.

Each day that you are gone,
A part of me has gone with you.
If you are never to return,
It will seem like I am gone, too.

I try to stay strong because I know that's what
*   you'd want your baby to be*
But mommy, I don't want you to leave me.

As she had done in the Eureka memorial, Carole Carrington turned up wearing bright spring clothes, not the dark skirts and shawls expected of those in mourning.

"I'm wearing happy colors," she said by way of explanation for her pastel blazer and light green pants. "That's the way Carole would have wanted it."

Her husband seized the opportunity to thank a community so far removed from his own for the "overflowing" love. Prior to February, he'd had little reason to visit Modesto, but once his daughter and grandchild vanished, the Carringtons and as many as 40 Sund-Carrrington relatives became an army of occupation at the local Holiday Inn, with nearly two dozen local volunteers operating phones, organizing search efforts, running errands, and distributing missing persons flyers.

"What a wonderful town," said Francis Carrington.

Again, Jens and his three surviving children did not make the trek to the Central Valley from Eureka, but several other relatives did, including his brother, Ken Sund.

"In this country, the best country in the world, with the best government in the world, we can find a way to make this a safe place," he announced, to loud applause. To that end, Sund read a petition he and his family had started that he planned to carry to the state capital, asking for tougher legislation aimed at parole violators and felons convicted of violent crimes. The Carringtons also established a $200,000 trust fund to offer rewards for information in other missing persons cases and to help families track down criminals responsible for similar abductions.

Once the song and ceremony ended, the local residents who turned out, never even having met any of the victims' families in many cases, gave their reasons to newspaper reporters as to why the Yosemite case had touched them so deeply—both in terms of sympathy and in terms of fear.

"You don't feel safe anymore," Rakkie De Guzman told the *Sacramento Bee*'s Marijke Rowlands. "Times change, and that's scary. We're here bringing out the goodness in people, despite some cruel people out there."

Peggy Rourke-Nichols said, "I want the families to know that there is good in these hills, not all bad."

And Modesto resident Kim Sauls, who came to the tribute with her parents, explained her sense of the Carringtons, the Sunds, and even the Pelossos as neighbors, not relatives of the victims of random violence who just happened to drive through town one day.

"They've become part of us," she said.

And, according to Carole Carrington, the feeling had become mutual. Following the benediction by the Reverend Paul Bodin of Emmanuel Lutheran Church, her stiff upper lip finally began to soften, as she and her husband made preparations to shut down their Holiday Inn command center and return for good to their retirement retreat in Butler Valley, near Eureka, and their three remaining grandchildren.

"I guess it's time to cry," she said. "I really can't say much. It's difficult. But I am glad we came."

VII

In Fresno, a Grand Jury began formally taking testimony on the Sund-Pelosso case during the first week of April. With a slowdown of the El Portal investigation and a general "no comment" on the FBI's findings overall, the benches outside the federal Grand Jury room became a regular Thursday morning stop for court reporters at the *Bee* as well as other newspapers. Even though proceedings were off-limits to the public and neither jurors nor prosecutors were allowed to speak about what went on behind closed doors, witnesses were not muzzled. Those who chose to talk began fleshing out a secondhand version of the FBI probe—a story that increasingly put Rufus Dykes and Mick Larwick squarely at the bull's-eye of the TourNap target.

"We will not comment on anything to do with the grand jury," said Assistant U.S. Attorney Carl Faller, chief of the Fresno office.

"Our goal is to build an airtight case," was all that the FBI's Nick Rossi would say about the investigation.

But the way the FBI and the U.S. Attorney's office seemed to be building their airtight case was by compelling an odd assortment of felons, addicts, molesters, and other pathological liars to either tell the truth to 23 sworn pillars of the community, or face the two harshest weapons in the grand jury's arsenal: contempt or perjury charges, either of which could land a reluctant or less-than-truthful witness in jail for months . . . even years. Still, investigators and prosecutors were dealing with regular methamphetamine users, many of whom could not or would not differentiate between fantasy and reality, and nearly all of whom suffered from some degree of paranoia. Getting them to talk was not easy, even with the threat of jail time hanging over their heads.

Rufus Dykes remained all too happy to talk, whether he was telling the truth or not. As he had from the beginning, he continued spinning tales for the FBI on demand—this time, from his cell in the medium-security Corcoran State Prison southwest of Fresno, where he awaited a hearing on his parole violations. The latest version of his frequently shifting story was that his half brother Mick had revealed to him that he had been the one who abducted and murdered the three tourists. Larwick had even gone so far as to give Dykes and some of the other Modesto lowlifes who comprised their crank clique several of the personal belongings of the victims, including stolen checks and a ring owned by one of the murdered women . . . or so Dykes said.

Further, Dykes claimed that the half brothers contacted a female associate—presumably Rachel Lou Campbell—and asked her to make a phony ID in Carole Sund's name so that they could cash the dead woman's checks. Another of the Dykes-Larwick group was given the task of getting rid of Carole's wallet insert by tossing it into the middle of a Modesto intersection, Dykes maintained.

But his interrogators became increasingly convinced that Dykes might have played a much larger role than he let on; that he, not Larwick, might have been the ringleader or at least his half brother's co-equal. During Dykes's lie detector test, the polygraph administrator asked if he had done any harm to Silvina. When Dykes answered "no," the machine indicated that he was lying. As the days rolled into weeks, investigators gathered further information that seemed to finger the parole violator and their star squealer as the chief predator, and not simply a voyeur who got caught up in the madness of the moment.

Adding to their theory was one of the first grand jury witnesses: Cathy Clay, a 36-year-old Modesto parolee whom authorities escorted into U.S. District Court in handcuffs and a green prison jumpsuit. Clay, who had been booked into Stanislaus County Jail on March 13 for alleged child abuse, drug possession, and a parole violation, told jurors that it was Dykes who had solicited her help in creating a fake

ID using Carole Sund's driver's license, according to the *Bee*.

Most of those subpoenaed during the first few Grand Jury sessions had roots in the Modesto crank community, huddled in dirt-poor housing near the Modesto Airport. It had become the focus of FBI activity and produced other witnesses like Cathy Clay who spoke of Dykes and Larwick giving Carole Sund's wedding ring and other jewelry to their girlfriends. When Jens told agents that his wife had left her ring at home during her Yosemite trip, the FBI switched their focus to Juli. They began confiscating jewelry and other property from Modesto-area pawn shops, as well as individuals like Terry Crabtree, one of Dykes's girlfriends, to whom he had given a diamond ring.

After investigators had finally recovered a ring that Larwick reportedly had given to the mother of his girlfriend, the investigators showed it to Carole Carrington. She said she was "80 percent sure" that it belonged to Juli. Gina Sund was even more certain, saying she was "90 percent sure" that the ring was her sister's.

Two of Dykes's other confidants, including girlfriend Maria Ledbetter, reportedly corroborated part of Cathy Clay's testimony. An acknowledged meth addict and 24-year-old mother of three, Ledbetter described how she spent much of February with Dykes, getting high and having sex. Rufus had plenty to hide, she told the news media.

"He came in and said to shut the windows and lock

the doors," Ledbetter said, recalling the day police came for Dykes, guns drawn, on his March 5 parole violation. "He handed me his gun and his knife. I went into my room and hid them in a pillowcase in the closet. I was so paranoid. We were both high."

During the two-and-a-half-hour standoff that followed as Dykes came down from his high, he phoned his father for advice on how he should surrender to police.

"I told him to go out real slow," recalled 67-year-old Burel Dykes, himself an ex-con. "No sudden moves."

Before surrendering, Rufus transferred his gun from the pillowcase to a backpack, which authorities seized after arresting Dykes, but they didn't get the switchblade which was still in the pillowcase, until they came back later with the FBI in tow.

"They waited all day to get that knife," Ledbetter said, explaining how her sister had given the knife to a friend and had to call him to get it returned before they could turn it over to the FBI. She said agents were also interested in whether or not she had seen Dykes with an ax or saw blades. Dykes usually carried another knife in addition to a gun, she told them, but nothing so cumbersome nor so gruesome as an ax or saw.

"They're trying to take our clique down," said Angelia Dale, 24, another female friend of Dykes and Larwick who was arrested for meth possession and testified only because she was threatened with jail. "They're going after us. We've all known each other for years. We all grew up on welfare. Some of us do drugs. They're trying to break us up."

She flipped reporters and photographers the bird as she entered the courthouse several weeks later to give her testimony. She flipped them off again as she was leaving, adding:

"You're all a bunch of liars."

"They've gotten a lot of people shaken up here," said another woman who emerged after one-and-a-half-hours of testimony before the grand jury, but refused to reveal her identity. "We all want to know what happened. These were three innocent people."

One potential witness who did not testify was 38-year-old Terry Ray, whose gray, waterlogged corpse was fished out of the Tuolumne River on April 6. An apparent drowning victim, he had been in the water three or four weeks, according to Stanislaus County coroner's deputies. But within hours of identifying him, questions began surfacing about Terry Ray's running buddies.

"Our investigation shows Terry Ray was associated with the cast of characters in the Sund case," Stanislaus County Sheriff's Detective Sergeant Jim Silva admitted upon some prodding from journalists. "But we don't know how close an association that is."

Federal sources confirmed that Terry Ray did business with Rachel Lou Campbell; that he made false identification cards and sold them to people like Larwick and Dykes; and that counterfeit mailbox keys that he also made allowed thieves to get into apartment mailboxes to steal bank checks and credit cards.

"Terry had about a three-inch stack of credit cards when I last saw him in February," said his 42-year-old brother, Dennis Ray. Ray described how a 17-year-old nephew told him that Terry might have been killed because he had information about Juli Sund's abductors—that Terry had seen the teenager being raped in Modesto before she died, he said.

(Like several other witnesses in the Sund-Pelosso case, Ray's 17-year-old nephew concealed his identity and remained in hiding for fear that the same thing that happened to Terry Ray might happen to him.)

"Terry went over to this house, walked into the bedroom, saw what was going on, turned around, and split," said Dennis Ray. "He wasn't into all that stuff."

Because Terry Ray spent nearly four years in prison for assault with a weapon and drug crimes, it seemed possible that he might have met Dykes, Larwick, or one of their friends in prison, according to Sergeant Silva. Ray had been on parole at the time of his disappearance in early March.

When asked if the FBI was aware that Ray was acquainted with the Modesto men, special agent Nick Rossi said: "We are in receipt of that same information, but we are treating it very cautiously. We are looking into it to see if there is a connection between Mr. Ray and this investigation. At this time we have no evidence to suggest such a link."

Terry Ray was fully clothed and there were no

punctures in the material, and an autopsy revealed no evidence of murder. A scan of Terry Ray's badly decomposed body showed no gunshot or stab wounds, Silva said.

"The most likely conclusion is that Ray tried to swim across the river and drowned before making it to the other side," Sheriff Les Weidman's office said in a news release.

Nonsense, said Dennis Ray.

"He wouldn't go swimming with his boots on," he said. "He was at the river and the lakes all the time."

More than a dozen witnesses testified during the first two weeks that the Grand Jury was empaneled, but all that emerged was a frustrating pattern of tantalizing hearsay. Investigators could not establish a solid link between the Modesto methamphetamine crowd and any credit card, checks, or other identification that belonged to Carole Sund. Some witnesses said that they saw Juli Sund and/or Silvina Pelosso being held captive in Modesto. Authorities didn't think much of these revelations, but dutifully checked them out just the same. They, too, did not pan out.

"We're not dealing with the most upstanding people here," one federal source told reporters. "But we have to do what we can with it."

FBI agents thought they had a promising lead when Maria Ledbetter's 18-year-old brother, David, an acquaintance of Dykes's, offered to tape-record a teenage girl who had been sexually involved with Dykes and claimed to have a lot of information on the case. Using FBI equipment, he taped 17-year-old Amy Wallace tearfully describing how Dykes admitted that he and another man raped and killed Carole and Silvina, took pictures of them, and kept a box of the women's possessions, including jewelry, which he gave to Wallace.

Juli, she said, may have been kept alive as a sex slave, she said.

"She was alive for a while, but the other two were dead at least a week before she was dead," said the girl.

Wallace had gone out with Dykes on February 13, spent most of Valentine's Day with him, but didn't see him at all on the following day. He showed up between 3:30 A.M. and 5 A.M. on Tuesday, February 16, Wallace said.

"We ended up partying a bit and he started cleaning his Jeep out at my brother's house," said Wallace. She claimed Dykes then told her how he had received a call from a Cedar Lodge Restaurant employee who told him about three women staying at the lodge, and they had money. Dykes called on a couple of friends and drove to El Portal, but what began as a robbery in the motel parking lot went sour quickly, he told her. After killing Carole and Silvina, he had one of his cronies dump the car and burn it, Wallace said.

But instead of simply giving the tape to investigators, David Ledbetter copied it and sold it to TV's *Hard Copy* during the second week of the grand jury investigation. He later made even more copies and sold them to other media outlets.

"Some of the stories have grains of truth," the FBI's Maddock told reporters. "Others are totally fabricated."

Cranksters began selling their stories to the highest bidder. David Ledbetter offered to trade *Hard Copy*'s taped telephone conversation to the *Fresno Bee*'s Matt Kreamer and Kimi Yoshino in exchange for a motel room and room service for him and a friend. Though the prospect of getting something more solid on Rufus Dykes than hot air was tempting, the two reporters declined. Besides upholding a long-standing *Bee* policy not to pay for information, Kreamer and Yoshino were also keenly aware that the Ledbetters did not make the most credible sources.

"I know in my heart he [Dykes] was involved," said Maria Ledbetter, who started out the morning with two 24-ounce "breakfast beers."

Others who had known Rufus all his life were not so sure.

"I don't believe my son had anything to do with it," said his father, Burel Dykes. But he added that his son might have heard stories from people who might have been involved. "He may know something, though."

When Dykes was only 3 years old his parents divorced, and he was raised mostly by his churchgoing grandmother and his truckdriver father, himself an ex-con who served twelve years in San Quentin during the 1950s for, as he put it, "everything short of murder." Once out, however, the elder Dykes never returned to prison.

A year after his grandmother died in 1980, 14-year-old Gene Dykes began his own criminal career with an arrest for burglary. He married, became a father, and divorced all before his 17th birthday. At 18, he was off to San Quentin for four years for having sex with a minor. Despite his constant run-ins with the law, neighbors who watched him grow up described the younger Dykes as a friendly kid and a hard worker—not a crazed killer.

"He's a nice guy," said 85-year-old Ellis Hopkins. "I haven't seen him in ten years, but he once did some work for us, put a pump in. We always got along."

"He's just not the type," said another neighbor. "He would have had to have been completely out of his mind."

While methamphetamine arguably had put him out of his mind when he was first taken into custody in March, Dykes was clean and sober when the FBI dropped by during their semiregular prison visits. An agent played the *Hard Copy* tape during one such visit and Dykes found the tape as laughable as the FBI man's contention that acrylic blanket fibers found on one of the victim's bodies matched fibers found in his half brother's car.

"I knew he was a liar," said Dykes, himself an expert when it came to stretching the truth so thin that it snapped.

At Dykes's suggestion, investigators had searched his Jeep Wagoneer, Larwick's Corvette, and a pickup truck that belonged to another friend. He was as surprised as they were when the FBI lab found tiny fibers that were microscopically identical to those found on and near Juli Sund's corpse, as well as on a San Jose Sharks jacket that Dykes owned.

Shortly thereafter, one federal source told the *Los Angeles Times*: "Physical evidence is going to drive this case."

Another told the Associated Press: "It was like the moon and the stars were lining up."

But Dykes kept changing his story. First, he said his only role in the murders was to take personal items from the victims. Later, he said he helped transport the bodies. After he said he killed Carole Sund with a knife, the versions became even more disparate— plausible, in most instances, but inconsistent.

The FBI believed the victims had to have been abducted or carjacked by as many as three assailants and that others, including some of the women called before the grand jury, might have been involved in a cover-up. But no one except Eugene "Rufus" Dykes would elaborate, let alone confess, and because he was unwilling or unable to lead investigators to hard evidence, doubt remained. The task force never charged Dykes, Larwick, or anyone else whom Dykes had implicated, and the investigation dragged on.

Silvina Pelosso made her final journey home to Argentina on Sunday, April 25, courtesy of Stockton philanthropist and San Diego Chargers owner Alex Spanos, who donated the use of his private jet for the flight. Carole Carrington invited a Sacramento *Bee* reporter and TV crews from *America's Most Wanted* and NBC's Sacramento affiliate KCRA-TV to join her, Jens Sund's brother Ken, FBI Chaplain Mark O'Sullivan, and the Los Angeles Argentine Counsel General Luis Kreckler in accompanying the 16-year-old's body on the overnight airlift to Cordoba.

The Pelosso family had already returned to Argentina on an earlier flight to begin arrangements for Silvina's funeral mass. With the bitterest irony, Raquel Pelosso told reporters before she left:

"The only thing I was afraid of for Silvina on her trip was earthquakes in California."

In Cordoba, Argentina's second-largest city, where the prominent Pelosso family operated a very successful soft drink distributorship, the sad occasion took on the trappings of a national tragedy. Police cordoned off downtown streets to accommodate the throngs as neighbors and Silvina's classmates crowded the funeral home to pay their respects.

"We're at the end of a very painful story for us all," Silvina's father Jose Pelosso told reporters. "But finally Silvina is going to be able to rest in peace. Having Silvina here is a huge relief."

The funeral itself was conducted on Tuesday, April 27, in Las Varillas, a tiny community of 16,000 about 110 miles from Cordoba. It was there that

Silvina's mother, Raquel, grew up. It was also where, a generation earlier, a teenager named Carole Carrington bonded with a young Raquel Cucco during the first six months of Carole's senior year in high school.

In 1973, the same year that Argentine dictator Juan Peron returned to power after an 18-year exile, Carole traveled to Argentina as part of a student-exchange program called Youth for Understanding. Despite political turmoil, frequent assassinations, and the Carringtons' lingering misgivings about Argentina's tendency toward military fascism, Carole fell in love with the pampas and the Patagonian outback.

Carole Carrington, who referred to her daughter in her premarried days as Little Carole in order to avoid confusion, said, "It was very traumatic for us to have her go away, but you know, you want your kids to grow up."

Little Carole found something else in Argentina—a lifelong friend. Raquel, the daughter of the Cucco family, who sponsored her Las Varillas sojourn, remained in touch with Carole long after each of them had married and become parents themselves. In 1984, a year after Juli was born, Carole and Jens Sund visited Argentina and took pictures while they were there of their daughter playing with Raquel's baby girl, Silvina Pelosso.

"Fourteen years ago, she had her personality already well established, at the age of eighteen months," Jens recalled. Silvina was sweet, shy, polite, and "far more bright and aware of what life demanded than our own North American teenagers," he said.

"Underneath this 16-year-old, shy, reserved teenager's exterior is a fiercely determined, ecologically aware, global-thinking Argentine, whose maturity surprises the average American adult. Yet she is only a normal high school sophomore."

Hours before the funeral began in Las Varillas, hundreds of mourners departed from Cordoba over rough roads in order to get there in time. Wearing their school uniform of blue skirts, white blouses, and red neckties, Silvina's classmates from the Villa Eucaristica school climbed into a covered truck for the two-hour journey. On the way, they passed around Silvina's picture and swapped stories about Silvina's fascination with going to America.

"She was like any young person thinking about all the possibilities," said her friend Mariana Costamagna.

She planned to study biology at a university in Argentina after her return. She planned to pick up where she'd left off, and continue her hobby, skating down at the Cordoba roller rink. She hoped to win more trophies in dance competitions, like the ones she'd won before she left, rocking out to the music of the Spice Girls and New Kids on the Block.

But her classmates who came to Las Varillas to grieve for Silvina understood that none of that was ever going to happen. Life would not resume as expected for Silvina or for any of those she left behind. Sixteen-year-old Clivia Claros said she thought constantly about how much she wanted Silvina's killers found and punished. The tattoo drummed in the Argentine press was an indignant demand for justice.

"This crime has the American seal all over. It has the perversity of crimes that are committed in this country. I don't think Argentines are used to this sort of crime," said Marina Gilbert, a reporter for *El Clarin*, one of Argentina's largest daily newspapers.

Argentine Consul General Luis Maria Kreckler echoed that same theme of angry and bewildered retribution in his eulogy.

"Silvina is resting with her grandfather now," he said. "Now the story is about the investigation. We hope it will finish as soon as possible. From the Argentine point of view, we want justice."

As cathedral bells tolled in the rural farming town, more than a thousand people packed the Nuestra Señora de Rosario church to pay their final respects. They spilled out into the town plaza as Silvina's white wooden casket lay before a vast tile mosaic of angels in clouds.

During the brief service, FBI Chaplain O'Sullivan prayed that the people of Argentina could "heal from all the pain that has been caused by the loss of this beautiful daughter."

Carole Carrington stood at Raquel Pelosso's side during most of the ceremony, wiping tears with a white handkerchief. Chaplain O'Sullivan held Raquel's arm as pallbearers carried Silvina's coffin, draped in purple, red, and white flowers, to the cemetery. The lead pallbearer, Jose Pelosso, wept gently as the crowd cleared a path to the Cucco family vault and Silvina Pelosso, 16, was laid to rest.

"They didn't deserve it," observed a tearful Carole Carrington. "They didn't deserve anything. Those two girls were the sweetest girls in the world. . . ."

VIII

After using the media for more than three months to spread the word about the FBI's unprecedented efforts in the Sund-Pelosso case, FBI Special Agent in Charge James Maddock had shut reporters completely out of the information loop by the first of May.

While strongly hinting that all the culprits had been rounded up and returned to prison on a variety of parole violations, there still were no indictments nor any promise as to when any would be handed down. The TourNap command center at Modesto's Doubletree Hotel closed, and most of the agents retreated to the main FBI offices in Sacramento or Fresno before month's end. The FBI's hotline, that invited tips and delivered a taped daily update on case developments to anyone who called, often went for days without being changed. Case spokesman Agent Nick Rossi, who once invited press inquiries now openly discouraged journalists from trying to milk him for new information.

The Grand Jury still met each Thursday morning at the Fresno Federal Courthouse, and the focus of the investigation still seemed to revolve around Rufus Dykes and Mick Larwick, the two half brothers from Modesto, but only Dykes was in a confessing mood. Larwick still maintained his absolute innocence.

Larwick's preliminary hearing on the attempted murder of officer Steve Silva and a host of other charges stemming from his 14-hour standoff went off as scheduled in May with no hint that the shaggy felon might have had any role whatsoever in the Sund-Pelosso murders. In fact, the attorney who appeared on Larwick's behalf told reporters repeatedly that his client was not involved in any way.

"Until they find who did it, everybody who has committed any violent crimes in this area is going to be a suspect," said Deputy Public Defender Gary Smith. "My client is innocent. I've talked to him. I've talked to his sister. I believe he probably is innocent."

With his bushy beard and tattoos, Larwick looked the part of an outlaw biker. He loved Harley-Davidson motorcycles, and even aspired to join the Hells Angels at one time, though he was never invited to become a member. When he was loaded, Larwick behaved like the irresponsible, reckless criminal that methamphetamine had turned him into, but those who knew him insisted he was not the kind of monster who could kidnap, rape, torture, murder, and burn three innocent women.

"That's not in Mike," said his cousin Patty Black. "That's not Mike. He's been in and out of jail for years. But like I said, those are things from his family. He wouldn't [cause harm] to a stranger and hurt anybody. He's more of a helpful person."

"He was good people," said Trudy Kay Northern, who had been acquainted with Larwick for several years. "I've seen him burn a lot of bridges, but that was because of the drugs."

The press was not appeased by the Thursday morning trickle of Dykes/Larwick news that occasionally dribbled from a Grand Jury witness. With the Carringtons guesting on a host of shows ranging from *Oprah* to *Good Morning America*, and *People* carrying the tragic disappearance of the three women as a cover story, the mystery had become a national obsession, and the appetite for tidbits about the FBI's progress became insatiable.

Three theories kept leaking from local law enforcement and finding their way into speculative stories that appeared in newspapers throughout the spring, from San Francisco to Los Angeles. All of them featured the Dykes/Larwick group in a central role, but each had them vanishing from a different place:

> #1 – the three women had been kidnapped or carjacked in Modesto, where they had been scheduled to catch their plane to San Francisco;

#2 – they took a wrong turn and veered deep into Tuolumne County, where they met with foul play and their bodies were ultimately found;

#3 – they were kidnapped from the Cedar Lodge in El Portal, where they left behind a few personal belongings in their room as if they planned to come back or were interrupted during packing.

In pursuit of this last and still most viable theory, the FBI returned yet again to El Portal, and the starting point for all the investigations that had developed to date: Cedar Lodge. Since they first arrived in February, agents had developed considerable skepticism about the regular patrons who ate at the restaurant and drank at the bar, as well as the irregular employees like Billy Joe Strange and Darrell Stephens, who worked in the pastoral setting but partied hard and heavy elsewhere in El Portal. Investigators began to understand what some residents meant when they referred tongue-in-cheek to Cedar Lodge as "Speeder Lodge."

"I'm sure the guy who owns the place doesn't have any idea what some are doing," one unidentified El Portal resident told the *Modesto Bee*. "If he did, they wouldn't be working there anymore."

The third week of May, agents were back in town, recanvassing, retracing and reinterviewing. On May 19, agents interviewed handyman Cary Stayner yet again, this time at his girlfriend's home. Again, he calmly laid out exactly where he'd been the week the women disappeared. No one noticed that he'd lost fifteen pounds since his first interview, that he was sweating, or that a cauldron of molten anxiety might underlie his bashful, easygoing exterior.

"He was the boy next door," one law enforcement source later said.

Investigators moved on to the next name on their reinterview list with the same nil result, and so on, and so on, and so on. . . .

A week later, Cedar Lodge's management asked Stayner to help agents with the investigation. He opened every door of the lodge with his universal maintenance key and stood by as investigators searched for a dark pink blanket with fibers similar to ones found on Juli Sund's body. The FBI wanted to see if those fibers were a match with fibers found in Rufus Dykes's Jeep Wagoneer or Michael Larwick's Corvette.

Stanislaus County Sheriff's deputies arrested Larry Duane Utley on Thursday, May 27, in what appeared at first blush to be a major break in the TourNap case. The tall, heavyset speed freak pal of Larwick and Dykes, who had been among eight witnesses called before the Grand Jury on April 15, was booked and held on $100,000 bail for alleged kidnapping and conspiracy . . . but not, as it turned out, in the Sund-Pelosso case.

During the same February weekend that the three women vanished, Utley and several friends took $200 and an ATM card from a man at gunpoint, and held him captive for three days at Utley's Modesto

quently, they rebuilt them with the use and sale of methamphetamine.

Morrison witnessed a close friend who did not run afoul of the law, but still died of the drug. The former lawman explained that methamphetamine "makes you lose all perspective."

"He was holding down three jobs at once," Morrison recalled of his dead friend. "He was paranoid, angry all the time, and he started shooting up because snorting it hurt his nose and made his teeth ache. Those are two of your body's frontline defense signals that maybe the stuff you're sniffing is toxic. But by shooting it into a vein, you bypass those natural defenses."

A crankster in a meth euphoria is convinced that his ability to concentrate has been raised exponentially when, in fact, the opposite is true, said Morrison. Addicts busy themselves irrationally, almost as if they suffer from a sped-up form of obsessive-compulsive disorder—washing dishes over and over, or buffing the same two or three tiles until they gleam while ignoring the rest of the floor.

"What'll happen is they'll keep finding spots that need to be cleaned up, even if the spots aren't there at all," said Morrison.

If Carole Sund, Silvina, and Juli were taken by cranksters, he said, there was no telling what might have happened to them, because a crank party can quickly escalate way beyond anyone's control, especially if sex is involved. In addition, their lack of sleep plays havoc with the cranksters' sense of time, as well as their version of reality, so that everything they recall during the time they were experiencing a meth high can be suspect.

"These guys are pathologically incapable of telling a straight story," said one federal official, echoing the FBI's James Maddock in his own explanation for why the Sund-Pelosso investigation began like a jackrabbit and seemed to be finishing at a tortoise's pace.

"The problem is that many of the people we are dealing with as potential witnesses are members of a crankster circle," he said. "They deal in the methamphetamine trade, and they have a lot of baggage."

But the FBI remained undaunted. As May turned into June, the crankster roundup continued.

On June 6, Modesto police aided a parole agent in arresting Rufus Dykes's ex-cellmate, Kenneth Alan Stewart. Known in prison by the nickname "Soldier," 24-year-old Stewart surrendered in a prearranged meeting at the trailer of one of his relatives at the Colony Estates Mobile Home Park. Soldier was held on two counts of attempted murder and a parole violation, stemming from a February 6 incident when Dykes stood by while Stewart allegedly stabbed a 37-year-old ex-con in the back. He also fired a pistol at the victim, but missed. The whole incident stemmed from a disagreement that the men had among themselves while they were in prison together.

The victim refused at first to cooperate with police, but other witnesses came forward and he eventually relented. Witnesses also named Dykes as at least an accessory after the fact. While investigators hoped Soldier's arrest would step up pressure for him to spill the beans on the Yosemite slayings, Stewart revealed nothing that helped. Family members later claimed that Stewart was in Idaho when the three women vanished—an alibi that apparently checked out, to the FBI's satisfaction as well as its frustration.

Two days later on June 8, 54-year-old Paul Candler landed in Jefferson County Jail in Birmingham, Alabama—a fugitive from California, where a warrant awaited him as a felon in possession of a firearm and making terrorist threats against his own mother. A second warrant from Tuolumne County charged Candler with arson and a second count of firearm possession.

A Fresno television station reported that Candler, who lived in the Merced suburb of Atwater, had property on Grizzly Road, approximately a mile from the spot overlooking Lake Don Pedro where Juli Sund's body was discovered. Again, the FBI reluctantly went public to rein in media speculation.

"The charges against Mr. Candler are not based on any information gathered in the Sund-Pelosso investigation," the FBI's Rossi assured the Associated Press. "He may be included in the very large pool of people that we wish to speak to in this case. But even if he is, that is not the reason for his arrest."

For his part, James Maddock refused to discuss any details, but said his agents had made significant strides in solving the murders of Carole, Juli, and Silvina.

"We're making substantial progress and have come a long way to putting this together. While we have a ways to go, I am completely confident that we'll have a prosecutable case against those responsible," he said.

With the seasons changing yet again—this time, from spring to summer—the TourNap task force had mounds of conflicting testimony from dozens of witnesses, but precious little hard evidence linking any of them to the abductions and murders. Outside of the many conflicting morsels of information that dribbled from the Grand Jury, their case rested upon a handful of matching microscopic fibers: a slender set of threads upon which to build a homicide indictment. Investigators still weren't sure where the kidnapping and killing occurred, what became of the murder weapons, what the motive might have been, exactly who their suspects were, and what precise role each might have played.

The FBI played a stalling game with the media.

"I do feel we have all of the main players in jail, but we are in no rush to charge them," said James Maddock.

Asked who those main players were, official spokesman Nick Rossi also tried to balance public optimism with the Bureau's private confusion.

"We've said from the beginning of this investigation that we're not going to identify suspects by name until all of the facts have been established and charges have been filed."

The investigators' chief guide through those murky few days in February between the tourists' vanishing act and their subsequent deaths at the hands of predators remained Rufus Dykes—and his story shifted more frequently than the San Andreas Fault.

"In his own warped mind, he's trying to shift the ultimate moral responsibility to someone else," rationalized one investigator who had tried pinning down Dykes's tale.

With his prison record, though, Dykes felt as though he had very little to lose by toying with his captors. The worst they could nail him for would be perjury and, given his violent past, that would amount to the lowest-octane brand of felony.

"I didn't kill anybody," Dykes told Associated Press reporter Christine Hanley from a glass booth at Deuel Vocational Institute, where he had been transferred into protective custody. "If I was involved, it wasn't through my knowledge. . . ."

While he was professing innocence to the news media, he still gave differing accounts to his FBI handlers. But even a malicious game player like Rufus Dykes grew weary of running the police around in circles. Finally, even Rufus threw up his hands.

"I gave you guys 80 stories," he told the FBI. "I don't have any more."

* * *

By July, a stolid sense of calm had settled over the Sund-Pelosso murder case.

Television and newspapers had generally moved on to other stories— the end of the war in Kosovo, the shocking death of JFK Jr. . . .

The Sund and Carrington families had accepted their own tragic losses with dignity and all the grace that their chronic grief would allow. Following through on their own activist philosophy, Francis and Carole Carrington put their full efforts into promoting the victims' rights foundation that they had created in their daughter's name. Carole accepted an invitation to testify before Congress on the issues raised by her daughter's and granddaughter's kidnapping and killing. She believed Carole and Juli died as a result of some random act of violence. They must have been surprised rather than lured into danger, surmised Mrs. Carrington. Her daughter would never have given in without putting up a fight. She and her husband remained confident that investigators were on the right track with Dykes and Larwick.

"As long as there's progress being made, I can't complain," said Francis Carrington. "We're going to go through hell when they arrest these people, and we're going to go through hell during the trial, but we still need it. We have to have it."

Following a family briefing with the FBI, Carrington said reports that those responsible might be in custody had made the wait for justice a little easier.

"In my own heart I feel it's them, and that it was

drug-induced," he said. "These guys take methamphetamine and stay awake for three or four days and then all of a sudden they just snap, and do something crazy. . . . You're dealing with dynamite."

Jens Sund had taken up running, both to handle the stress of single parenthood and to assuage his personal pain from the cosmic body blow that Fate had dealt him and his family. He no longer talked much to the press.

Then, just as everything appeared to be winding toward a conclusion, an unsettling news bulletin roared out of El Portal and into living rooms across America during the last few days of July: the body of pretty blond naturalist Joie Armstrong was found partially submerged in a drainage ditch outside her home, just inside the gates of Yosemite National Park, no more than five miles from Cedar Lodge. She had been decapitated.

IX

Her parents divorced when she was still a toddler, her half brother was dealing cocaine by the time he turned 18, but in her own life, Joie Armstrong seemed to be doing just about everything right.

"She made boys swoon and girls want to be her friend," Orlando artist Kim Fox recalled in speaking of the effervescent young strawberry blonde with the big brown eyes, who felt equally at ease scaling the sheer granite face of El Capitan during a hot summer's day or toe-dancing to *Swan Lake* on the vast front lawn of her ramshackle Yosemite cabin.

Tara Reinertson, who worked with Armstrong in Marin County just before Joie joined the Yosemite Institute, remembered her dancing through life.

"Oh, it's *so* good to see you!" Joie would say whenever a friend showed up on her front porch. Then she'd finish off the greeting with a bear hug, an offer of a goblet of red wine, and a seat on her front steps, beneath a blanket of stars. On birthdays, it was Joie who reciprocated with her own neighborly visit, turning up on her friend's front porch bearing a blazing chocolate cake. When there was the inevitable breakup with a boyfriend, pitched battle with family over some imagined slight, or disagreement with a boss at work, it was Joie who offered solace either over the phone or simply by popping by with her patented apple-cheeked grin, scratching at the screen door.

"One time when I was feeling sad she came over with a present," recalled Tara. "It was a handmade magic wand, a green velvet star on the end of a stick."

It wasn't much different after she took the job with Yosemite Institute in December of 1998 and moved into the tiny but tight community of Foresta a few months later, situated in a secluded alpine valley a few miles from El Portal, at the western entrance to Yosemite. On a clear night, she could be glimpsed on her front lawn, dancing beneath the stars, spinning like the planets, according to Reinertson.

She remained a sprite who faced up to her deepest fears but still loved to act a little wacky. She wore rings on nearly every finger and a dark green malachite pendant around her neck. She'd confound her dates by wearing pink retro dresses with Red Wing combat boots.

Earlier in July, Armstrong had climbed a third of the way up the face of El Capitan, slept suspended overnight, and then told her mother afterwards that it had been only the fifth time she had ever gone rock climbing. She had practiced dangling from a sling in a tree in her yard, suspending herself like a cocoon to get the hang of it. Once, she spoke to her mother about reading up on how to keep from sliding down the side of an ice mountain.

"Joie, are you scared?" Leslie Armstrong asked her daughter.

"Oh yeah!" she answered.

But she remained undaunted, according to Mrs. Armstrong.

"She just tackled everything," she recalled.

No goody two-shoes, Joie could hold her own with the guys, either pounding down shooters at the Cedar Lodge bar or trekking through the wilderness wearing a full backpack, as she had done in the spring when she hiked up the snowy north-facing side of Mt. Shasta. But she could also buck the tomboy image and knock the boys out of their socks when she chose to dress up for a night out. Her long blond hair, high rosy cheeks, and ever-present smile made her glow in a crowd.

She was also a teacher—a passionate environmentalist who naturally gravitated toward the ecological crucible that is Yosemite Valley, accepting a job there just before Christmas.

"I have nothing but superlatives to describe Joie," said John Carlstroem, executive director of the Marin Headlands Institute, where Armstrong taught for two years before going to work for its sister organization at Yosemite. "She was an amazingly good science teacher and naturalist."

After several months of living in temporary quarters at Yosemite, she had taken up permanent residence in May, intent on staying there and branding the land and its visitors with her own love of nature. During her brief life, Joie Armstrong soared like the hawks and falcons she could easily identify by Latin or laymen's terminology for her students at the Yosemite Institute.

"She said that because she taught young women and encouraged them to be independent and strong, she wanted to be independent and strong," said her new neighbor, Ann Abbott Matteson, who counseled her to embrace the vast Yosemite wilderness where she had chosen to settle and not to fear it.

Her friend Kim Fox, who first got to know an urban Armstrong years earlier when they both worked together behind the counter at Barnie's Coffee & Tea at Orlando's Florida Mall, recalled a transformed Joie sending e-mail from the Sierras. On July 16, she raved to Fox about the vegetable garden she had planted outside her wood-frame cabin.

"You should come see this place. I love the big meadow with all its daisies and incredible history. . . . I also love my garden and living in Yosemite—one of the most beautiful places in the whole wide world."

Joie and her live-in boyfriend Michael Raffaeli had recently made a romantic trip to a waterfall in the park.

"It was straight out of a dream," she had written.

Five days later, Joie Ruth Armstrong's dream had turned into a nightmare.

On Wednesday evening, July 21, the 26-year-old biologist left her job in Yosemite Valley about 5 P.M., driving to the three-bedroom cottage with the broad front porch that she shared with Raffaeli and another roommate. The three lived in an enclave of about 30 cabins on Foresta Road in an area not frequented by tourists, south of the Crane Flat campground, but her two roomies were away—Michael, preparing to take some youngsters on an Outward Bound wilderness experience, and another roommate, on other business.

Home alone for the first time since moving there, Armstrong had been invited to sleep over at a friend's place, but decided to conquer her own irrational fears and stay there by herself. She'd gotten through one night just fine and now planned to make a little trip to the coast to see an old friend during the rest of Raffaeli's time away. She flipped on the stereo, began packing her white Toyota truck for a weekend in Sausalito, and phoned her boss's wife to say she would drop by with some work files before she left for the town across the bay from San Francisco. But something happened between 6:30 P.M. and 7:30 P.M. and Joie never showed up with the files.

Sonny Montague, who was married to Joie's supervisor at the Yosemite Institute, got a little worried and made the five-minute walk to Armstrong's cabin. The stereo was still on, the front and back doors were ajar, and Joie's truck was still parked out front, but Joie was nowhere to be found. The fading sun cast shadows among the stand of fir trees at the back of the cabin, and the faint, dewy odor of burnt pine wood hung in the air—a daily reminder of a seasons-old forest fire that once nearly consumed this provincial sanctuary.

As a billion stars began gathering and glittering in the evening air, the hundreds of acres of knee-deep dry grass and forest answered with silence each time Montague called out Joie's name. The area was so still that the occasional approaching car could be heard a half mile away. Anywhere else, the vacuous quiet might be interpreted as spooky, but this was Yosemite.

As Sonny stepped from porch to road to yard, the solitary sound of her own footsteps brushing through the grass or crunching the gravel at nightfall held a grand resonance of the forest in each echo—comforting, not forbidding. After a few minutes of getting no answer, Montague gave up and returned home. A wide open front door and the fact that Joie left the stereo blaring were no reasons for a neighbor to panic in the laid-back atmosphere of Yosemite.

A member of the Yosemite Fire Department, who happened by Armstrong's cabin at around the same time as Sonny Montague, recalled the following day that he had seen a white-over-light-blue International Scout parked nearby. He had no reason to stop to see who it might be though, so he drove on.

A few hours after Sonny had dropped by for the

work files, another Yosemite employee recalled picking up a hitchhiker several miles away on Highway 140, east of El Portal but just outside the park itself. The hitchhiker stood next to a white-over-light-blue International Scout that he said had broken down on the way back from Yosemite Valley. He'd gone there to get some "decent food," he said. The park employee told the young man to hop in and drove him to Cedar Lodge, where he said he lived.

Another Cedar Lodge handyman recalled seeing Cary Stayner come in a back door near the swimming pool at about 9 P.M. Later on, around midnight, when the handyman got off work, he drove home on Highway 140 toward Mariposa. As he passed the Two-Five curve of the Merced River, where many of the El Portal nature lovers often went skinny dipping, he noticed Stayner's distinctive white and blue International Scout parked at the side of the road. A bright moon was out, and the fiery July weather still hung warm and heavy in the air, even after midnight. As he passed by, Stayner's coworker figured Cary must be down at his watering hole, washing his naked body cool and clean by the light of the moon.

Joie's Sausalito friend, who had come to know her when they both worked at the Headlands Institute, grew sufficiently worried when Armstrong had not shown up by 3 A.M. She called the Sausalito police, assuring them that it was not like Joie to dawdle or fail to call to warn that she might be late. Her friend filed a missing persons report and later called Joie's mother, Leslie Armstrong.

"As soon as it got light, we were able to begin mounting a search where her residence is," said National Park Service spokesman Kendell Thompson on Thursday.

By 7:30 A.M., a dozen park rangers had been dispatched to Armstrong's cabin, and encountered the same scene that Sonny Montague had found the night before: her truck was packed for the trip, her front door was open, and her stereo was still on. Though there was no sign of a struggle or forced entry, a pair of men's sunglasses were found on the floor of her living room, bent and damaged as if they had been crushed. The sunglasses, they would later learn, did not belong to Armstrong, Raffaeli, or the third roommate.

About 1:30 P.M., searchers stumbled upon Joie Armstrong's body, partially submerged in a drainage ditch just a few hundred yards from her cabin. A wound on her right wrist "appears to be a cut indicative of a defensive wound," investigators wrote in their reports, but while they were fairly certain Joie had put up one hell of a fight before she died, there was a gruesome problem with the body that had to be dealt with before any other evidence was gathered. Her head was missing.

Joie Armstrong had about 80 neighbors up and down Foresta Road, living in 35 different housing units. Park rangers who were shortly joined by Mariposa County sheriff's deputies and FBI agents for a total of about 50 investigators, began by questioning those who lived nearby while they continued to comb the area around the cabin for clues.

One of the first to speak up that morning was the fireman who had seen a blue-on-white sport utility vehicle parked near the cabin the previous evening. A "Be on the Lookout" alert was broadcast to law enforcement agencies in an effort to locate and identify the driver. At about 4:30 P.M., Yosemite park rangers Bonnie Schwartz and Ruth Middlecamp found him.

The pair had been dispatched to investigate a report of an International Scout matching the SUV's description, but because it was parked by the side of Highway 140 at a sharp bend in the road just beyond their Yosemite Park jurisdiction, the two rangers called on the Mariposa County Sheriff's Department for assistance.

While Middlecamp played the backup role and waited behind, Sheriff's Detective Cathi Sarno joined Schwartz, and the two women edged down the gently sloping escarpment to the bend in the Merced River known around El Portal as the Two-Five. There they found a tall, athletic, sandy-haired man sitting on the riverbank like a self-absorbed Adonis, nude and smoking a joint. They confiscated his marijuana and began questioning him.

His name was Cary Stayner, he said. Yes, he had ID and was happy to share it with the two officers. He worked at Cedar Lodge as a kind of jack-of-all-trades, repairing everything from light fixtures to broken windows. He'd been there for nearly two years. His credentials would check out. He was no drifter who had simply floated in and out of Yosemite. This place was his home, and Thursday was his day off. He was kicking back, enjoying the sun, relaxing, getting an all-over tan . . . something he did often enough, to which anyone would readily attest back at Cedar Lodge.

He hadn't been anywhere near the Crane Flat area either on this day or on the previous evening, Stayner told the officers. He was confused as to what they might be looking for, but was perfectly happy to let the two women inspect his truck. But, he said, he drew the line at his dark green Jansport backpack. They could not look in there.

Sarno and Schwartz were adamant: they would take the backpack now and simply obtain a search warrant later if he refused to cooperate. Exchanging glances, both officers were thinking the same thing: the backpack was just about the right size and weight to contain a human head.

Stayner finally relented. He let them look, but instead of Joie Armstrong's incriminating head, the two officers found only an eclectic collection of items suited to a day trip to the river: a Polaroid camera, an X-Acto knife, a harmonica, a Corona beer, a package of sunflower seeds, Visine eyedrops, a package of Zig-Zag cigarette papers, a lighter, and a red Tupperware container.

There was one more item tucked inside that might have been the cause of Stayner's high anxiety. It was a paperback copy of *Black Lightning*, a bestselling 1995 novel by horror and mystery author John Saul, about a serial murderer who stalked women in Seattle. Had either officer been more familiar with Saul's generally horrifying plot lines and graphic descriptions of hideous violence, they might have arrested Stayner on the spot and held him for further questioning. A summary of the 438-page *Black Lightning* reads like a preposterous and skillfully contrived, but absorbing blueprint for serial murder (don't finish reading the summary if you don't want to know the book's ending!):

The novel begins with the story of intrepid Seattle newspaper reporter Anne Jeffers, who is present at the execution of serial killer Richard Kraven, a highly respected college professor/mad scientist who stands accused of brutal murder across several states. Kraven anesthetizes his victims, then slices them open with a power saw to extract their still-beating hearts in a clumsy attempt to see if life can continue minus the key organ.

For five years, the heroine Anne Jeffers doggedly details Kraven's killing career, intent on seeing him executed for his misdeeds. When he is finally caught clear across the country in Connecticut, Kraven insists to Jeffers that he is innocent. Further, he tells her she will suffer once he's gone. At the very moment Kraven is executed on the East Coast, Jeffers's husband suffers a near fatal heart attack back in Seattle. To Anne's horror, Glen Jeffers returns from the hospital literally a new man: he has been possessed by the black soul of the newly executed Richard Kraven.

Soon thereafter, power saw murders just like Kraven's begin happening once again. Because they occur near Jeffers's Seattle home, suspicion falls on Glen. But the copycat killer turns out instead to be Richard Kraven's younger brother, Rory Kraven, acting out a lifelong grudge because his mother idolized Richard and never paid much attention to him.

Sarno and Schwartz kept the backpack, shot photos of his International Scout, and sent Stayner on his way. At about the same time, back in the park where Joie Armstrong lived, investigators discovered her missing head. About 40 feet away from the spot where they had located her body, the pretty young naturalist's lifeless face stared up at them from the bottom of a spring-fed pool in a trickling streambed.

Inside Joie's cabin, the growing crew of cops and FBI agents were carefully cataloguing and drawing some early conclusions. She appeared to have been bound with duct tape and, judging by the vacuuming that the forensics team did in the front room and bedroom, her assailant left behind hair and possible fibers, as well as body fluids on the bedsheet. He had at least attempted to rape as well as kill her.

Outside, there were fingerprints on Joie's truck, footprints, and a fresh set of tire tracks near the spot where the fireman had seen the blue and white SUV parked. Yosemite ranger Mark Fincher, a professional tracker, noted that the impressions were distinct enough to reveal a different tread pattern for each tire, which would make tracking down and identifying that particular truck much easier. They shot rolls of photos and made plaster impressions.

By nightfall, despite FBI denials that the two incidents were connected, television news producers had already begun speculating that a link might exist between the slaying of Joie Armstrong and the Sund-Pelosso case. In early-evening newscasts, stations from Miami to the Sunds' hometown of Eureka began topping the news with the Armstrong decapitation. The story was treated as if it were the latest grisly development in the Yosemite murders, followed by a feeble FBI disclaimer that the two incidents could not be related.

"The beheaded body of Joie Ruth Armstrong, a 26-year-old naturalist who worked for the Yosemite Institute, was found yesterday," began one San Francisco television reporter. "There appears to be no link between yesterday's discovery and the deaths of Silvina Pelosso and Carole and Juli Sund. The area where the naturalist was found is about five miles from El Portal."

Back at Cedar Lodge, Cary Stayner was quietly making preparations to hit the road. He packed some camping supplies, clothes, and a few belongings, and sold his 27-inch Sony Trinitron television and its companion Zenith videocassette recorder to another lodge employee. Before he drove off into the night, however, investigators were back for a second round of questions. At about 9 P.M., Stayner was tracked down to his place over the Cedar Lodge Restaurant and asked again: Where had he been the previous evening and could anyone vouch for him not being in the vicinity of Foresta Road around 7 P.M.?

Cary maintained his blank composure, just as he had done when he was first questioned back at the Two-Five by the two female officers. He repeated his assertion that he hadn't been anywhere near Joie Armstrong's cabin and that he knew nothing about the unfortunate unfolding tragedy that had occurred there. Investigators may have had their doubts, but they also had no search warrant and no further cause to put him under arrest. So they moved on to other potential suspects at the lodge.

But in the meantime, Yosemite ranger and tracking specialist Mark Fincher had made a comparison of the photos that had been taken of the tire tracks left outside Joie's cabin and the snapshots of impressions made by the tires on Stayner's Scout. The photos left little doubt in Fincher's mind: both sets of tracks were made by the same truck. The next morning, investigators headed back to Cedar Lodge. This time, they intended to bring Stayner in for questioning.

Stayner hadn't lied to the police about one thing: Thursday had, in fact, been his day off. But Friday was not, and for the first time in roughly 18 months, the good-looking handyman with the penchant for nude sunbathing had not reported to work. Frustrated, the FBI went door-to-door in the Cedar Lodge employees' living quarters above the lobby, showing Cary Stayner's coworkers and neighbors a bent pair of sunglasses and asking if Stayner owned such a pair.

"Everybody thought it was over with the other case," complained a cashier at Cedar Lodge. "We're not used to this stuff around here. All of the sudden, it's here again."

Lodge workers called Stayner's father in Merced. When he heard what had happened and how Cary might be implicated, Delbert Stayner phoned the police himself and officially reported his son missing. He was convinced that Cary was not directly involved, but he had heard enough about cases like that of Terry Ray—found drowned after he allegedly had seen Juli Sund being raped by a gang of cranksters— to fret about his son.

"What I'm worried about is he might have seen something he wasn't supposed to," said Cary's 66-year-old father, who added the poignant observation:

"We lived through this before and it's not very funny. My little boy Stevie Stayner went missing for seven and a half years. That is my middle son, and now my oldest son is missing. I'm kind of torn up over that."

Friday morning and evening, telecasts up and down the Central Valley led once again with the Joie Armstrong story. They continued to get canned comments or no comment at all from the FBI, but workers at Cedar Lodge were talking, and what they passed on to the news media was that agents had been nosing around after a maintenance worker who had failed to show up for work—a man who apparently had not been employed by the lodge at the time of the disappearance of the three tourists.

At the first of two hastily convened news conferences that the FBI felt obliged to stage on Friday, a positive and self-assured James Maddock warranted that he had "... absolutely no reason to believe there is a connection" between the slaughter of Joie Armstrong and the Sund-Pelosso murders.

"We have no reason to believe there is a continuing threat," he added in a booming voice that sounded like calming confidence, but came across as the most disturbing kind of uncertainty. "I have reason to believe that there's a killer loose somewhere, but I don't believe the killer is planning another crime."

Television, radio, and newspaper reporters were not mollified. Stations began a nonstop alert late in the day, piecing together details as quickly as they could be gathered about the missing maintenance man, as well as his missing International Scout. It became the lead item in several newscasts that he was wanted for questioning by the FBI. Before most of California had even sat down to dinner, Maddock's early damage control attempts to play the Joie Armstrong investigation low key had been utterly obliterated. There had been yet another horrible murder in

Yosemite, one of the most beautiful places on earth. Newscasters read viewers' minds when they stared into the camera and asked: How could that be?

The *San Francisco Chronicle* broke the story Saturday morning about the identity of the mystery maintenance man, but apparently that news came too late for the Saturday morning editions of many newspapers, including the *Sacramento Bee*. That and the fact that Cary Stayner had no access to television turned out to be a blessing, according to Patty Sailors, manager of the Laguna del Sol nudist camp.

"I was drinking coffee in bed when one of our members called me and told me to turn on the TV," she recalled. "It was about seven-thirty in the morning. They were talking about this guy that the FBI was looking for and our member says, 'He's here! It's the guy, and he's here!' I said, 'Not the *guy* guy!' and she says, 'Yes! It's the guy!'

"And I said, 'Oh fuck!'"

While Cary Stayner's name, picture, and license plate number were flashing into thousands of homes all over California, the wayward handyman himself had camped out beside the artificial lake that is the centerpiece of the 100-acre Laguna del Sol nudist resort near Sacramento.

He had checked in Friday afternoon under his own name and paid for a two-night stay. He was alone and seemed to want it that way. Jan Ronne, the Laguna del Sol member who had phoned Patty Sailors, said she recognized Stayner from the previous evening, wandering through the resort's clubhouse near the dartboard area. She had seen him before at the resort, several months earlier, and knew him by name.

"He was easy to remember," Sailors said. "In the world of you-don't-know-what-you-know, you must admit that he's a very good looking guy."

Patty's husband, Steven Sailors, checked Stayner's license plate numbers against those that were being reported on TV while Patty contacted the Sacramento County Sheriff's Office. Jan Ronne phoned the FBI hotline 800 number that had been flashed on her TV screen. Cary Stayner was to be considered armed and dangerous, they were told, but if the resort's meager security staff could hold him there without endangering anyone, the FBI would soon be on its way.

One line Jan Ronne recalled from her brief conversation with Stayner the previous evening worried the Sailors.

"He just said, 'Things are just getting weird. A lot of things have changed recently and I need to get out of Dodge,'" Ronne remembered.

Laguna del Sol's support staff were called into service, given walkie talkies, and told to keep tabs on Stayner, as he was packing up and appeared to be preparing to leave. Steven Sailors ordered two trucks to be hastily driven to the narrow arched entrance to the Laguna del Sol parking area. They were parked with their hoods up in such a way that they would appear to be broken down when Stayner tried to drive away. The trucks blocked the only way in and out of the resort, and the Sailors planned to lock the inside gates to the resort itself once Stayner passed through, so that he would effectively be boxed in the parking lot until the police arrived. But Stayner saved them the trouble. Clad in jeans and a T-shirt, he went to the resort restaurant for breakfast instead of simply leaving. Trying to behave as normally as possible, his waitress seated him away from other mainly nude diners.

The Sailors and their now very nervous staff felt a momentary reprieve from the morning's tension, assuming that the FBI would soon be showing up. Their only fear was that there might be a line somewhere in the copy of the *Sacramento Bee* that Stayner was reading, identifying him by name or, worse, by photo. If Stayner's suspicions were aroused, the Sailors had no desire to test the sheriff's office admonition that he might be armed and dangerous. But there was nothing about Cary Stayner on the front page and nothing about him inside. He leisurely leafed through the rest of the paper until shortly before 9 A.M., when FBI agents and Sacramento County sheriff's deputies arrived.

As he put down the newspaper, Cary Stayner was told that he was not under arrest. There were no handcuffs or Miranda rights read. The agents who stood at his table said that they only wanted him to accompany them back to FBI headquarters in Sacramento so that they could talk.

The imagined scene of mayhem, gunplay, or hostage taking in the Laguna del Sol dining room that

Patty and Steven Sailors feared might happen never materialized. Stayner neither bolted nor threatened, but merely pushed himself away from the table and quietly marched off between the agents. Many of the customers, sitting in the buff at nearby tables and leafing through the same edition of the *Bee* that Cary had been reading, didn't know what had even transpired until after Stayner and the agents were gone.

News of his apprehension at a Sacramento nudist colony spread like wildfire, with reporters racing off to Wilton, where Laguna del Sol is located, as well as to Cary's hometown of Merced to grab off some sound bites from the citizens.

"I have no idea what's going on," Kay Stayner said when told that her son had been arrested. "As far as we know, they just wanted to question him after he didn't show up for work. I have no idea why he didn't show up for work."

Cary Stayner had a good reason for failing to report to Cedar Lodge the previous day, as it turned out. Agents noticed a fresh cut on his hand on the ride back to Sacramento and speculated that he might have been injured in a recent struggle—perhaps a struggle with someone like Joie Armstrong. They made an appeal to Cary's conscience: if it were true that he had been the man who stalked and murdered the young naturalist, his confession would at least offer some peace of mind to the victim's family.

After some initial denials, Cary surprised his interrogators by bursting like a dam. A top FBI interrogator got him to confess in a calm matter-of-fact tone over several hours, spilling detail after detail in a taped interview about how he did, in fact, attack and slice the head off of Joie Armstrong. He even told them where to recover the knife. The voices in his head, Stayner said, goaded him into killing the young woman.

After waiving his rights to an attorney, Stayner even agreed to make the two-hour trip back to Yosemite and actually reenact the murder at Joie's Foresta Road cabin. Late Saturday afternoon, Cary Stayner demonstrated where he parked his truck, how he approached Armstrong, where he took her inside the house, how he struggled with her, where and how he beheaded her, and where he disposed of her body and her head—all for the FBI's video camera. The powerful and extraordinary taped evidence would become the centerpiece of the prosecution's case.

Within hours, FBI Special Agent James Maddock told reporters during a Sacramento news conference that investigators were confident they had the man they believed killed Joie Armstrong. Cary Stayner "provided details not generally known outside law enforcement" that supported his confession, said Maddock.

What his agents were not ready for—and did not at first believe—was Stayner's further confession to the kidnapping and murder of Carole Sund, Juli Sund, and Silvina Pelosso. The same dam that had burst with details about the Joie Armstrong killing also exploded with details about the abduction, rape, and murder of the three tourists and, as in the case of Joie Armstrong, the grim details he provided were not generally known outside of law enforcement.

X

By Sunday, the FBI's conviction that the Armstrong murder and the Sund-Pelosso case were unrelated was rapidly crumbling. With Stayner's hideously unbelievable tale taking on more and more credibility by the hour, the TourNap task force's confidence in Rufus Dykes's various murder confessions did a fast fade. The investigators held on to a belief in the scientific evidence that had been gathered to prove that Carole, Juli, and Silvina had died at the hands of a crank gang, but Cary Stayner's knowledge of the most intimate inside details of their investigation, coupled with his increasingly brazen declaration that he and he alone committed all four murders, left their working theories about the crimes in total shambles.

Besides impounding Stayner's Scout for search and analysis, agents quickly sealed off Stayner's studio apartment above the Cedar Lodge restaurant so that when the inevitable press corps showed up in

El Portal on Sunday morning, they were stopped at the dark green side door which bore a sign reading EMPLOYEES ONLY.

Previously garrulous waitresses, desk clerks and other lodge employees were now mum. Only Yosemite Motels owner Gary Fischer or his official spokesman, Jerry Rankin, a former journalist who managed a motel in nearby Mariposa, were allowed to speak to the press, and they had little to say beyond "no comment" and how shocked they were by the news.

"He was well-groomed, well-mannered, and well-spoken, friendly without being effusive," Rankin said, describing Cary Stayner. "You just don't expect this type of thing in a rural atmosphere. Essentially, this is an urban crime that happened in a rural area."

A bartender at the lodge restaurant summed up the paranoia among the rest of the Cedar Lodge staff in two sentences: "I can't say anything. I'll get in trouble."

On condition of anonymity, one hotel worker volunteered, "It's really amazing to me. Cary was really mellow and laid-back. I guess he didn't let anyone else into that other world."

Just down Highway 140 at Indian Flat RV Park, where the Cedar Lodge gag order was not in effect, employee Bob Reed articulated the collective skepticism that had developed in El Portal toward the somber swagger and specious omniscience of James Maddock and the Federal Bureau of Investigation.

"Lots of people here know [Cary]," said a tight-lipped Reed. "I'm not going to believe it until it's proven. They have been wrong about people here before."

Sixteen-year-old Aaron Ludwig, an El Portal native who knew and liked easygoing, dope-smoking Cary Stayner, was not shy about observing that Cary "was a cool guy." Letty Barry, manager of the Yosemite Redbud Lodge, said Stayner frequently stopped in for a candy bar on his way to the Two-Five nude beach.

"Everyone knew his car,"said Barry.

Jake Youngdale, another local teen, remembered a summer social at El Portal's Carroll N. Clark Community Center during which he and others were discussing the meth gang from Modesto. Stayner happened by and interrupted with what, in retrospect, seemed an ominous statement:

" 'For all the FBI knows, it could have been two punk kids in El Portal who did it,' " Youngdale recalled Stayner telling him and his friends. "And then he laughed and smiled at us."

Outside the Sacramento County Jail, where Stayner was being held pending a Monday appearance in federal court, James Maddock staged a noon press conference on Sunday, during which he admitted that his agents had interviewed Stayner as early as a few days after the three women disappeared back in February, but that the handyman was never considered a suspect. Instead, he acknowledged, the FBI turned its attention toward a gang of Modesto speed freaks.

"That was my sincere belief based on the results of intense investigative efforts," said Maddock.

Maddock's press briefing, which was detailed on the FBI's newly reinvigorated media hotline, was a terse, face-saving summary of the explosive developments of the previous 24 hours:

". . . Following Stayner's detention, investigators developed specific details about the crime that led to his arrest. This morning, a criminal complaint against Stayner was signed by a federal magistrate in Fresno, California. Stayner is being charged with violating Title XVIII of United States Code Section 1111, which makes it a crime to commit murder within the special territorial jurisdiction of the United States, such as a national park. . . ."

When it came to eating crow on the Sund-Pelosso investigation, FBI spokesman Nick Rossi was far more circumspect, equivocating, and long-winded on the media hotline's taped message than his boss had been in public:

As suggested at an earlier press briefing, we now believe there is a connection between Armstrong's murder and the murders of Carole Sund, her daughter Juli, and their family friend Silvina Pelosso, all of whom were last seen on the night of February 15. During the last 24 hours, we have developed specific information linking Stayner to the Sund-Pelosso murders. We will continue to work closely with our task force partners from Tuolumne County, Stanislaus County, and the Modesto Police Department to complete the Sund-Pelosso investigation. We will also be working closely with the district attorneys of Tuolumne and Mariposa County and the Mariposa County Sheriff's office to coordinate any eventual prosecutions. With Stayner's arrest, we believe that no other person involved in any of these murders is still on the loose. The possible involvement of other individuals aside from Stayner in the Sund-Pelosso case is still being evaluated.

Before today, we had not identified any other individuals by name as potential suspects in the Sund-Pelosso case. We have previously expressed the belief that the key players in that case were already in custody on unrelated matters. That was a sincere belief based on the results of intense investigative efforts and the best information available at the time, and was expressed in part to discourage the dissemination of numerous rumors concerning what may have happened to the victims. In light of yesterday's arrest, the possible involvement of others in the murder of Carole, Juli, and Silvina is being reevaluated. We still have a great deal left to do in this case, therefore; we will not be discussing the specific investigative steps that are still under way. Our mission is clear. We will work with our task force partners of the United States Attorney's office and the District Attorney to insure that Cary Stayner is successfully prosecuted for the murder of Joie Armstrong and to see that charges are filed as soon as possible in the death of Carole, Juli, and Silvina. . . .

At present, investigators have not established any link between Stayner and other individuals who may have been considered as potential suspects in the Sund-Pelosso case. In the near future, we will meet with prosecutors from the U.S. Attorney's office, Tuolumne County District Attorney Nina Deane's office, and the Mariposa County District Attorney's office to discuss prosecution strategies for the Sund-Pelosso case. At this time we cannot predict exactly when charges will be filed in that case. We have no further information available at this time, and we will not be doing any exclusive interviews in the days ahead. We do not anticipate any additional press briefings until further charges are filed.

Francis and Carole Carrington felt both consternation and closure with the announcement of Stayner's arrest.

"It was really startling, because we had not heard this name at all before," said Carole Carrington. "This was not one of the people we were thinking was involved, and he seems like such a normal kind of guy. It's really amazing. . . . It's better to know than let your imagination work on you. We hope this is brought to a just end. That's all we can ask for."

Her husband registered incredulity equal to that of his wife, as well as dubious, faint praise for the FBI.

"Like Mr. Maddock, I feel bad we couldn't resolve this sooner, and perhaps save someone," he said soberly. "We all wish that he [Stayner] could have been found much sooner. . . . It seemed like he almost wanted to be caught at the end here. There's a lot of questions that need to be answered about the logistics. How he did this . . . it seems very difficult for one person to do all of that with three women. . . . I'm sure that the FBI can check all of these things out."

Contacted in Argentina by the Spanish-language Univision TV network, Silvina's mother, Raquel Pelosso, was not so forgiving.

"This man was questioned so many times. He is either a very astute person or there was carelessness," she said bluntly.

And most confused as well as devastated of all the bereaved parents of Stayner's victims was the latest one: Joie Armstrong's mother, Leslie.

"I was under the impression that there had been a person or persons already arrested in regard to the previous murders," a tearful Leslie Armstrong said from Yosemite during an interview on NBC's *The Today Show* just days after Stayner's arrest. "I had the good pleasure of being with Joie some time this summer and I asked her about it, and I don't think that she was afraid here. I had concern when I heard the first news last spring, but no, it was not a preoccupation with me that I should be afraid for her."

Cary Stayner's remarkable confession to the tragedies in Yosemite provoked a negative national reaction to the FBI's handling of the case. Exploding just before the revelation of another internal Bureau scandal, revolving around FBI lies about using flammable tear gas projectiles during the 1993 Branch Davidian standoff in Waco, Texas, the Yosemite case elicited a rare public castigation from Sen. Charles Grassley, the Iowa Republican who chaired the Senate FBI oversight subcommittee.

"The dismissal of Cary Stayner as a suspect earlier this year by the FBI means that the latest killing may have been preventable," Grassley said flatly. "Homicides have never been the FBI's strong suit. Perhaps the FBI should stick to what it does best: complex white-collar crime. Incidents like these by the FBI tend to undermine public confidence in the federal law enforcement."

But local law enforcement that worked side by side with the FBI on the case weighed in, for the most part, on the side of Maddock's agents.

"There was not one shred of evidence or suspicion to link him as a suspect in the Sund-Pelosso homicides until he became a suspect in the homicide of Joie Ruth Armstrong," said Tuolumne County Sheriff Dick Rogers.

"He's got a story simply because he baffled and blustered his way through the FBI and a steel dragnet, and somehow was able—with a moderate amount of basic intelligence—to pretty much outwit everybody," said Commander Bill Blake of the Merced County Sheriff's Department.

But for Leslie Armstrong, who called her daughter simply "my greatest accomplishment," finger pointing at the FBI was an exercise in futility—something she would have to postpone at the very least, if not dismiss altogether. She could not even bring herself to express any of her rage toward Cary Stayner in the first several days after the murder.

"I know that there is a lot there and I will have time to probably be real angry a little later," she said. "Right now I am just soaking up every bit of Joie that I can from her friends and her surroundings here. He's not worth too much of my energy right now, but I did explode the other day. I know the anger is there."

Unlike memorials for the three previous Yosemite murder victims, there was no public celebration of Joie Armstrong's passing, only very private grief. The media were kept at arm's length. During the earliest hours following her murder, her uncle even refused to confirm for reporters that her last name was Armstrong.

"What I hear about Joie is she was just a wonderful gal," remarked Francis Carrington.

"Joie reminds us a lot of our daughter—a younger version," Carole Carrington chimed in.

Both Carringtons bonded instantly with Leslie Armstrong, who spoke of a kind of all-consuming loss that only parents of murder victims can really comprehend.

Juli Sund, a fifteen-year-old member of the Eureka High School cheerleader squad, pictured in a missing persons bulletin during the last weeks of winter in 1999.

Carole Sund, Juli's forty-two-year-old mother, featured in the same missing persons bulletin.

Silvina Pelosso, the Sunds' sixteen-year-old family friend from Argentina, who disappeared along with Juli and Carole following a Valentine's Day outing to Yosemite National Park.

Silvina Pelossa and Carole Sund mug for the camera next to the Merced River on the floor of Yosemite Valley. Less than a day after this photo was taken, the pair would vanish along with Carole's daughter, Juli.

Friends Silvina and Juli cut a cake together . . .

Courtesy Carole Sund/Carrington Memorial Reward Fund

. . . and pose side by side with the majestic Upper Yosemite Falls as a backdrop to their final adventure together in Yosemite National Park.

Makeshift memorial at the side of the road on California State Highway 108, where the burned bodies of Carole Sund and Silvina Pelossa were recovered from the trunk of their incinerated Pontiac Grand Prix.

Photo by Corey Mitchell

Photo by Dennis McDougal

Card left at the Highway 108 roadside memorial.

Photo by Dennis McDougal

Teddy bear and other mementos left near the site where Juli Sund's body was found, overlooking Don Pedro Lake.

Photo by Greg R. Hubbard

Cary's younger and more famous brother, Steven Stayner, posing beside the Merced intersection where he had been abducted as a seven-year-old in 1972 and held for seven years by convicted pedophile Kenneth Parnell. This was the final photo of Stayner before he died in a motorcycle accident in 1989 at the age of twenty-four.

Photo by Marci Stenberg

Wearing one of his ever-present baseball caps, Cary Stayner comforts his father, Delbert, also wearing a cap, on the August afternoon in 1990 when Cary's uncle, Jerry Stayner, was shot to death during a still-unsolved Merced murder case.

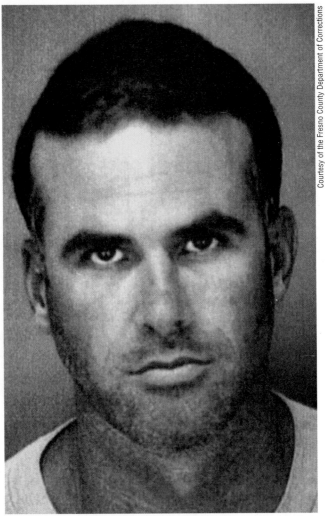

Cary Stayner's booking photo, taken shortly after he was arrested for the July 21, 1999, murder of Joie Armstrong.

"You can sympathize, but when you empathize it's a whole different thing," Mrs. Armstrong said, with a blend of emotion and trembling eloquence.

During the third week of August, Leslie Armstrong's 26-year-old daughter was cremated and privately buried near a waterfall at Pleasant Hill Cemetery in Sebastopol, California. If there were eulogies, they were heard only by close friends and family. Paparazzi and TV crews were not invited. Days before the final goodbye, however, Leslie Armstrong had her own public statement to deliver about her daughter, in part to counter the publicity—however negative—that her murderer was receiving at the hands of the press.

"I started thinking about our American tragedy, and it has to do a lot with the violence and crime that we see today," she said. "It seems like [there's] an obsession with it. I know that there are more good people than there are bad. We are just filled with so much news about the bad. One of the reasons I wanted to talk was because we were hearing nothing about how good Joie was and everything about this man."

Her daughter had made a career of overcoming self-doubt and her own private fears, she said. Her first name not only described who she was; it was also how she approached living.

"Joie was so full of life and had so many interests and passions, and she went for everything," recalled her mother. "She often thought that she wasn't good enough or couldn't do things well. So she studied and pursued and worked out and tried and—just in trying to do her best—I believe she excelled in just about everything.

"She related well to all kinds of people. She was good with her family, with her friends, with her bosses, and with the children that she taught. I have been overwhelmed by the number of people that have told me how she has touched their lives. She was an utter, utter, utter delight, brought joy to every occasion and any room she walked into."

Her short résumé was flawless, and spelled out how Armstrong packed more into 26 years than most women do given three times the life span.

Joie was born in Germany while her Air Force father was stationed there, and though she remained close to her dad throughout her life, her parents divorced by the time she celebrated her third birthday. She was raised by her mother, who remarried and lived for several years at the heart of California's Wine Country in Sonoma County, near her own parents. Divorcing for a second time, Leslie moved herself and her daughter across the country to Orlando when Joie was nearly in her teens. There, Joie attended and graduated from high school before returning to California in the early 1990s for college.

Because her mother lived in Florida and her father in Nevada, Joie found herself spending most of her off-campus time at her grandparents' home in Santa Rosa. But most of the time, Joie was an activist, standing at the front line of a generation frightened as much by a hole in the ozone, the Greenhouse effect, and the destruction of the global rain forest as her parents' generation had been cowed by the threat of thermonuclear warfare. Her aim was to become a teacher and to strike a blow for environmental causes. She earned a bachelor of science degree in parks and natural resource management from Chico State University, interned with the National Audubon Society in 1996, and launched her career at Stanislaus County's Foothill Horizons program, teaching weeklong nature courses to children with an emphasis on preserving the receding American wilderness.

Hiring on with the Marin Headlands Institute in 1997 and moving to Yosemite two years later were the consummation of a young career.

Two days before her death, Joie had dinner with Ann Abbott Matteson, a 63-year-old neighbor who had lived in Foresta for many years, and after dinner, they visited Yosemite historian Shirley Sargent, where they had cherries, cheesecake, and conversation.

Joie apologized for driving over in her truck rather than walking—the more environmentally sanctioned form of travel in the woods. But she was afraid, she told the two older women. She was staying alone in the cabin for the first time and had seen a predator she'd known from her college days in Chico wandering around in the Yosemite Valley. She had been afraid of him back in school and she was afraid of him now, though she would not specify why.

"She said, 'I'm afraid to walk home in the dark,'" Matteson recalled.

Matteson advised her to face her fears in much the same way a legendary 19th-century Yosemite pioneer woman did. Elizabeth McCauley Meyer lived for many years by herself in the wilderness after her husband died, in a home built on the same spot as Armstrong's cabin.

"I was encouraging Joie's feeling of safety there, telling her that it was a benign place, a benevolent place—that the spirit of Elizabeth would be about. I think I'll be haunted for the rest of my life," said Joie's nearest neighbor in the loose-knit Foresta community. "I was lying in my hammock and she was being killed down there. We did not hear anything."

Joie's memorial at Yosemite began with a $10,000 contribution to an environmental protection fund in her name, and grew rapidly. She had no headstone, plaque, or obelisk marking her time on earth, but the same kind of random roadside monument that commemorated Juli, Carole, and Silvina grew just as rapidly as her memorial fund. At the corner of Foresta and Old Coulterville Road, near the house and meadow where she was killed, a kiosk is decorated with purple flowers, ivy, corn husks, bows, a medicine bag filled with charms and herbs, a necklace bearing a small Aztec emblem, and Miwok headdresses swathed in feathers. There is an article about Joie's life, letters addressed to Joie, and poetry.

* * *

"I obviously never thought anything like this would ever happen to me," said Leslie Armstrong. "Next month she was going to go to Costa Rica, spend a month studying Spanish, and then volunteer in the rain forest for two months after that. I had the highest regard. . . ."

Mrs. Armstrong paused, swallowed, and changed from past to present tense.

"I *have* the highest regard and respect for her. She was exquisite."

XI

Cary Stayner didn't say a word during the first of his many days in court.

On Monday afternoon, July 26, the tall, trim, tanned, and confessed killer of four women entered U.S. Magistrate Peter A. Nowinski's courtroom in manacles, with strands of silver in his close-cropped hair and his eyes as blank as the expression on his tight-jawed face. He radiated an utter absence of emotion as he listened to the charge leveled against him: the first degree decapitation murder of Joie Ruth Armstrong. In posture and bearing, Stayner resembled a full-grown G.I. Joe doll in an orange Sacramento County Jail jumpsuit. The only sign he gave that he even heard the magistrate was an affirmative nod each time he was asked if he understood his rights.

In less than three minutes, Nowinski ordered Stayner held on the charge and transported as soon as possible to Fresno, where all future proceedings were to be conducted.

The media glut eight floors down, in front of the brand new Sacramento Federal Court building, was reminiscent of the Cedar Lodge parking lot in February or Modesto's Doubletree Hotel in March, only now, FBI Special Agent in Charge James Maddock brushed by the microphones and video cameras, refusing to answer any press questions at all.

Later, on the telephone, FBI spokesman Nick Rossi also refused, rejected, and declined, as did U.S. Attorney Paul Seave and Federal Defender Quin Denvir. The public servants mandated to hunt down evil and mete out justice were being as mute about this newest twist in the increasingly bizarre Sund-Pelosso—and, now, Armstrong—murder case as the press had been voluble.

Maddock had other reasons than the unwelcome Joie Armstrong surprise to scorn the media. His other high-profile Northern California case during the summer of 1999 had also just blown up in his face, giving added resonance to Senator Charles Grassley's stinging remarks about the FBI's limited competence in solving homicides.

Two white supremacist brothers accused of murdering a gay couple near Redding, 165 miles north of Sacramento, turned out to be the probable suspects in a string of synagogue fires in and around the state capital—a revelation that Maddock preferred to keep mum until after he and his agents had had an opportunity to interview the brothers and get a look at the evidence against them.

Maddock's problem was that local law enforcement—not the FBI—had nailed Benjamin Matthew Williams, 31, and James Tyler Williams, 29, after the brothers tried picking up merchandise they'd ordered from a Yuba City store using one of the dead men's credit cards. After weeks of bellowing to the press that the FBI had entered the synagogue burning case because setting fire to three synagogues constituted a hate crime under federal law, Maddock was forced once more to acknowledge that old-fashioned local police work had succeeded where swarms of his well-dressed, well-educated, politically correct agents had come up empty.

Shasta County sheriff's investigators had searched the brothers' homes following their arrest and found a list of people associated with the incinerated synagogues, along with hate literature from the Illinois-based World Church of the Creator. They also found a veritable arsenal of 26 guns, including two assault rifles, a shotgun, 9 mm pistols, and a .22 caliber semiautomatic that the Williamses allegedly used in the brutal July 1 murder of Gary Matson, 50, and Winfield Scott Mowder, 40. After forcing the gay couple to record an answering machine message saying they were ill and leaving town for medical help, the brothers proceeded to shoot Matson and Mowder to death in their bed, according to police. Prior to the murders, the Williamses hadn't even been considered among the pool of possible suspects in the synagogue fires.

When the *Sacramento Bee* got wind of the break in the case and planned to publish a story, Maddock contacted editor Ron Rodriguez to ask him to hold off. When Rodriguez refused, Maddock threatened to cut his newspaper off from information about the Sund-Pelosso case—a threat Rodriguez found empty, given the FBI's lack of cooperation all along. The synagogue arson story was published over Maddock's objections, and the FBI's tenuous relations with the media in California's state capital eroded even further, leaving no one surprised when Maddock cast an even darker pall over his agents' investigation after Cary Stayner's arrest and confession.

Investigators remained dubious about Stayner. They knew they had their man in the Joie Armstrong murder, but they were not ready to believe the entirety of Cary's story about the Sund-Pelosso killings—especially his contention that he had acted alone. While the details of his confession were being analyzed, the FBI remained confident that they had many of the right suspects in custody already.

Then it all began to crumble.

Two investigators and a polygraph specialist from the Attorney General's office were dispatched immediately to Deuel Vocational Institute, armed with 14 questions for Rufus Dykes. Among them were yes-or-no questions about Dykes's complicity in the murder of any of the three Yosemite tourists and the incineration of their rented Pontiac. Dykes rolled up his sleeves, strapped on the lie detector wiring, and passed with flying colors. His previous confession to the murder of Carole Sund was as worthless as he knew it to have been when he first gave it—and that's when Maddock appeared to finally throw in the towel.

"Now our mission is clear," Maddock said. "We will work with our task force partners, the U.S. attorney's office, and the [Mariposa and Tuolumne] district attorneys to ensure that Cary Stayner is successfully prosecuted for the murder of Joie Armstrong, and to see that charges are filed as soon as possible in the deaths of Carole and Juli Sund and Silvina Pelosso."

But he had nothing further to say to the men and women of the press.

Cary Stayner knew nothing and cared less about the FBI's renewed gag order. Thus, when a 32-year-old San Jose TV reporter asked to speak with him during the last few hours that he was in the Sacramento County jail before being shipped off to Fresno, Stayner readily agreed.

In the biggest scoop of his career, KNTV correspondent Ted Rowlands did the news media's first untaped interview with Cary Stayner, during which the 37-year-old handyman/nudist publicly declared for the first time that it was he and he alone who stalked, murdered, and disposed of the bodies of Carole Sund, her daughter Juli, and family friend Silvina Pelosso. Broadcast exclusively that same evening over KNTV Channel 11 in San Jose and sister station KBWB in San Francisco, Rowlands's televised report about his through-the-plexiglas interview with the accused killer roughly paralleled Stayner's confession to the FBI—with a few notable differences.

To begin with, Cary Stayner let Rowlands know that if anyone was interested in producing a miniseries or a TV movie about his life story, as had been the case with his younger brother Steven, he would be more than happy to entertain offers. Stayner's startling proposal so jarred the nation's broadcasters that hardly a report was delivered about the Yosemite murders over the ensuing weeks without mention of Cary's Hollywood hopes. Networks and newspapers alike saw his movie-of-the-week suggestion as a bizarre twist on the old Andy Warhol adage that everyone is entitled to his fifteen minutes of fame.

But Cary's curious admissions did not end with his lust for celebrity. He also told Rowlands he'd dreamed of capturing and killing women since he was seven years old. On the day after Valentine's Day, his "dream" finally came true. He'd been watching Carole Sund and the two young women in her charge throughout their stay at Cedar Lodge, tracking their every move. Their room in the isolated 500 building, a hundred yards or so from the motel's main lobby was visible from Stayner's room above the restaurant. He knew when they arrived and he knew when they left. He watched and he waited.

Sometime after 10 P.M. on February 15, Cary Stayner knocked at their door and talked his way inside

Room 509 on the pretext that he had to make a repair in the bathroom. Once Carole Sund let him in and closed the door behind him, things went very quickly. He pulled a gun on Carole Sund and told her he was there to rob them. If she and the two girls complied, no one would get hurt. All he was looking for was money.

Towering over Carole by nearly a foot, Stayner could have overpowered the supermom from Eureka even if he'd had no gun. He was strong, had at least 60 pounds on her, and could have made short work of disabling her and probably doing the same to the two girls, though there might be considerable screaming had he done so. But Stayner was apparently so convincing in his role as an armed and desperate but amiable thief—perhaps a junkie looking for quick cash—that Carole quietly did as she was told and her two girls followed suit. According to Stayner, he bound and gagged all three women without a sound or a struggle.

Next, he separated them from one another. Juli and Silvina were consigned to the bathroom. He shut the door on the two girls, plucked up a length of rope that he had brought with him, and wrapped it around Carole's neck. As she lay helplessly on the bed, bound and gagged, he methodically strangled the life from her, then stuffed her corpse into the trunk of the red Pontiac.

Silvina was his second victim. Again, he told Rowlands, he choked the young woman to death. He murdered his second victim in the bathroom while he kept Juli in the adjoining bedroom of the single room suite. As Juli still cowered, ignorant of the fate of either her mother or her friend, he then carried Silvina to the trunk of the car and put her next to Carole.

It was long after midnight when he wrapped Juli in a blanket and put her in the front of the car with him. Then they drove west down Highway 140, past Mariposa and a host of Gold Rush towns with quaint names like Mount Bullion and Coulterville. After more than an hour of twisting mountain roads, Stayner pulled into a parking area at Moccasin Point, overlooking Don Pedro Lake. With daylight already starting to dimly glow in the east, he dragged Juli from the car, up a narrow trail, over a rise, and beyond the reach of any headlights.

There, he slit her throat with a savage cut, almost severing her head from her body, and left her lying in a heap beneath a clump of poison oak. Then he drove further, past the junction of Highway 49 and Highway 108 to the New Melones Reservoir, where he planned to dump the car. But an early-morning fisherman was already out and about that day, and Stayner decided to drive on, high into the hills of Tuolumne County.

As he climbed higher through the Sonora Pass, the sky grew lighter and the patches of snow became larger, brighter, and more frequent. At a tree-lined stretch of the highway some 30 miles east of Sonora, he found a dirt logging road and began driving down deep into the woods. He did not get far. While he had intended to dump the car, with the bodies still in the trunk, into another nearby isolated reservoir, the car wedged on a tree stump just a few hundred feet from the highway and refused to budge. As dawn approached, Stayner fled. He walked back down the highway to a convenience store, phoned for a cab, and rode back to Yosemite, paying the $170 fare with cash he'd taken from Carole Sund's billfold.

A couple of days later, he said, he returned to torch the rental car, which remained undisturbed in the same spot where he had left it.

"I am guilty," Stayner declared to Rowlands. "I did murder Carole Sund, Juli Sund, Silvina Pelosso, and Joie Armstrong."

But whether his jailhouse confession was entirely candid remained wide open to question. Not only did his naked craving for notoriety leave Rowlands flabbergasted, at least part of his matter-of-fact recitation of the facts of that horrifying homicidal night would quickly be exposed as a flat-out lie: that he had neither raped nor molested any of his victims in any way.

In addition, Stayner's oddly offensive attempt at offering words of comfort to the Sund, Pelosso, and Armstrong families landed with a thud.

"I am sorry their loved ones were where they were when they were," he said, according to Rowlands. "I wish I could have controlled myself and not done what I did."

With Cary's sanitized version of the killings now

made public in a very dramatic fashion, the novel he had been carrying in his backpack the day before his arrest took on additional meaning. After all, John Saul's *Black Lightning* was as much about hunting for headlines as it was about hunting for heads. The sibling rivalry detailed at the very heart of the story of murdering brothers Rory and Richard Kraven resonated with several uneasy parallels to the real-life drama that would characterize Steven and Cary Stayner's late relationship—even though Steven hadn't achieved his own celebrity status through chainsaw massacre.

In one of several chilling and telling passages detailing the internecine conflict between the famous mad professor character Richard Kraven and his second-rate serial murdering brother Rory, John Saul wrote:

> Richard must have been eating at Rory all his life, even if he'd never shown it. Richard, who had remained newsworthy even after he'd been executed. And suddenly it made sense.
>
> He wanted the attention. . . . All his life, everything was focused on Richard. And even after Richard was dead, it didn't stop.

In *Black Lightning*, Rory Kraven believed that even their own mother favored Richard over himself. Still, he would never utter a negative word about his brother:

But Rory had been nothing—the kind of man who plodded through life, using all his resources just to get by. Rory hadn't wanted to talk about Richard—all he said was that they didn't get along very well, they weren't close, they weren't very much alike.

In light of Ted Rowlands's interview and the well-thumbed copy of *Black Lightning*, the FBI was getting an early bead on Cary Stayner's possible motives for his string of murders, but there was still no news to be had from Maddock and company. Even when Jenny Paul, a driver for Sonora's Courtesy Cab Co., went public later in the week with her recollection of Cary Stayner paying $170 for a two-hour ride from Sierra Village to Yosemite on the morning of February 16, the Bureau remained officially silent.

While the FBI had once again pulled the shade down on its investigation, more stories begin filtering in, along with grisly details of Armstrong's decapitation and the curious manner in which Cary became a prime suspect. Joie had struggled mightily with her attacker, who was apparently as sloppy at the crime scene as he had been meticulous during his overnight murder melee in February. Still, it took three interviews—one at the Two-Five nude beach, one later the same day at Cedar Lodge, and one more two days later at the Laguna del Sol nudist resort—before he was actually arrested.

After KGO radio's Mary Ellen Geist went public with her story about her near-miss encounter in the

Cedar Lodge hot tub with Stayner, others began coming forward. Hollywood agent April Rocha described a similar eerie experience to *Daily Variety* columnist Army Archerd, which had taken place at Cedar Lodge just a short time before Joie Armstrong was murdered.

It was after 10 P.M. and the pool had closed, but a lodge worker told Rocha and her daughter if they gave the pool area supervisor a beer, he'd let them soak for a spell in the motel hot tub. The women climbed in, the only two people left in the pool area, and after a bit, Rocha returned to their room, leaving her daughter behind. Thinking herself alone, the young woman began singing in the tub. The lights in the pool area then flicked off and on a couple of times, which she took to mean that the pool was finally closing for the night. Then she heard a male voice behind her.

"You have a lovely voice," said the pool attendant. "What room are you staying in?"

"I don't know the number," said Rocha's daughter. "I'm staying with a friend." She quickly climbed out of the tub and returned to her room.

Cary Stayner turned off the lights and shut the pool down for the night.

Cary Stayner was voted "most creative" by his classmates at Merced High in 1979, but for all his creativity, he left little in the way of a lasting impression. The one recurring theme in their description of the confessed serial killer who now seemed so out-spoken about his crimes was that he was "quiet."

"He was very nice and quiet, especially around the time his brother disappeared. I felt very sorry for him," said classmate Terri Cromwell.

"I knew him enough to say 'Hi' to," said Renee Terry, who lived around the block from him. "He seemed very nice and quiet."

Former teacher Dan Baladad remembered Cary Stayner as "a very nice young man [who] didn't have any discipline problems at all. He seemed like a quiet young person."

"He was quiet, and an above-average student," said Robert Evans, another former instructor.

"I remember him as a nice guy . . . pretty quiet, shy, and reserved," said Christy Hoffknecht, editor of the Merced High *Statesman* student newspaper. "He got along with everybody."

And so the litany continued. Teachers and class-mates alike rattled off interchangeable impressions of the "aw shucks" persona that Stayner wore during the years he was growing up in Merced. His ineffable ability to melt quietly into the background was as re-markable as the ever-present baseball cap that he wore throughout his high school career. The hat was to hide the fact that Cary tore his hair from his own skull—a habit he'd had since preschool and which had advanced to a point that he ripped whole clumps from his head in a single pull by the time he was a teenager.

"Cary has pulled his hair out from the roots since

he was a little kid," said his mother, Kay Stayner, who tried everything short of psychotherapy to get him to stop. "I thought it was just a habit, like people that grind their teeth," said his aunt Lori Stayner. But most people outside the immediate family didn't know about Cary's odder behavior. They knew him merely as the nice guy in the back row who kept to himself, didn't cause a fuss, never excelled, but generally met all the requirements, and always wore a baseball cap. Quiet. That was Cary Stayner. The quiet man.

Most lost track of him soon after graduation. He was on the missing alumni list 20 years later and had not signed up for his high school reunion on September 18, 1999. By the time his classmates heard the Armstrong murder news, it was clear that Cary Stayner would not be in attendance.

"I thought the next time that I would see his name in the paper was when he became an editorial cartoonist at some newspaper or when he got his own comic strip," said Jack Bungart, who worked on the Merced High School student newspaper at the same time that Cary Stayner was its editorial cartoonist. "Even his doodles were great."

His cartoons were remarkable, if a little dark in their humor. His caricature of the balding Merced High principal captured the administrator's egg-shaped noggin perfectly. Another graphic gag depicted the cafeteria chef dipping her ladle into a steaming cauldron of human skulls.

Matt Cone, who grew up in a house just down the

street from the Stayners, remembered a cartoon flip book that Cary drew in high school, that animated a bomb blowing up a palm tree. His art wasn't just comic figures either. He drew life portraits straight on, in two-thirds profile, and from the side—all views done with both uncommon skill and nearly photographic detail.

In the days that followed Cary's arrest, his family withdrew. Delbert and Kay stopped answering the phone and soon had the number changed. When reporters came to their door, they spoke through the screen at first, saying only that they believed in Cary and could not believe what was being reported about him in the press. Later, they stopped coming to the door altogether.

In his final public statement following the arrest of Cary, Delbert recalled a time when he was happy to give interviews.

"Thank you for all your support since December 4, 1972, when you helped look for Steve," he said before going into seclusion. "You helped celebrate his return in 1980, you helped mourn his death in 1989. Now we must ask you for our privacy during this terrible tragedy."

Yet, to hear those few family members willing to speak out about the accused killer, young Cary was anything but bloodthirsty. He was . . . quiet.

"My son, I talked to him yesterday," said his aunt Anna Jones, whose own son Ronnie was not just Cary's cousin but also one of his closest pals growing up. "He said, 'Mom, I remember that when we were kids and I had the BB gun and we'd go out in the orchards . . .' and my son would shoot every bird and everything else that ran across the ground. And Cary would never do that. He enjoyed nature."

Cary was rambunctious as a child, according to Matt Cone. They were on the church softball team together. They did some streaking in the early 1970s, when it was fashionable to shock one's elders by racing by wearing only tennis shoes. They pulled stunts like setting a paper dummy in the middle of Yosemite Parkway during Halloween, then laughing like hell when some unsuspecting motorist hit it, thinking he or she might have run over a body. In Matt Cone's opinion, Cary Stayner didn't become the quiet nature-loving wallflower everyone recalled in high school until *the* watershed event in both the lives of the Stayner family, and the history of Merced, California: the 1972 kidnapping of his younger brother, Steven.

"The whole family suffered," said Cone. "The parents were obsessed with finding Steven. I remember when I was over there [at the Stayners' house] one day and a lady came to the door who, it turns out, said she was a psychic. She tells them, 'Your son's dead. He's in a garbage dump.' That's when I left."

And Cone—as well as most of the rest of the neighborhood kids—rarely returned during those seven years between Steven's abduction and his return to Merced. Kay Stayner, the mother, seemed to shut down, becoming distant and cold. Delbert, who had a down-home wit and had always loved his role as family patriarch, lost his job as well as his sense of humor when he lost his younger son. He would occasionally disappear into Steven's room, and Cary would find him there, digging through the drawers, sniffing at the missing seven-year-old's clothes.

As for Cary, he reacted to the loss of his little brother with silence.

"Cary was very close to Steven," said Matt Cone. "In some way, he may have thought it was all his fault. He was the older brother and he should have been watching out for his little brother, even though there was absolutely nothing he could have done about it."

Cary Stayner became more and more quiet through junior high school, until he nearly faded from view altogether. By the time they were in high school, Cone said, Cary kept to himself almost all the time. Instead of hanging out with the other students or sharing in mischief the way he had before December 4, 1972, Cary went to school, did his schoolwork—quietly—and then went straight home without dawdling. His parents got angry with him if he dawdled. But if Cary got angry, he wouldn't show it. He imploded.

"The way I remember it, his face got bright red and he'd walk away," said Cone. "Mostly, he was just quiet."

XII

The oldest of five siblings, all born at the same community hospital in the same central California farm town in the same tumultuous decade, Cary Stayner was delivered August 13, 1961, to Delbert and Kay Stayner.

The impact of the 1960s would have a delayed effect on the Stayner family. Assassinations, the drug culture, and student violence only penetrated Merced through the growing power of television, but TV was still grappling for a stranglehold on rural America during the Stayner children's earliest years. The Stayners were working class, but not poor. They certainly could afford a TV set, but the still novel medium had scant impact on their daily lives. With much more frequency than they watched *Ozzie and Harriet* or *Gilligan's Island*, Cary and his brother and three sisters grew up performing farm chores, exploring the Bear Creek and Merced tributaries for frogs and salamanders, or hunting four-leaf clovers and field mice in the vast stretches of grassland at the base of the Sierras.

Of all the national news bulletins unleashed by a televised Pandora's box during the '60s, only Vietnam immediately touched lives in the San Joaquin Valley. Thousands of local lads were lured by the video romance and patriotic duty of foreign military service, but not all returned. Dozens of their number came back home to nearby Castle Air Force Base in coffins. Married and a father before the Southeast Asian war began gobbling up his neighbors, Delbert was neither drafted nor threatened by conscription. He seemed to live a charmed if simple life. He started out his career working in the canneries which dominated the local economy, and spent most of a lifetime there operating, fixing, or maintaining the heavy equipment that kept the conveyor belt commerce running.

Delbert Stayner was a guileless man with humble dreams who worked the fruit and vegetable factory farms of Central California until his mid-twenties, when he landed a job in a northern California sawmill, met a pretty, dark-haired teenager, and brought her home to Merced to marry. The former Margaret Mary Katherine Augustine was something of an archetypal Merced match for her amiable, easygoing husband. She was eight years his junior, but nearly as tall as Delbert and she never stood in his shadow. Strong-willed and even a bit fiery, Kay Stayner insisted on correct posture, clean living, and firmness of purpose. She had as good a sense of humor as her husband, but with a bit more of a sardonic edge. She spoke clearly and in a forthright voice, yet she could lapse into smoldering stoicism when she felt silence was warranted.

Kay Stayner came from a Roman Catholic family in a small lumber town and, attended an all-girls parochial boarding school. In her teens, she even considered becoming a nun at one point. Along with Delbert's Dust Bowl forebears, Kay's rural Portuguese/Mediterranean relations comprised the seed population of the second wave of growth for the tiny Gold Rush–era village which grew during the first half of the century into the county seat of Merced. In a variety of ways, the Stayner family represented a consummation of the two blue-collar cultures, nurtured by the family values preached by the Mormon church and fueled by an agricultural zeitgeist at a time when the rest of the country was moving in droves to the big cities.

The marriage of mild-mannered Delbert to tough but tolerant Kay made absolute sense. While the rest of the country seemed to be going crazy, the Stayners raised their youngsters right there in Merced, where the American dream of home ownership and two cars in every garage was not only still possible— it was practically mandated in the municipal charter. There were absolutely no external signs in those early years that the Stayners of Merced were destined to become as cursed in their own fashion as the Kennedys of Massachusetts.

Cary's birth was followed at roughly two-year intervals by Cindy, Steven, Jody, and Cory. By 1967, the Stayners had outgrown their modest home in Merced. Financially, they were well enough off that Kay and Delbert made a grab for their version of the brass ring: their own almond ranch in Snelling, which is located along the banks of the Merced River, actually some 20 miles north of Merced itself. At 35, Delbert was at the peak of both his earning power and energy. After purchasing the ranch, he worked a full 40-hour week at the Consolidated Canners & Growers packing plant in Merced, in addition to farming 20 acres of almond trees virtually all on his own. When he wasn't repairing machinery at the cannery, he was driving a tractor through his orchard, tending his trees.

For almost four years, the Stayners lived the farming life, only driving into Merced for staple supplies, visits with relatives, and church services twice each week at the Merced Mormon Stake. Out on their ranch, they were as self-sufficient as the almost mythic family of Laura Ingalls Wilder in their *Little House on the Prairie*. Cary and his younger brother and sisters had cows, pigs, and goats to tend, and wide-open spaces to explore. If Delbert hadn't pushed so hard to keep his agrarian dream afloat, they might never have had to leave.

While shaving one morning in 1970, Delbert's back gave out and he fell to the bathroom floor in agony. Kay called the same hospital in Merced where all five of their children had been born and an ambulance was soon on its way. The diagnosis: a slipped disc. Treatment: back surgery. Though he was out of the hospital and back on his feet in just a few weeks, Delbert was never quite the same, and certainly not as fit to tend, harvest, and market 20 acres of almond trees all by himself. He took on a partner, Mac Scoggins, who also worked at the Consolidated Canners & Growers cannery. Scoggins moved his own wife and three children out to the Snelling ranch, but one more year of trying to make a living left both the Stayner and Scoggins families on the ropes. Following the especially dry summer of 1971, they left the ranch. They weren't ready to sell their dream yet, and held on to the mortgage in hopes that the weather and the market for almonds would turn around, but for the time being, both families moved back to Merced, closer to the breadwinners' day jobs.

The Stayners' new home was a single-story tract home on Bette Street in a modest neighborhood in southeast Merced. Unlike the ranch, where they could roam free, the Stayner children now lived in town, with neighbors and fences and all the attendant hazards that go with an urban existence, including crime and traffic accidents. While their home was midblock, in a safe, unpretentious part of town, it was located two blocks from the busy four-lane Yosemite Parkway, which becomes state Highway 140 at the city limits and winds its way for 40 miles through Cathey's Valley, Mariposa, and El Portal, into the western entrance to Yosemite National Park. Every year, there were accidents on the parkway, and occasionally deaths.

When Cary's little brother Steven first disappeared, that's what everyone in the family feared had happened to him.

Those who knew the Stayner family before December 4, 1972, recalled the kind of tight-knit clan for which phrases like *heartwarming* and *salt-of-the-earth* seemed to have been coined. To hear friends and neighbors tell it, the family could have moved out of Merced and right into a Disney movie. Not only did they work and play and worship together, they also filled their weekends with fishing and boating trips at nearby lakes and streams. Yosemite was a home-away-from-home for the Stayners, and camp-outs were a way of life. For all his workaholic tendencies before his back surgery, Delbert never forgot what it meant to be a father, sharing what little free time he had with his family in the great outdoors. He felt a particular affection for his second son, Steven.

Born April 18, 1965, Steven Gregory Stayner was only seven years old, four foot eight inches tall, and 60 pounds when he disappeared. With a shaggy brown mop of hair, freckles, big brown eyes, and a bucktoothed grin, he could have been a body double for the Beaver. Both parents described Steven growing up as practically a puppy when it came to dogging his dad's footsteps. He followed Delbert everywhere and basked in his affection whenever his father had a spare moment to jostle him or curl up with Steven on the couch to watch TV.

Delbert had never had so close a relationship with Cary. Steven and his older brother Cary were not exactly the Smothers Brothers; there was a mild sibling rivalry even in the earliest days—an unutterable sense, especially from Cary's point of view, that both mom and dad liked Stevie best. Under normal circumstances, they both might have outgrown that early competition for their parents' affection—but destiny had a different outcome in store for the Stayner brothers, as well as the whole family.

In addition to being the little prince of the Stayner home, Steven was also the little dickens. He found himself in hot water with some regularity. He wasn't malicious—just curious, unrelenting, and a little too creative at times.

"He never did anything really out of line," said Kay Stayner. "He was just normal . . . an ordinary boy who would drive you crazy asking can he please do something."

When he was only three, he and his older sister Cindy dumped sand in his father's gas tank to see what would happen. Even though the truck wouldn't start, Delbert just laughed that one off. But Steven's childish experiments and pranks grew less humorous the older he got. While Kay was the day-to-day disciplinarian, swatting the errant kid who got out of line, the time-honored phrase *Wait until your father gets home* had special resonance in the Stayner household—particularly as it related to Steven, who all but worshiped his old man. Delbert was no monster given over to fits of rage, and there was definitely a mutual admiration between father and son, but Delbert did not hesitate to take his belt off when the occasion merited it.

Steven was due for a spanking when he came home from school on December 4, 1972. The previous day, he'd been to a birthday party and when he came home, he scrawled his name across the garage door—an offense deemed paddleworthy by his parents. When he didn't show up from school on time, one of his mother's first thoughts was that her dreamy third child had gotten caught up dawdling on the way home as a convenient means of delaying, or perhaps ducking, his punishment altogether.

Cary and his sisters didn't think much about their brother's tardiness at the time. Steven loitered, it was a fact of life. If he showed up late from school again, it would probably mean a couple more swats from Delbert or Kay, and he'd get home on time for a few weeks until he forgot again. That's pretty much how his little brother was.

Only as the hours ticked by and darkness began to fall did anyone begin to assume anything more sinister might have befallen Steven.

The truth was that a man had approached Steven in the early afternoon with a fistful of religious pamphlets. It was at the corner of Jean Street and Yosemite Parkway, halfway between Mrs. Walsh's second grade class at Charles Wright Elementary School and the Stayners' Bette Street home. Another man was parked nearby, waiting behind the wheel of an old white Buick.

"A guy asked me if I wanted to donate something to a church," Steven later told police. "I said, 'Sure. I think my mom might want to . . .' He asked me if I wanted a ride home."

And thus began one of the strangest odysseys in the annals of modern American criminal history—a rupture in the life of a small boy as well as the lives of his family, with such tragic repercussions that they would continue to reverberate through hundreds of other lives and still not fully run their course for decades to come.

The man with the pamphlets was one Ervin Murphy, a dim-witted misfit who worked as a night janitor at the Yosemite Lodge in Yosemite National Park. Earlier that autumn, another social misfit named Kenneth Eugene Parnell came to work at the lodge as a night bookkeeper and the two men struck up a friendship—so close a friendship that Parnell quickly came to confide in Murphy that he had a dream. He was tired and lonesome living alone, he said. He wanted a son. Parnell asked Murphy's help in "picking up" a child.

At first, Murphy declined, but Parnell was relentless. After several refusals, Murphy finally agreed to help his new friend. The slow-witted Murphy later maintained that, if he had known the toxic temperament of Parnell's intentions or the true nature of his manipulative friendship with the bookkeeper, he would never have become Parnell's willing stooge.

Kenneth Parnell was a child molester—a court-certified predator and pedophile with bona fides dating back more than two decades. Born in the Texas panhandle in 1932, Parnell never really knew his father, who abandoned him, his older half brother, and two half sisters to his stern fundamentalist Christian mother when he was five years old. His desertion so upset him that Kenneth Parnell spent several hours on the day that his father left with a pair of pliers, pulling four teeth out of his own jaw in protest.

Parnell's fragmented childhood whipped him from Texas to Bakersfield, California, and back twice, as his thrice-a-week churchgoing mother tried to find a permanent place to nest. While moving her children back and forth across the country, Mary Parnell did not fail to drive the fear of God into her children. They knew their Bible and they said their prayers, on their knees, with rigid regularity. When she bought a boardinghouse and finally did settle down for good in Bakersfield, her damaged younger son suffered further trauma when he befriended one of his mother's boarders and got a firsthand lesson in forced fellatio at the age of 13. This time, instead of pulling teeth in protest, Parnell set fire to a pasture and wound up in juvenile hall.

Released from juvenile custody a few months later, he next stole a car and wound up back in a correctional institution for youthful offenders for two more years. It was there, away from the nonstop

Bible banging he endured at Mary Parnell's boarding-house, that Kenneth Parnell perfected the nuances of sodomy and oral sex. In the unenlightened 1940s, the California Youth Authority and juvenile hall was a buggery and blow job buffet for all but the strongest and most resolute adolescent inmates, regardless of their sexual orientation. Whether Kenneth Parnell took to it naturally or developed a taste for anal and oral sex, he acknowledged in later years that he cut his teeth on sexual fantasy fulfillment while growing up inside the joint.

At 16 he was out of jail. At 17, he married his high school sweetheart. At 18, he got her pregnant. And at 19, Kenneth Parnell became the proud father of a little girl during the very same week that he abducted and molested an eight-year-old boy. At Parnell's trial, a court-appointed psychiatrist pronounced him a "sexual psychopath" and the judge sentenced him to a psychiatric hospital, while his wife vowed never to let him see his daughter again.

That was 1951, a watershed year for Kenneth Parnell. He spent the next year in and out of state hospitals for the mentally ill. The time that he actually spent in such institutions was the time between his escapes. Following his last escape—all the way to New Mexico, where he was working as a fry cook when he was caught and returned to California—Parnell was sentenced to an institution from which there was no escape. Beginning in August of 1952, Parnell did a three-and-a-half-year tour at California's maximum security penitentiary at San Quentin.

He violated parole in less than a year and wound up back behind bars at California's other maximum security prison outside of Folsom, near the state capital of Sacramento.

He twice attempted suicide. He was later convicted of armed robbery and grand larceny in Utah and jailed for another six years—nearly three times the sentence he received for raping an eight-year-old boy. Between his California and Utah prison terms, he remarried and fathered a second daughter, again ending the marriage and fatherhood with divorce. He was released from Utah State Prison in 1967 with the proviso that he leave the state and never return. Parnell went to Arizona, married and divorced a third time, and came home to California in the winter of 1972.

At the age of 40, lifelong loser Kenneth Parnell moved back in with his mother in her Bakersfield boardinghouse. She had lost none of her domineering Holy Roller fervor and, unrepentant sinner that he was, Parnell found the better part of valor to be seeking sanctuary elsewhere. He chose Yosemite.

When he filled out his application with the Curry Company, which operated the concessions within the National Park, he neglected to mention his career as a felon, a convicted sex offender, and a mental patient, and apparently, the Curry Company never checked. In May of 1972, he was offered the night auditor's position at Yosemite Lodge. There he met Ervin Murphy and cooked up his scheme to hit the streets of Merced and select himself a son.

Murphy's first couple of attempts to entice children into Parnell's car had been unsuccessful: the children said they had to go home, and Murphy simply stood back and let them go. But Steven was different—more trusting, perhaps a bit more naive than the others. Steven Stayner suited Parnell's purpose just fine. When Murphy brought the boy to the Buick idling at the curb, the man behind the wheel told Steven he was a minister and ordered the boy to climb in the backseat. Murphy climbed in the front and they drove toward Steven's house, ostensibly to ask his mother for a donation to Parnell's ministry.

But Parnell drove on by Bette Street. Indeed, he drove in a circle, back toward Yosemite Parkway and out of the city, onto Highway 140 and into the hills that lead to Cathey's Valley. When Steven pointed out his misdirection and that they had left Merced far behind, Parnell ignored the boy at first. But as they left Merced behind, he told Steven not to worry. They would stop and call his mother once they spotted a pay phone.

In Cathey's Valley, they pulled over. Murphy and Steven waited in the car while Parnell made the call. He was out of earshot, but when he returned to the car, he had a smile painted on his face. Steven's mother had given him permission to let Steven spend the night with him.

Back in Merced, the panic began to set in—first with Kay and Delbert and, soon thereafter, the rest of the family. By 6 P.M., Boy Scouts and police reservists were canvassing the area where Steven had last been seen. Cary and his sisters knew there was big trouble brewing when their parents packed them all off to Mac Scoggins's house for the night.

The seven-year search for Steven Gregory Stayner had begun.

After the kidnapping and the phony phone call to Kay Stayner, Parnell drove to a trailer park in Cathey's Valley, where the two men took the boy to a rented cabin. There were already toys scattered on the floor in anticipation of a successful abduction, and Steven showed some mild interest.

That night, each clad in only a towel, Parnell and his new "son" slept in one bed while Murphy slept on the couch. Though Murphy stuck firmly to his statement years later in court that he never knew a thing about Parnell's true intent toward the boy, Steven reluctantly admitted under repeated questioning that his nonstop horror story as Parnell's permanent rape victim began that very first night. Over the next seven years, Parnell boasted that he forced Steven to submit to both anal and oral sex over three thousand times, by Parnell's own estimate.

Back in Merced, Delbert and Kay stayed up for the first of many sleepless nights drinking coffee, trying to come up with likely places that Steven might have gone . . . while alternately nursing each other's worst dread. The following day, the other Stayner kids were back home, wanting to know if Steven had returned. He had not, they were told, and they were once again packed off to the Scogginses' while a citywide investigation of the boy's disappearance continued.

Two days passed. The grandparents had to be told. Delbert's parents lived nearby in Merced and knew about their missing grandson immediately, but Kay's parents were divorced. Her mother lived near the coast in the Salinas Valley town of Hollister while her father, Robert Augustine, lived at Judy's Trailer Park in Cathey's Valley. They drove up to deliver the bad news to him. Not a hundred yards away, in a rented red cabin on the trailer park property, Kenneth Parnell and Ervin Murphy were holding their boy captive, but no one knew.

Inside the cabin, Parnell was breaking bad news of his own to the seven-year-old boy: his parents couldn't afford to take care of him anymore. A court had named Parnell as Steven's guardian. He flashed Steven an official-looking document that Parnell claimed awarded him Steven's sole custody. Steven broke down in tears, prompting the first of Parnell's regular tantrums about his whining and weeping. No son of his was going to be a cry baby, or lapse into incessant tears. Whether out of fear or numb despair, Steven's sobbing fits slowly dissipated over the next several weeks until, eventually, they stopped altogether.

With no one yet the wiser, the two men left the cabin and drove the boy to Parnell's quarters at Yosemite Lodge. There, Parnell gave the boy sleeping pills to keep him from making a break for it while he was off at work. When Steven was awake, Murphy kept an eye on him. His new "guardian" dyed Steven's hair so that he would not be recognized, and warned Steven that he was never to tell anyone his true identity. If he did, he'd get a spanking.

At one point, Steven recalled trying to phone his parents, but he didn't know how to dial information. On another occasion, he tried running away but got lost, became frightened, and returned to Parnell.

"I'd ask myself, 'Mom and Dad, where the hell are you?' It somehow reinforced the lie that Parnell told me they didn't want me," Steven recalled later.

Kay Stayner had her recollections of those first days and weeks too, and they were not dissimilar from her missing son's.

"I can remember sitting there one day thinking, 'I don't think I can stand it. If he's missing for a week, I'm going to go crazy,'" she said. "At that point it had only been three days, and I could hardly take it. Then the week ended and he was still gone. And then when a month went by and he was *still* gone, I realized that this was something we were going to have to live with. After a month, I thought, 'This can't go on any longer,' and then after a year . . . It was like the earth opened up, Steve fell into a chasm, and the earth closed up with nothing different except Steve wasn't there."

For a full year, Kay Stayner refused to leave the Bette Street house, convinced that Steven would return and that someone should always be waiting there for him when he did.

Meanwhile, after only a few weeks at the Yosemite Lodge, Parnell and Murphy parted company. Murphy remained in the National Park while Parnell quit his job and hit the road with Steven in tow. They moved 150 miles northwest, to a trailer park in the coastal valley town of Santa Rosa. Renamed Dennis Gregory Parnell by his new "guardian," Steven enrolled in Santa Rosa schools for the next three years, utterly unaware of his real family's vigil back in Merced.

Steven had no way of knowing that, night after night, in a ritual that his brother Cary shared with no one, the 10-year-old older brother of the kidnap victim stepped out into the dark and stared up at the sky. Cary stood in the same spot at the same time each evening and scanned the heavens until he found his lucky star. Then he whispered the same prayer:

"Wherever my little brother is tonight, bring him home safe and sound. Please bring Steven home."

But neither God nor the stars heard him, or they had some other plan in mind. Cary continued the ritual for years, but eventually Steven gave up on his former family entirely. He forgot his telephone number, his parents, and even his own name, and began calling Kenneth Parnell "Dad."

XIII

In 1974, the Stayners sold the almond ranch in Snelling. Hail destroyed the crop one year and frost did it two more times.

"The Lord just hadn't been on my side for quite a few years," said Delbert.

Even though the two adults and four remaining children of the Stayner family had outgrown the small frame house on Bette Street, Delbert and Kay nixed a plan to move back to the ranch or even to find larger quarters in town, for fear that Steven might return someday and not know where his family had gone off to.

The garage door upon which Steven had scrawled his name was repainted . . . all except for the name "Steven Stayner," which remained as both a constant reminder to the Stayners of just what they had lost and as a memory jogger for a prodigal Steven, who the Stayners believed might someday return, only to have forgotten which tract house belonged to him.

The Merced Police still had detectives assigned to the Steven Stayner case, but time and not even a single clue put it farther and farther into the back of their active files. According to Delbert, the police explained to him early on that children missing more than three months are presumed dead.

Several months after Steven's disappearance, a deranged drifter confessed to the kidnapping and killing of Steven in what he later admitted was intended to be a perverse act of kindness, designed to put the family's loss behind them. A search for a body where the drifter said he'd buried the boy, in the hills east of Merced, revealed nothing, and he finally conceded that it had all been a hoax.

The Stayners put out the kind of "missing child" flyers that have become all too routine in recent years at local post offices, community bulletin boards, and roadside rest stops. It read:

Missing Juvenile—Steven Gregory Stayner— male, caucasian, age 7, DOB 4-18-65, 4' 8", 60 pounds. Lt. Brn. Hair. The hair is shaggy and collar length. Brn. Eyes. Missing since 12-4-72 from this city. Steven was on his way home from school when he was last seen. He was last seen wearing a tan coat, blue jeans, multicolored flower shirt with a zipper in the front. Steven has never run away in the past. This may be a case of foul play or kidnapping. Any information on the above juvenile, please contact Sergeant Moore, Merced Police Department.

Ironically, flyers were eventually distributed throughout central and northern California, including to several of the schools that Steven attended. No teacher, student or parent ever made the connection.

For a time, Delbert and Kay both went crazy.

"It changed our lives to the point where my husband Del and I could only project into the future by saying, 'When Steve comes home and when we're a whole family again, we'll do this . . .' The event pushed us apart. We didn't do anything because we were always waiting for Steve to come home," said Kay Stayner, who admitted that she "more or less closed up" during that period.

"My strength came from not showing any emotion, because if I ever let down that wall, I'd go to pieces," she said. "I always felt that if I ever let go, I'd never be able to pick myself up again."

Delbert feared for his son's soul as much as for his safety. In the Mormon faith, a child isn't baptized until he reaches the age of eight, and Steven had been six months shy when he vanished.

The trauma took its economic toll on the family too. Delbert, the man who once worked 60-hour weeks to support his family and to build an almond orchard dream in the Sierra foothills, could not hold on to his job. Kay had to support the family as a hospital cook. For two years, the couple split up and contemplated divorce. Once the Rock of Gibraltar, according to elder son Cary, Delbert collapsed into a weeping shell of his former self.

"All of a sudden, this one day, December 4, 1972, my little brother is gone and my dad is crying all of a sudden," Cary told an interviewer years later. "Never saw my dad have a tear in his eye in my whole life. All of a sudden, life changed."

Delbert once put a gun to his head and threatened suicide, according to a neighbor.

"I'd ride around in my pickup with a sawed-off shotgun on the seat in case I saw someone with Stevie," said Delbert. "I began to suspect everyone had something to do with it—friends, neighbors, even family members. If a child dies, you bury the child. With a missing child, you have a knot in your chest that never leaves."

The Stayners hired a psychic to explore the fifth dimension for their boy, and though the seer claimed to have had a vision of Steven's body in a cave somewhere near Cathey's Valley, both parents rejected the idea. Neither Delbert nor Kay could be convinced that their son was dead.

Every Christmas, beginning with the first one, just three weeks after Steven's disappearance, each of the Stayner children would shop for a gift, wrap it, and attach a label bearing Steven's name. The gifts went under the tree, just as if Steven were still a part of the family, and still very much in each of their lives. When he didn't return home by New Year's, the gifts would get packed off into a closet.

After seven years, there was no room left in the closet. Every time the door was opened, unopened presents for Steven spilled to the floor in an avalanche.

By age nine, Steven realized "things weren't right—my parents wouldn't have hired a guy to pick me off the street," he said, relating his story to *Newsweek*'s David Gelman years later. He scanned newspapers and watched TV to see if there was any mention of him. But by then, the brouhaha over his disappearance had cooled, and Steven had become a statistic, not a story. Kenneth Parnell told him that his parents had died—a lie that was easier to accept than the idea that the Stayners might simply have given up on him.

Besides, Steven had developed a curiously caring ambivalence about his new "father," who treated him well enough when he wasn't raping him.

"The two developed a close relationship," said one prosecutor involved in the case. "Apparently the man was kind to him. At some point, he [Steven] decided to stick with what he had."

But theirs was a life continually on the move, chiefly because of Parnell's nomadic career as an on-again, off-again bookkeeper. By refusing to put down roots, Parnell was also able to preserve the secrecy of the true nature of his relationship with his "son." In 1975, he pulled Steven out of fifth grade in

Santa Rosa and moved farther north to the rural town of Willits. A month later, they moved again—this time, to the coastal town of Fort Bragg, where Steven got into some minor trouble setting fires and starting fights at school.

Once during their Northern California odyssey, police picked Steven up for shoplifting, but he never took the opportunity to reveal to them who he really was. They returned him to his father, Kenneth Parnell, with an admonishment never to steal again, and Parnell took the cops' lecture as a sign that it was time to hit the road once more. In September of 1976, "Dad" and "Dennis" moved again, settling a few miles to the east on the remote outskirts of the dirt-road settlement of Comptche in rural Mendocino County. There they remained, living alternately like Rabelaisian libertines and guilty hermits, for the next three years. At one point, their "family" was joined by Barbara Mathias, an addict and ex-wife of one of Parnell's former neighbors who apparently had no problem with joining Ken and Steven in an occasional ménage à trois, according to court records. A toxic parent herself, Mathias came and went over the years, introducing her own children to Parnell, who allegedly attempted sex with them just as he had with Steven.

Parnell was not much of a parent as Steven grew up. He behaved toward Steven more like a permissive older brother who had never learned abstinence or self-discipline himself and passed his lax ways on to his young charge. By the time the boy turned ten, he'd already become addicted to tobacco. He was drinking whiskey in the sixth grade and, when Parnell scored any marijuana, Steven slunk off into the woods to enjoy a joint or two of his own while the Old Man toked his doobie in the front room.

The older Steven grew, the less interest he showed in trying to find his way home to Merced. It was not for lack of escape opportunities. Steven had his share of baby-sitters during Parnell's infrequent absences, and he began staying overnight at the homes of friends before he entered junior high. Once, while in the sixth grade, he and 60 other students spent several days away from home in San Francisco on a field trip. By high school, he was making out-of-town trips as a member of the football team.

Sarah Beach, one of Steven's classmates during his years in Comptche, remembered him as Dennis Parnell, "a shy kid with a goofy sense of humor and a big, toothy smile" who rode around on a friend's motorbike.

"I went to the Parnell place twice, both times on the back of the little motorcycle," Beach recalled. "It was a dingy trailer, surrounded by a chain-link fence. Steven would run in to get his coat and run back out, and we'd patch out of there down the dirt road. He wouldn't let me come in."

Steven lived a furtive, schizoid existence. He phoned friends when Parnell wasn't around and he frequently hitchhiked to the movies, friends' houses, or home from school. Steven also had access to bicycles. He even learned how to drive Parnell's car and sent letters to his friends without "Dad's" consent or knowledge. But ironically, as stated in the flyer his parents distributed after he first disappeared, Steven was never one to try to run away—and he never did.

In August 1979, the Parnells moved once more, to a secluded one-room shelter with no running water, indoor plumbing, or electricity at an overgrown ranch in the mountains near the town of Manchester. Each weekday morning, Steven hiked up the hill from the cabin he and Parnell shared to the main road, where he caught a ride with sheep rancher Bill Piper to Point Arena High School.

"He used to talk about things on the way to school, like movies, but he never talked about his family," recalled Piper. Once, when Piper asked him about his mother, the teenager simply sat mute and wouldn't answer.

"He never said a word, so I figured he didn't want to talk about it," said Piper.

At Arena High, Steven was a quiet C student who played briefly on the junior varsity football team. Parnell had taken a job as a night auditor at Ukiah's ornate Victorian-era Palace Hotel and he often took "Dennis" with him so that his teenager could watch TV in one of the hotel's empty rooms.

They were an odd couple, but oddly amiable too—at least in outward appearance. Steven's teachers never saw any problem between father and son, and neither did any neighbors. One of Parnell's coworkers described their relationship as "nice and easygoing . . . a real model parent-son sort of thing."

Steven might have remained with Parnell forever if Parnell had been able to contain his lust. But for whatever sick reason, Kenneth Parnell's fetish was narrowly focused upon little boys, and the plain fact was that Steven was no longer small. He was, in fact, getting to be as tall as Parnell himself. His voice was changing, he was on the verge of shaving, and he had hair growing in places where there had been none before.

Each day Steven came closer to becoming a man, Kenneth Parnell lost a little more interest. He wanted new meat—even tried enlisting Steven into playing the Ervin Murphy role and helping him snatch another youngster from the streets of Ukiah. Steven reluctantly pimped for Parnell a couple of times, but conveniently failed to get any of the boys that Parnell targeted into the waiting car. Parnell saw he was getting no real help from Steven, so he solicited the help of Sean Poorman, a 16-year-old neighborhood teen.

On Valentine's Day, 1980, Poorman and Parnell played out a scenario hauntingly akin to the one Parnell and Ervin Murphy had used to abduct Steven Stayner seven and a half years earlier. Five-year-old Timothy White was on his way from school to his baby-sitter's house clutching a handful of his classmates' valentines when Poorman attempted to woo him into Parnell's car. When wooing failed, Poorman grabbed him, tossed him in the backseat, and Parnell punched the gas.

Later that day, at the cabin he shared with Steven, Parnell attempted to assuage Timmy's terror the same way he had successfully seduced Steven: by surrounding him with favorite toys and foods—to wit, spaghetti and tacos. In another replay of the original abduction, Parnell dyed Timmy's blond hair dark brown to throw off anyone who might come searching for him.

For his part, Steven delighted in having a little brother. Over the next two weeks, TV newscasts and local newspapers carried the youngster's photo and stories about the lack of progress in the search for Timmy White. But in the televisionless cabin, Steven was showing the five-year-old how to play tag, reading him comic books and even teaching Timmy some basic arithmetic. Between the fun times, Timmy would lapse into homesick tears, reminding Steven of his own futile spells of despair in his early days with Parnell. Timmy so touched Steven that he finally decided to act—not for himself, but on behalf of the kidnapped boy.

Bad weather prevented execution of Steven's plan for nearly a week but, late in the evening of March 1, 1980, while Parnell was working at the hotel, the boys walked and hitchhiked 40 miles from Manchester to Ukiah. Steven knew the risks. When he saw slow headlights heading their way on the highway, he would grab Timmy and leap off the pavement until he was sure it wasn't Parnell home early from work and out on the road, looking for them.

Once they got to Ukiah, Steven tried first to follow Timmy's directions to his parents' home and to his baby-sitter's house. They were unable to find the Whites' home and the baby-sitter wasn't home. It was not part of Steven's original game plan, but he finally decided to take Timmy to the police. He coached the boy on how to enter the station to turn himself in, then he led him to the front door and stepped back across the street, into the shadows.

A light rain was falling as Timmy peeked through the glass door, but he did not enter. Instead, he turned and ran crying down the street. Officer Bob Warner saw him dash off into the dark and stepped outside in time to see the little boy catch up to an older boy. Warner radioed a squad car to intercept the pair and then followed after Timmy, catching up with him and Steven two blocks away.

"What's going on, guy?" asked Warner.

"We're just trying to find this kid's home," said Steven.

"What's your name?" the cop from the squad car asked the younger boy.

"Timmy White," he said.

"Do you know how long we've been looking for you?" asked the cop, before turning to the older boy.

Asked his name, Steven gave his real name for the first time in seven years, and told the officers he had been missing from his home in Merced for over seven years. (For dramatic purposes, Stayner's biographer Mike Echols took poetic license and changed that answer to the authorities' first question to "I know my first name is Steven," which became the title of Echols's 1991 book.)

But Steven still would not immediately identify his "guardian" as Kenneth Parnell.

"He was visibly shaken that his father was going to get into trouble," said Ukiah police chief Donald Johnson. "You could tell he thought this man was his father."

After some coaxing, police finally got a name. They arrested the stocky, balding bookkeeper Kenneth Parnell at once—and not a moment too soon, as it turned out. He had been preparing to pull up stakes once more and take his two young "sons" with him—this time, to Arkansas.

"I brought Timmy in because I didn't like what was happening," Steven said. "It happened to me and I didn't want to see it happen to anyone else."

But there were at least three other motives for Steven's altruism to which he admitted in later years.

One was as base as simple jealousy. Whether he was being sardonic or simply cruel, Parnell had flatly told Steven that he was getting long in the tooth. He had picked himself a new chicken because he had grown tired of Steven.

A second reason was the "do-or-die" moment Steven felt in the way of opportunity: if he had Timmy with him, and two voices testified to Parnell's kidnapping instead of just one, the likelihood that some adult might listen and free them both would climb exponentially.

But the third reason was, perhaps, darkest of all in its way. In two weeks' time, Timmy had come to regard Steven as his hero—a "god," as Steven put it. Delivering Timmy from the hands of perdition into the grateful arms of his frantic parents instantly gave Steven hero status well beyond the community of Ukiah or the White family. Steven Stayner was no longer a half-willing abductee or a pedophile's plaything. He would return home a celebrity.

"I also would be coming home for doing something positive," said Steven. "Maybe get some congratulations."

It didn't turn out quite that way.

XIV

On March 2, 1980, a Merced police officer knocked at the front door of the small frame house at 1655 Bette Street and asked Delbert and Kay Stayner if he could talk to them about their son. Kay blanched. She leaped to the conclusion that Cary, who had just gotten his driver's license and was off on his first trip away from home, had been in an accident.

"We assumed it was our oldest son, Cary, because he was up in Yosemite on a camping trip and we were very worried about him," Kay Stayner recalled nine years later, in a first-person memoir for *TV Guide*. "We figured maybe he'd slipped off a cliff. It never even occurred to us that it could be about Steve. When the officer said, 'No, this isn't about Cary—it's about Steve,' it floored us."

Within twenty-four hours of his reappearance at the Ukiah police station, Dennis Gregory Parnell had magically metamorphosed back into Steven Gregory

Stayner, and was on his way back to the home he'd left behind in the San Joaquin Valley seven years and four months earlier. He arrived in Merced on a Sunday to a media horde swarming on the Stayners' front lawn. Amid strobe lights, tears, fanfare, and every sort of kudo short of a ticker tape parade, Steven Stayner was reunited with Kay and Delbert, his three sisters, and his older brother, Cary. It became international news, later ranked by Associated Press as one of the top ten stories of the year.

"My mom made chili verde for all the newsmen," said Vicki Tatum, who grew up next door to the Stayners and continued to live there for another twenty years after Steven returned. "There were TV trucks from one end of Bette Street to the other, and the other streets in the neighborhood were all blocked off."

But the picture-perfect ending of the Steven Stayner story had a peculiarly hollow ring. While there was no denying the rush of emotion and the heartfelt embraces captured on national network TV, the full truth of Steven's years with Parnell had yet to emerge. He wouldn't even reveal the sodomy secret to police until after nearly two weeks of questioning. Interrogation at the hands of the media became very nearly as uncomfortable.

"At first he ate up all the attention and was impressed by it," said his older sister Cindy Stayner, "Then it got old and he tried to get out of the light."

One newspaper reported the ordeal as the story of "the boy with two dads," almost as if it were some quirky tale about a kidnapping victim who couldn't make up his mind between his abductor and his real father. The Steven Stayner story took on a much more serious and darkly terrifying tone when, reluctantly, over time, Steven began to confess to the incessant array of journalists who came knocking at his door for interviews that he had, indeed, been routinely defiled by Kenneth Parnell. While Steven didn't like to talk about how he had been used to sate the aging pederast's lust, he seemed better able to deal with the ugly truth of his relationship with "Dad" Parnell than either his community or his own immediate family. He even joked about how his nonstop recitation of the details to the newspaper interviewers was actually therapeutic and saved him and his family the cost of years of psychological trauma counseling. He absolutely refused to get professional help, and his parents encouraged him not to do so. They told the world that they were convinced there would be full healing from his abduction and sexual abuse in the closeness and love of a family reunited.

"I never reached out to talk about it with my parents and they never pushed to find out," said Steven. "I returned almost a grown man, and yet my parents saw me at first as their seven-year-old. After they stopped trying to teach me the fundamentals all over again, it got better. . . ."

But not by very much.

Indelible changes from years of living with a pedophile, as well as Steven's normal maturation into an occasionally rebellious adolescent put him at odds with a family who remembered him only as a buck-toothed, shaggy-haired innocent. The older, toughened survivor who returned to Merced after seven years with Parnell stood out boldly and somewhat uncomfortably beside a family and a whole way of living that had receded like so many faded memories. The changes became painfully apparent when the Stayners gathered around to watch him open up seven years' worth of Christmas gifts. By the time Steven returned, the G.I. Joe doll that his parents had wrapped for him during the first Christmas after he vanished served only as a painful reminder of just how much time had passed.

"He's not our little seven-year-old anymore that you can cuddle and paddle on the fanny and send out to play," said Kay Stayner, who characterized the homecoming as bittersweet. From the viewpoint of the rest of the family, Steven's return was seen as simply overwhelming.

"When Steve came home, everybody else all got shoved in the background," Kay added.

The Steven Stayner whom Kenneth Parnell had raised was a hard-drinking, chain-smoking, foul-mouthed young stud who liked fast cars, fast living, and kicking back.

Still, Steven was also a genuine local hero. It probably did not help that Timmy White had come to regard him as "a human god," as Kay Stayner put it. The adulation heaped upon her prodigal son by the media, his hometown of Merced, and Timmy's eternally grateful parents, made Steven difficult to live with.

"He did poorly in school from the start," his mother said. "He wouldn't do his homework, and was more interested in girls and hanging around than he was in schoolwork."

Steven was a poor fit as a freshman at Merced High. On the one hand, his years with Parnell, who had never graduated from high school himself and cared little about education, left Steven ill-prepared to keep pace with students his own age. On the other hand, Steven had both a furtive wariness and a sexual sophistication that was light-years beyond his classmates, making close relationships among his peers exceedingly difficult. He was envied and even revered as a celebrity, but was also the subject of sniggering gibes by those who assumed that pedophiliac rape automatically made Steven himself a homosexual.

"How could the media put that kind of label on a human being?" asked Vicki Tatum, who watched Steven dissemble over time, alternately welcoming, then tolerating journalists, and ultimately shying away when the overattention became unbearable. While there seemed to be a constant open season on his sex life among the town gossips and even in the national media, the subject was taboo in the Stayner household. When people asked Steven's older sisters about the sexual abuse, they had no answer.

"I never really talked to him [about the abuse]," said Cindy Stayner. "*No one* talked about *it*. My parents really wouldn't talk about it."

Cindy and her sisters were not the only Stayner children affected by the trauma of Steven's disappearance and dramatic reappearance. Next to Kay and Delbert, his older brother Cary probably suffered the most.

The night that Steven first returned to Merced, Cary had a hard time sleeping. He sneaked into the living room where Steven was dozing peacefully and stared at him.

"I stayed up a long time just looking at Steven while he slept, and listening to him breathe," Cary told one writer. "I just couldn't believe that my brother was finally back home again.

"You know, I went outside that night and I walked several blocks and then looked up at the stars and started to wish on one again. But then I remembered that Steve was back home and so I thanked the star instead."

The shock of Steven's victimization was especially hard for his older brother to take, as it became clear to the proudly heterosexual Cary Stayner that Steven had regularly engaged in homosexual activity. As a Mormon and a recent high school graduate in a community that still viewed gay sex as blasphemy and gay men as freaks of nature akin to cannibals or vampires, Cary saw it as his brotherly duty to cure his kid brother by getting him laid—with women, this time—as quickly and as frequently as possible. As the dutiful 18-year-old brother who had to have felt some of the same irrational guilt for Steven's kidnapping that Delbert and Kay suffered from, Cary even made up a slut wish list for Steven during those first few months—the names of easy women on the

Merced High campus whom young Steven could quickly steer between the sheets.

If he was flattered or grateful, Steven didn't show it. Though a "normal" life was virtually impossible by any definition, it was what Steven sought. But it was not what Cary wanted, either for Steven or for himself.

"When Steven returned, Cary stood completely in the background. He didn't want to be in the spotlight. Ever. Not during that time, or after," proclaimed Kay Stayner.

But Kay Stayner was wrong. Cary was drawn to the spotlight like a moth, even if he was forced to stand mutely at the edge of it with his sisters and parents while Steven basked at its center. He harbored jealousy at Steven's nonstop notoriety while at the same time feeding off of it. He professed a false modesty that apparently fooled everyone, even his own mother. He took to introducing himself to new acquaintances as "Steven Stayner's brother" instead of using his own name, and he hovered nearby whenever a journalist or video crew showed up for yet another interview. Further, although he claimed to be proud of Steven's heroism when speaking about his kid brother, Cary also came to resent Steven's libertine and occasionally disrespectful behavior at home—in part because Cary felt as though he could never have gotten away with the kind of coarse and brazen behavior that Steven often exhibited.

As Dennis Parnell, Cary's little brother Steven had grown up without family rules. He was "basically on my own," as he put it, while Cary was forced to follow the standards of a devout Mormon household. Cary, who had been the Stayners' only son for seven years, was instantly shoved into the family background the night that Timmy White and 14-year-old Steven Stayner walked into the Ukiah police station. In his own way, at the age of eighteen Cary Stayner was just as much adrift and outwardly unfocused on his future as his kid brother. Cary had become "very much a loner and very angry at the world" in the years following Steven's abduction, according to Kay Stayner.

Instead of helping to resolve that anger, Steven's unexpected return raised the temperature on Cary's smoldering resentment even higher by adding a measure of envy to his feelings about Steven's abduction and return as the favored son.

"It was just that, 'I'm Steven Stayner,' and his head was all bloated out," Cary told screenwriter J. P. Miller, who traveled to Merced in 1987 to meet the Stayners as part of his research for an NBC miniseries on the Steven Stayner story. Besides having to share a bedroom with his little brother, Cary also got a front row seat as gifts, rewards, and adulation poured in for Steve.

"I guess I was jealous. I'm sure I was," said Cary. "I was the oldest and all that. Then all of a sudden it's gone. I got put on the back burner, you might say."

The brothers became Cain and Abel, quarreling more often and more bitterly than Steven did with his parents.

"When Steven came back at age fourteen all the family's attention turned a hundred and eighty degrees from that which had been focused on Cary during those previous seven years," observed one family acquaintance.

Cary faded deeper into the background.

The miracle of Steven Stayner's reappearance as a teenager vanished the same way the innocence of Steven Stayner's childhood disappeared—just not so dramatically nor so abruptly. After the TV cameras shut off and the media left, Steven's life returned to normal . . . or rather, to as normal a life as a raped young media star could expect in the tiny, gossipy farm town of Merced.

Steven was not just taller and heavier, with more hair on his face. Steven was no longer little Stevie. He was still a teenager, but he had already acquired many of the traits of a very troubled adult. He kept his emotions in check and held certain truths to himself, no matter how many times he was interviewed. He even considered suicide once after his return to Merced.

"I don't cry," Steven told one journalist. "In seven years, I built a wall around myself. If I could [cry], I might not be able to stop."

Three years after his triumphant homecoming, Steven stood six feet tall, sported a mustache, drank Jack Daniel's, smoked pot, and took up shooting pool and roller skating. Steven was restless, to put it mildly. He couldn't hold a job, but with part of the option money that producers paid the Stayners for TV rights to their story, Steven bought a '76 Mustang as soon as he was old enough to drive. Two weeks later, he hit a parked car. He got his first ticket and was awarded his first forty-five-day driver's license suspension.

He liked driving fast. By the age of nineteen, Steven had piled up $1,100 in unpaid traffic tickets. He paid them off by raking leaves and splitting logs for the county, but that didn't end his problems on the road. He continued his speeding ways. Before he turned twenty-one, he'd crashed three cars. There were similar scofflaw problems at home and at school. He was a lousy student, an angry son, and a moody brother.

He and Delbert had screaming matches over what Steven was allowed to do under Delbert's roof. The Stayners kicked him out of the house twice after they quarreled with him and Steve finally dropped out of Merced High in his senior year after a rash of bad grades. He opted instead for what would be an unsuccessful experiment at home schooling. He had no attention span for, nor interest in, schoolwork, whether it was doled out in books and classroom lectures or spoon-fed to him at home. Ultimately, he did pass the test for a high school equivalency diploma, but the signals of a very troubled youth continued to hover all around him. Yet Steven and his parents still refused to get him professional counseling.

Instead, he wondered aloud about all that had gone awry in his life to the parade of reporters who showed up incessantly from as far away as New York and Australia and Switzerland and Germany. All the television networks and magazines, every wire service and most major newspapers, wound up sooner or later at 1655 Bette Street, pencils poised and cameras whirring to capture each nuance of Steven Stayner's miraculous life after Kenneth Parnell.

"Why doesn't my dad hug me anymore?" Steven complained. "I guess seven years changed him too. We used to go to the lake fishing. [Now] he just sits in the house. Everything has changed. Sometimes I blame myself. I don't know sometimes if I should have come home. Would I have been better off if I didn't?"

Delbert tried too late to impose his own Mormon ethics on his prodigal son, but all his lecturing did was increase the generational friction. It didn't help that Delbert was no longer the strong, masculine role model that he had been prior to Steven's abduction, and that he had been unemployed with "emotional problems," leaving Kay much of the responsibility for earning an income. For a time, she operated a day care center.

"You can't expect to go through life unless you work for it," Delbert blustered shortly after Steven quit school. "I think he's starting to learn that. I don't want him to be a welder all his life, but it's a start."

Steven did enroll in two welding classes at Merced Community College after he earned his high school equivalency diploma, but soon lost interest and dropped out, just as he had from high school. He expressed an interest in law enforcement, but never applied for work with any police department. He sold fried chicken, delivered pizzas, did chores for the city parks department, worked as a security guard and a janitor, and labored in a meat-packing factory—but never at any job paying higher than minimum wage.

Whether it originated from his shattered childhood or his detached adolescence, Steven Stayner had no focus nor lasting enthusiasm for anything that might amount to a career. The one constant in his life after his years with Kenneth Parnell was the media. Reporters kept coming. The story of the little boy stolen who came home a man was regurgitated incessantly still. During Steven's first adult fishing trip with his father to nearby McClure Lake. During the family's first picnic and Christmas together. On all of the anniversaries of his abduction and his return. When Kenneth Parnell was tried and sentenced for kidnapping Steven and Timmy White in 1982. And again on April 5, 1985, when Parnell was released from prison.

A book was inevitable. A former social worker named Mike Echols began peppering Delbert and Kay Stayner with requests to write such a chronicle about Steven's ordeal shortly after Steven's return to Merced in 1980. Echols described himself as an antipedophiliac activist, yet ironically, in the course of writing his book, Echols eventually came to know Kenneth Parnell as well or better than he did the Stayners. According to the couple, Echols seemed far too close to the avowed child molester to make them comfortable, and while the Stayners at first agreed to let Echols tell their son's story, they later declined to give him either their permission or their cooperation. Most of *I Know My First Name Is Steven*—the book that Echols eventually published in 1991, two years after the airing of the NBC miniseries of the same name—came from court records involving Parnell's two trials, and the appeal of his convictions for abducting Steven Stayner and Timmy White. After initially cooperating with him, the Stayners shut Echols out of their lives, but he would return before the close of the 1980s.

"He waited until Stevie was eighteen, then he went to him," said Delbert. "Stevie came to me and his mother, crying that he wanted us to sign a paper giving that man permission 'cause he [Steven] said otherwise they wouldn't make a movie about it. So we did."

His wife was even more blunt, using the same damning epithet to describe Echols that she used when speaking of Parnell.

"I have his book, but I will not open it," said Kay Stayner. "I don't know why I keep it around. That man is despicable."

While understandably fractured and dysfunctional in any number of ways, all of the Stayners remain unified on the twin subjects of the television version of *I Know My First Name Is Steven* versus the book that Echols wrote. While it took some dramatic license, the miniseries was excellent and evenhanded, they believe. The book, however, which dwelled on the most lurid details of Parnell's perverse sexual appetites and Steven's forced submission, was pornographic, according to several family members. Steven's wife Jody (whom he married in 1985), who does not see eye to eye with Kay and Delbert on most things, agreed with their assessment of Echols as "despicable." She described the reading of Echols's book as the kind of experience that makes the reader want to shower immediately after finishing it. She was pleased to participate in the making of the TV miniseries, however.

Steven met his future wife in 1984, when Jody Edmonson was a junior at Atwater High and Steven, already a high school dropout, was working as a packer at the Richmond Meat Company. They dated for a year, then married in 1985, when Jody got pregnant. He was 20. She was 17.

In the beginning, Jody seemed to have a profound effect on Steven. She believed later that it might have been simply that she was the first person in his life who simply listened to him without either condemning or exalting him. He was a handsome prize for a young girl, and she liked to party just as much as he did, but at the end of the day he was just Steven—neither the hometown hero nor the hometown homo. In her adolescent naïveté, Jody became his sounding board. He opened his heart to her—or at least as much as it was possible for him to do so.

Steven converted to his parents' faith, joining the Merced Stake Center of the Church of Jesus Christ of Latter-Day Saints, and took his new role as family man quite seriously. On December 23, 1985, Jody gave him Ashley Lewella Stayner. Eighteen months later, on May 11, 1987, Ashley had a little brother: Steven Gregory Stayner Jr.

"They don't go out unless I go with them or there's someone outside watching," Steven told yet another interviewer after the children were born. "If they're just out on the porch, the door is always open. As long as I can see them and hear them."

But there was a time when Steven didn't see his children. Passion and patience aside, Jody fought frequently with her husband over his free spending and low wages. They separated, reconciled, and separated again, and the children remained with Jody. They also did not see their paternal grandparents—at least, not with any frequency. The Stayners were experiencing their own lack of domestic bliss in the late 1980s.

In 1986, Delbert and Kay split up without warning just weeks after an Easter weekend camping trip that the entire family enjoyed at Lake Shasta in Northern California. All the Stayners were there, including Steven, who remarked that it was "sorta like old times."

But that may have been just the problem. Old times had not always been good times. Whether aggravated by the disappearance of their seven-year-old son or due to far deeper and more enduring psychological issues, Kay and Delbert Stayner had "personal problems" that brought county social workers into their lives, according to one family member. While the precise nature of those problems was not revealed, Kay mysteriously opted to pull up stakes, move to Gold Hill, Oregon, and take her young daughter, blond, blue-eyed Cory Stayner, along with her. Kay and Cory remained in Oregon for more than two years, until Cory graduated from high school and came back to Merced as an adult. Like Steven and Jody, Kay and Delbert reconciled just in time for the miniseries.

Screenwriter J. P. Miller recalled a family that was "emotionally dysfunctional."

"I found no affection between the parents and the children," he said, writing Kay Stayner as a cold and distant character over the objections of his bosses at NBC. "They said she wasn't sympathetic enough."

Miller, whose credits included the Oscar-winning *Days of Wine and Roses* and TV's *Helter Skelter* miniseries about the Charles Manson case, stuck to his guns. The result was a script that concentrated on the horror of Steven Stayner's abduction, his years with Parnell, and his happy return to Merced, but did not overlook the nuances of an oddly out-of-synch family that seemed to pose as normal.

"It was weird," Miller said years later. "I had the feeling something bad was going to happen again."

XV

On May 21 and 22, 1989, NBC premiered the four-hour miniseries *I Know My First Name Is Steven*, based on the longest known case of kidnapping in modern U.S. history. The sensational tale of the Mormon Stayner family, whose younger son Steven had vanished December 4, 1972, while on his way home from school, was the stuff of enduring TV reruns, and had a life well beyond its initial network run. The drama earned several Emmy nominations and a Golden Globe nomination as best miniseries, and was one of the top-rated TV movies of the year. It went on to similar success in Europe, Asia, and around the world, and continued to pop up on American television with some regularity ten years later.

Steven Stayner himself had a small role near the end of the first segment of *I Know My First Name Is Steven*, appearing as one of the police officers who took the kidnapped 14-year-old back home to

Merced to be reunited with his parents. Cary Stayner, however, had no part in the film and remained hidden where he had always been: in the background. Even the actor who portrayed him had very few lines.

After interviewing him for his screenplay, J. P. Miller described Cary as "shy, withdrawn . . . he felt he was a loser. He was very polite; he had dreams of being an artist."

Indeed, Cary's successful stint as the student newspaper's editorial cartoonist briefly motivated him to pursue a career as an artist. That dream went nowhere though, becoming a victim of Cary's own negative view of himself. He refused to apply to college or art school because "it'll never happen," he told one interviewer. Instead, he confined his sketching and cartooning to an occasional exercise in self-expression for himself, or for the enjoyment of his family and friends.

"He wanted to do books [as an illustrator] but couldn't find no writer to do it with," observed Delbert Stayner.

One member of the Stayner family who did recognize Cary's talent and encouraged him to do something more with his art was Delbert's youngest brother, Jerry. Cary's uncle was sixteen years younger than Delbert and considerably different from his older brothers and sisters. Not content to work in the canneries like many of his relatives, Jerry started his own glass business with a partner, Steve Cox, and their C & S Glass Co. eventually grew prosperous enough to give Cary a job for a few years as a window installer and glazier.

But Jerry also took his nephew under his wing as an artist. Far from pooh-poohing his sketches as idle doodling, Jerry vowed to help Cary with formal schooling if he could. Never very big on formal education beyond high school, the Stayner family could have had its first bona fide technically trained commercial artist in Cary. And Cary recognized that upbeat, inspiring uncle Jerry might be just the means to that end.

Cary liked drawing women, and occasionally impressed a girl with his talent for portraits as well as caricature. While he could draw the female form expertly, however, he had trouble relating to the real thing.

"He never had a steady girlfriend, but I know he had sex with girls, and he'd always doodle in his notepad and make these naked women," recalled his cousin, Ronnie Jones. Jones also recalled Cary's reticence to go skinny-dipping with willing women. When Jones once spotted a bevy of babes bathing in the buff along the Merced, Jones readily accepted their invitation to come join them. As Jones shed his skivvies and hopped in the water, Cary remained on the beach, staring.

Throughout the many years she had known Cary, Steven's wife Jody couldn't recall a single conversation of more than a few mumbled words that she had ever had with her brother-in-law. Other female cousins or close family friends described their own relations with Cary as cordial, but hardly close, and never much deeper than a "Hi, how are you?" Even when he took them camping or hiking in the Sierras with him, the dialogue rarely got deeper than warnings about poison ivy patches or directions to the closest spot to find drinking water. If he had any confidants among the opposite sex, neither the men nor the women in Cary's life seemed to know who they might be.

If anything, Cary never seemed to have outgrown the adolescent tendency to objectify females. There were incidents when he was in his teens, before Steven returned home, in which Cary acted out some of his apparent fantasies, according to next-door neighbor Vicki Tatum.

Tatum was in seventh grade at the time of the first incident, when the two older Stayner girls, Cindy and Jody, had asked her to sleep over. She remembers that she was wearing red shorts and a candy-cane-striped tube top when she went next door to the Stayners', and she wondered later if that had any-thing to do with setting off Cary's strange behavior.

The girls stayed up late, gossiping and eating pop-corn, and all of them slept together in one big bed. Shortly after the lights went out, Cary crept into the room. He was stark naked. Unlike the prospect of taking his clothes off to go skinny-dipping with strangers, apparently stripping in front of girls over whom he exercised some control as an older brother or next-door neighbor had more appeal to him.

"I said, 'Cary, either you leave or I'm gonna scream and tell my parents!' " recalled Tatum.

Cary left the room.

Later that year, Tatum said Cindy Stayner came to her with the upsetting news that Cary had not ended his nudist ways. He would call Cindy to the bathroom when he was getting out of the shower and ask for a towel. When she handed it to him, Cary would merely stand there, dripping and naked, and stare at her. Cindy asked Vicki to run away from home with her, according to Tatum.

The two girls, who were about two years younger than Cary, sneaked out of their respective houses, rendezvoused on the street, and slept that night in a haystack a mile or so from their homes. They breakfasted on a sumptuous meal of bologna and bread that they bought from a nearby convenience store, but tired of the runaway life by the end of the day. They returned home to spankings and thankful parental tears—particularly in the Stayner household, where the very real panic and haunting pain of a missing child still had especially uncomfortable currency.

When Vicki turned 17, Cary left her with yet another naked memory. This time, she and a girlfriend accompanied Cary and another young man on a camping trip to one of the nearby lakes. That evening, the girls cooked and the guys cleaned up. When the campfire was out and the only light came from the stars and moon overhead, Vicki noticed something moving beneath her cot. It was Cary, nude. Vicki warned him away just as she had several years earlier, promising a scream if he tried anything funny.

"Maybe if I would have gone out with him . . ." she said a little wistfully many years later, sounding like a guilty nurse who failed to diagnose and treat a patient's disease.

Corin Nemec, who played Steven as a teenager in the NBC miniseries, recalled the one big scene in *I Know My First Name Is Steven* in which Cary's character seemed to offer up yet another testimonial to his frustrated sexuality. In a revealing moment in the second half of the miniseries, the older of the Stayner brothers goaded the newly returned Steven to find himself a loose young tart and get laid as soon as possible.

"Cary gave him a list of all the girls who would 'put out,' " recalled Nemec. "The scene didn't mean much to me then. . . ."

Steven tried it his brother's way for a while. He led a promiscuous sex life that began with losing his virginity shortly after his 15th birthday on a playground in Merced's Applegate Park. Seven years later, however, while 28-year-old Cary was still without a steady girlfriend, Steven had long abandoned fast women and free love in exchange for his rocky one-woman romance with the former Jody Edmonson. If only he had been able to give up his love of fast vehicles as easily as he had given up fast women, the lives of everyone near him, including his brother Cary, might have turned out very differently.

When *I Know My First Name Is Steven* finally aired, the real Steven Stayner was a manager trainee at Pizza Hut. His salary was low, but the job had promise. Though he had already blown most of the $40,000 he had earned for selling his story to television, he still had enough for a blue and white Kawasaki EX-400 motorcycle, which he drove—fast—to and from Pizza Hut each day.

At 24, Steven seldom drank hard stuff the way he once packed whiskey away, and while he enjoyed a joint from time to time, he could not accurately be described as a pothead. He did not sleep around. Although many things had changed in his life for the better, he still sped through intersections, along passing lanes, and around blind curves with the same reckless abandon that he exercised in his younger days. As a mark of his more responsible growth to a new level of maturity, however, he did wear a helmet most of the time. Unfortunately, the evening of September 16, 1989, was not one of them.

Less than four months earlier, the NBC miniseries had premiered, trouncing ABC's epic *War and Remembrance* in the ratings. Now the miniseries was up for an Emmy and Steven was once more the Prince of Merced. It was a good time in Steven's life. In addition to the renewed adulation for saving Timmy White, it also looked as though Steven might actually be putting his life back together. He and Jody remained separated, but they were talking, and Steven was seeing the children.

But it was not to be. Just before 5 P.M. that day, he climbed aboard his motorcycle and rode down an Atwater highway into eternity. Stayner, who had a suspended license, was not wearing a helmet. Two months earlier, his helmet had been stolen.

Migrant laborer Antonio Loera borrowed a dark gold 1976 Plymouth Volare from a friend that afternoon and was driving south down a dirt road toward Santa Fe Drive, the main highway that connected Atwater with Merced. As the 28-year-old packing house worker pulled out onto the rain-slicked highway, the Plymouth's engine stalled and, try as he might, Loera was unable to choke enough gas into the car's faulty carburetor to spark the pistons back into action. When he looked up from the dashboard to the motorcycle hurtling toward him, accompanied by the sound of squealing tires and metal raking sparks across the asphalt, it was already too late.

Steven Stayner skidded into the door on the driver's side of the Volare. Frightened, Loera finally managed to fire up his engine, and backed away from Steven and the wrecked Kawasaki. He fishtailed down the highway away from the accident.

Loera ran away that evening, as far as Tijuana, before his conscience and pressure from the Mexican government got the better of him. He turned himself in several days later, but that would not bring Steven back from the dead. Riggs Ambulance arrived minutes after the accident, hauling Stayner's broken body to Merced Community Medical Center, and just forty minutes later, at 5:35 P.M., Dr. Clair Pattinger declared Steven Gregory Stayner dead of a fractured skull and massive head injuries.

The night after Steven died, *I Know My First*

Name Is Steven lost the Emmy for best miniseries to *War and Remembrance.*

Delbert and Kay were off on a camping trip at the time of the accident and got the news by phone. On September 20, they buried Steven alongside Delbert's own parents at Merced District Cemetery. Like the price of the motorcycle that killed him, the $4,250 in bills from the hospital emergency room and the Stratford & Evans Funeral Home came out of the money Stayner had earned for selling his story to television.

"It's final this time," Delbert said at the funeral, which drew 450 news reporters from around the globe. "I know where Stevie's at now."

"I'm so glad that he went as Steven Gregory Stayner, our brother," said his middle sister who, like his widow, was named Jody Stayner.

Antonio Loera was charged with felony hit-and-run driving, but three months later, the farm laborer pleaded no contest and Merced Superior Court Judge George C. Barrett gave him ninety days in jail, a $100 fine, and suspension of his driver's license for a year. Already angry over the court's refusal to give Loera the maximum sentence of four years, Stayner's estranged wife hired San Francisco's celebrated "King of Torts," lawyer Melvin Belli, and sued Merced County for $5 million, claiming that the stretch of highway where Stayner died was unsafe, and unmarked as a hazard. She settled with Loera for $15,000 and the county paid $100,000.

Ten years later, in an ironic postscript to the story

of Steven Stayner's life and death, Jody had become co-owner and operater of a farm labor contracting service. She noticed one day that Antonio Loera was on her payroll and ordered him to the front office to pick up his check. When Loera stood in front of her, he recognized her and began trembling, remembering the furious lioness he'd faced in the courtroom, who demanded Loera be sent to prison for killing the father of her infant children.

"I told him to relax and not to worry about his job," she said. "I gave him an extra one hundred dollars and told him I forgave him."

Jody Stayner did not recall Cary appearing as one of the pallbearers at Steven's funeral. To her knowledge, he didn't even show up. As usual, he'd faded into the background, recognizable only by his everpresent ball cap, which hid his ravaged patchy scalp from public view.

Around the time of Steven's accident Cary lived with his Uncle Jerry. They shared a tiny frame bungalow on industrially zoned Brantley Street on the west side of Merced, just half a city block from C & S Glass. It was the only residence on a street lined with businesses, in a particularly poor part of Merced, but it was within walking distance of the glass shop, and the rent was dirt cheap.

At 42, Jerry Stayner was closer in age and interests to his 28-year-old nephew, Cary, than he was to his 57-year-old brother, Delbert. He was also more tolerant, and simply easier to live with than the occupants of the tumultuous household where Cary had grown up. At any given time, the already overcrowded house at 1655 Bette Street could, and did, brim over with relatives. Kay's father Bob Augustine moved in with the family for a while after Steven's return, and Steven himself lived there with Jody for several months while Kay and Cory had gone away to Oregon. Kathy Amey, a cousin from Delbert's side of the family, came there to live one summer, and Delbert had to expand a closet just to give her room for a bed.

The small frame house, constructed in the post–World War II building boom as a starter residence for a small nuclear family, had come to serve as a temporary settling place for what seemed like every relative who was between either jobs, marriages, or places to live. Thus, even though the Brantley Street house was hardly more than a shack itself, it was a welcome landing pad for Cary during the year before and the year following Steven's death. Jerry had just ended his own second marriage and the two bachelors—uncle and nephew—made a perfect odd couple.

Cary's contemporaries from that period of his life remember a doper whose fondness for weed had grown since his graduation from Merced High in 1979. There was some talk that he had even turned to harder drugs, and that he combined his love of the outdoors, especially Yosemite, with his love of controlled substances. Matt Cone, who lived around the block from Bette Street and graduated with Cary from Merced High, recalled Cary stopping by Taco Bell, where Cone worked in the early 1980s.

"He told me he was tired of organized religion," Cone recalled. "He said he was going to start his own religion."

If so, marijuana would have been its sacred herb. His Uncle Jerry didn't speak of his nephew's drug use, even after they had become roommates. All he raved over was Cary's artistic abilities. Yet despite Uncle Jerry's encouragement, Cary still hadn't done anything beyond occasional sketches. He set up a drawing table in the front room of the Brantley Street house for doodling, but his art began and ended there. Cary had evolved into a classic Central Valley type: the artsy stoner, whose ambitions are anesthetized by a dime bag of really good shit, whose dreams remain boxed inside his head, and whose frustrated existence never reaches far beyond the city limits. Cary was quirky, but universally praised as a nice guy. He was just . . . quiet.

One of his contemporaries remembered witnessing a very different Cary Stayner once during a party at the Brantley Street house while Uncle Jerry was away. The Cary Stayner he saw was perfectly capable of murder.

It was Cary's birthday party, according to Fernando Echevarria.

"There wasn't any food, but there were chips and a birthday cake," he said.

There was Cuervo 151 proof white tequila, and grass too. And, for those who cared to adjourn to the bathroom, there were also lines of cocaine. When the party moved into high gear, the tiny front room of the tiny house became packed with people—mostly guys, like Echevarria, who had tagged along with his friend Jeff, an acquaintance of the Stayners.

Echevarria didn't know most of the people there, but he did notice two young women—standouts because, as Echevarria remembered it, they were the only two females at the party. While Echevarria was immediately interested in the shorter blonde who went by the name of Kendra, the taller brunette appeared to be Cary's date. Both of the women wasted no time getting wasted, however, and mingling with every guy at the party.

When it came time to cut the birthday cake, the women were spinning on tequila and coke, alternately dancing, making refueling trips to the bathroom, and smearing cake icing on their noses, crotches, buttocks, and breasts. Jeff and Echevarria joined them in the bacchanal, daubing cake on the women as they danced, and getting daubed in return. The whole while, Echevarria noticed in his drunken peripheral vision, Cary Stayner stood rigidly at his drawing table, wearing a baseball cap and eyeing the brunette. He made a comment about not getting cake on the floor, but it was ignored. It appeared to Echevarria that Cary was drawing furiously, but Echevarria paid little attention and kept on rocking, until the fury suddenly spilled over onto the dance floor.

The brunette was so loaded that she taunted the men with a suggestion that they drop their inhibitions along with their underwear and see how a ménage à trois might work out. She wasn't interested in waiting to adjourn to the bedroom either. As Echevarria remembered it:

"She said, 'Let's get it on, if the two of you are man enough! Right *now*!'"

At that point, he said, Cary Stayner snapped.

"He went into his room, came back with a pair of nunchakus. His eyes were pinpoints, fixated on my friend Jeff, me, and the two girls, and he just began beating my friend Jeff to the ground."

Expertly whipping the chain, rope, and metal ninja weapon through the air like a deadly bolo, Cary Stayner used the nunchaku to knock his victim to the floor, then leaped on top of him and began to choke him with it. Fearing for his friend's life, Echevarria said he grabbed the knife that had been used to cut the birthday cake, leaped on Cary's back, pulled off his baseball cap, and grabbed him by the hair. He brought the blunt edge of the knife up against Cary's throat.

At six foot one, Cary was much taller and heavier than Echevarria, who said he would probably never have attempted anything so foolhardy had adrenaline not mixed with the coke and Jose Cuervo in his system. Cary reached up to grab the knife away, but cut his hand when he sliced it against the sharp edge.

The two women were crying and holding on to each other, huddled together in a corner as the tension of the moment began to ease. Cary's cousin Ronnie Jones pulled him away, and moments later Echevarria helped his friend Jeff to his feet and dragged him out of the house. Echevarria said they left and never returned, but did not file a complaint with the Merced County Sheriff's Department either. The whole horrifying incident went unreported.

"I just get sick and tired of hearing people around here talk about how quiet Cary was and what a nice guy he always was," said Echevarria, who went on to become a Merced County Health Department employee. "As far as I'm concerned, he was an asshole. He tried to kill my friend Jeff. I have no doubt about that."

From that point on, he and Jeff referred to Stayner as "Scary Cary" whenever they recalled the incident.

Cary's cousin Kathy Amey, who said she was there that night too, remembered the incident quite differently, claiming that the trouble began with Jeff—not Cary. She accused Echevarria's friend of pulling a knife after harassing the two women in the bathroom. Only then did Cary resort to using his nunchaku, she said.

Regardless of which version of the party tale is accurate, it seems clear that Echevarria and Jeff may not have been the only people who felt the heat of Cary's wrath around that time. In later years, even friends and his own family began to reluctantly suspect that Cary might not be the benign wallflower he appeared to be.

Still, in 1990, he was the last person on earth that anyone suspected might go so far as to kill his own uncle.

Jerry Stayner sold his interest in C & S Glass to his partner, Steve Cox, after his second marriage went sour in 1987 and he needed money for lawyers, alimony, and child support. He went to work as a dispatcher for Leavitts Trucking and had been there for about a year. When he went home for lunch on the day after Christmas, 1990, something went terribly wrong in the hallway of the Brantley Street house that he shared with his nephew Cary.

A neighbor passing by who noticed the front door wide open stopped in to see if Jerry was home and found the body. He called 911. Uncle Jerry had been shot three times with his own nine-shot .22 caliber pistol before his killer drove away in Jerry's company truck.

Cary covered his face and wept in the front yard when he came home to the news.

"I think it was just a lowlife bum who was in town and didn't have any money and was caught in the act," Cary told the *Merced Sun Star*. Cary did recall seeing a drifter in the front yard, picking oranges off of their tree a few days before the shooting. He was so sure about the looks of the possible suspect that he even volunteered to draw a composite sketch for police which was later published in the newspaper.

The facts faced by sheriff's detectives and the coroner were these:

Jessy Jerrold Stayner, 42, left work at 12:45 P.M. to get some lunch. At 1:15 P.M., the 911 call came in. When the ambulance service brought Jerry Stayner into Merced Community Medical Center thirty minutes later, there was a bullet in his chest and two in his head. There was a hole in his hand as if he'd made the futile attempt to fend off a bullet, but there was no sign of struggle at all in the house and no defensive scratches or other wounds on his body or clothing. At 2:16 P.M., Jerry Stayner was declared dead.

The story, as Cary guessed it, was that Jerry must have surprised the burglar when he walked into the house. The killer made off with his wallet, as well as the .22 pistol and his company truck. And one more thing. The burglar also took the company dog: a three-year-old schnauzer named Digger.

Surprisingly, all but the wallet turned up, and in less than twenty-four hours to boot. The truck was found with the keys still in the ignition, the pistol on the front seat, and Digger the dog—curled up on the floorboards but in perfect health—locked inside the cab. The truck was parked just a little over a mile away behind a Beacon Gas station.

Despite an initial flurry of activity and an APB for any drifters resembling Cary's composite, the case went unsolved. Two months after Jerry Stayner was buried, Merced County Sheriff's Lt. Don Cline speculated that the dead man might have known his assailant.

"The killer killed Stayner to avoid detection," he declared.

Cary took on the role of comforting his aunt and looking after her three young daughters, just as Uncle Jerry once had done. Cary was almost like a substitute father to Jesslyn, the youngest girl, according to Uncle Jerry's ex-wife Lori.

"The holidays were always hard on Jesslyn, because Jerry died at Christmas, and Cary was always around to help her out," said Cary's cousin Kathy Amey.

As the years passed, none of them gave too much thought to the killer who got away. And certainly they never suspected their cousin. Cary was too nice, too supportive, too quiet a young man to have done so foul a deed. The coincidence that the murderer abandoned Jerry's truck at the intersection of Jean Street and Yosemite Way—the same spot from which Steven Stayner had been kidnapped eighteen years earlier—was completely lost on them.

In the years following the deaths of Jerry and Steven Stayner, Cary receded further into the landscape than ever before. He was seldom home even for family get-togethers, as illustrated by his absence from most of the snapshots in the Stayner family photo albums. He did not attend class reunions. The few friends that he had made in high school on the student newspaper and yearbook staff went on to jobs in journalism, advertising, or photography, and frequently in bigger cities, far away from Merced. But Cary remained an underachiever and a home-town boy.

Instead of becoming an artist, he was satisfied being a glazier, first for C & S Glass, and later on with Merced Glass & Mirror Company. When the owner of Merced Glass pissed him off once, Cary "wanted to jump in a truck and drive through the boss's office and jump out and kill everyone there," said coworker Michael Marchese. Instead, Stayner punched a piece of plywood until his knuckles bled. He eventually left to become a freelance glazier, his boss none the wiser that he and his wife had been the fantasized target of Cary's wrath. If anything, they remained complimentary about his work, and gave him special praise for the caricatures he had drawn of them.

Cary later explained to Marchese that he'd exploded that one time because he was having a nervous breakdown brought on by a chemical imbalance.

There were drugs, of course, and their effect on Cary became increasingly apparent the older he got. He told Matt Cone once that he had been in rehab, and while records of voluntary commitments are deemed private under state law, it was generally acknowledged among the Stayner family that Cary's recreational use of grass had gotten far out of hand.

In March of 1997, he was arrested for the first and only time for drugs. Stayner and 31-year-old Michael Sean Osborn were caught up in a narcotics sweep conducted by the Merced–Mariposa Narcotics Task Force. Both were arrested at Osborn's Atwater house, not more than a mile from the Crestview mobile home park, where Delbert and Kay had finally moved after their latest reconciliation, just before Steven's death.

Cary's car had been spotted parked out in front of Osborn's place on at least three separate occasions, according to the police. Inside, cops found 253 potted marijuana plants under cultivation and, outside in a shed, another 85. Osborn waived his Miranda rights, but Stayner refused to talk to police. Both men were arrested for possession of marijuana for sale.

During his interview, Osborn said he'd earned about $5,000 during the previous year from selling pot, and that Stayner had no role other than helping him water and fertilize the plants from time to time. Osborn defended his crop on grounds that he was growing it for medicinal purposes, but Merced County didn't buy it. He was charged, and in August of the following year received a seven-month jail sentence, followed by four years of probation.

Despite his own arrest, Cary was never charged. Osborn had already confessed, clearing Stayner of any blame beyond being a hapless helper. Deputy DA Ash didn't believe there was enough evidence to prove to a jury that Cary was guilty beyond a reasonable doubt.

Following that brush with the law, Cary decided it was time to finally leave his hometown. At the age of 36, he pulled up stakes and moved to El Portal, where he got himself a job at the Cedar Lodge, far from the city where so much trouble had befallen his family and himself, and nearer the indescribable beauty of the Yosemite Valley that he had always loved so much.

XVI

During the first weeks of August 1999, the news of Cary Stayner's arrest and confession to the murders of Joie Armstrong, Carole Sund, Juli Sund, and Silvina Pelosso hit the Stayner family like a meteor.

"The Cary we know is not capable of these crimes," sobbed Delbert through the rear screen door of the Stayners' gray mobile home, located on a crushed gravel corner lot in the working-class suburb of Winton. "We love you, Cary. You will always be loved by your family."

"We really don't think Cary did this," said Kay Stayner, peeking out from behind a set of round reading glasses at yet another onslaught of TV cameras and tape recorders. "It goes against everything he is about. It's totally uncharacteristic."

Committing such crimes in Yosemite "was sacrilege," she added in a strong, clear voice. "The place is beautiful."

Facing the media together, the Stayners bore a faint resemblance to *American Gothic*, Grant Wood's famous portrait of a hardscrabble Midwestern farm couple. Like her husband, Kay Stayner vowed to stand by her child, right or wrong. Unlike her husband whose unconditional belief in his son's innocence simply did not waver, Kay also grudgingly offered a caveat in the event that Cary did turn out to be guilty.

"Cary may have done it," she offered. "If Cary did do what they're saying he did, it had to have been a psychiatric thing. You know, he did have that obsessive-compulsive thing where he pulled his hair out all the time. That might be something to do with it. . . ."

She stood very erect, but not stiff, shaking hands firmly and retaining a wry sense of humor, even in the face of such tragedy. While her bent, bald, and crushed husband broke down at yet another unbelievable Stayner family catastrophe, Kay remained strong—a survivor who had seen it all and could not be shocked by anything that Fate sent her way.

"It's a terrible shock to us all, everyone who knows Cary," said Sandy Cox, who comanaged C & S Glass with her husband Steve. "None of us ever thought this was possible. The Cary who's being portrayed on the news, that's not the Cary we've known for many years. My heart bleeds for his family. They have been through so much heartache, and now to go through this . . ."

Sandy's grown daughter Sarah was not so supportive. She recalled a scant two months prior to Joie Armstrong's murder when Cary kept harping to Sarah and her friends that "he was already famous," but that no one knew it yet. Pressed for details on what he was talking about, he merely smiled a knowing smile and would say nothing more on the subject.

While she had grown up with the Stayners and even lived in one of the houses that Cary had formerly occupied, Sarah tempered her unabashed affection for the man she characterized as "almost like an uncle" with new fears that she had been duped about his true identity her entire life. She never felt threatened by Cary growing up. But his arrest put her in a pondering frame of mind, as it had all of the female cousins and close family friends who had known Cary as the kind, gentle, easygoing outdoorsman of the family. She shuddered at the thought: Could she, too, have ever become one of his victims?

Cary's niece Jesslyn felt the same sense of violation.

"Cary was around every day after school," she said. "He only lived three blocks away. They lived on Bette and we lived on Ellen Street, which is just four streets over. I used to hang out with Cary, you know. We'd go to the malls and hang around."

Once, just two years earlier, in 1997, Jesslyn had gone on a camping trip with Cary back into the mountain wilderness east of Coarsegold.

"We hiked back to a waterfall about a half an hour

away from everything," she recalled. "We were all alone, just the two of us."

He could have done anything, and Jesslyn would have been powerless to stop him. The key to her own safety, as well as that of Sarah Cox and all of the other young women that Cary knew, seemed to be that he really *knew* them. Like a predator in the wild that refuses to kill its own kind, Cary apparently selected victims at random, whom he did not know and with whom he had no familiar bond. Until Joie Armstrong, he had been clever, clean, and even ingenious in his killing, leaving no trace of physical evidence behind. More importantly, he left no trail whatsoever of any familiarity with his victims. To him, it appeared, the women he selected for murder had all the humanity of mannequins.

During the first week of August, law enforcement up and down the state began to focus on other unsolved murders, particularly where the victims did not appear to have any previous relationship with their killers. The same day Armstrong's body was discovered, even before Cary Stayner was arrested, an FBI agent was already on the telephone to Calaveras County Sheriff's Det. Robert Mortimer speculating about a connection to the 1994 murder of 23-year-old prostitute Sharalyn Murphy.

"The fact that he [Stayner] cut her head off makes me wonder," reflected Mortimer, whose department had found the prostitute's body around Christmas near a one-lane mountain road a little over a hundred miles north of Yosemite. Like Joie Armstrong, Murphy had been decapitated, but authorities had never been able to find her head.

"He has nothing left to lose now," said Mortimer. "He already admitted to those other ones. If he did this one, he might as well admit it."

Another fifty miles north, in El Dorado County, authorities began looking at Stayner as a possible suspect in the 1992 decapitation murder of 19-year-old Veronica Martinez, a Sacramento waitress. Likewise, Placer County—the next county north on the map—had the unsolved abduction and murder of Cinthia Wanner. Sutter County, west of Sacramento, also had a murder case involving a beheaded woman, and Sacramento County itself had a series of deaths dating back to the early 1980s in which women were abducted and their throats slashed.

Down south in Santa Barbara, police were trying to determine Stayner's whereabouts in April of 1985, to see if he might be connected to the murder of model Kim Morgan, also a decapitation victim.

"We would be remiss as a law enforcement agency if we didn't take a look at this case," commented Santa Barbara Police Sgt. Brian Abbott.

In nearby Tuolumne County, detectives began to investigate any connection Stayner might have had to the 1994 stabbing murder of an unidentified woman whose body was torched in a barrel at Don Pedro Lake, near the place Juli Sund's body had been found.

In Merced, police were reopening the case of two

small girls who had been killed by an ax murderer in the 1980s. And even closer to home, just a few blocks from Kay and Delbert Stayner's double-wide trailer, a friend and neighbor of the Stayners refused to believe what the Merced County Sheriff already suspected: that Cary might know what had become of 11-year-old Vanessa Smith.

Beverly Smith, who had spoken at Modesto's "Vigil of Hope" rally for Carole, Juli, and Silvina the previous March, hadn't lost her own hope in a crusade to find her missing daughter, who had vanished right outside her Winton home almost three years earlier.

All that remained of the young blonde after she went for a walk down by a country highway one afternoon in 1996 was her walking stick, found by the side of the road. Because dogs were unable to pick up her scent beyond the road's edge, it was widely assumed she had climbed into someone's car and been whisked away.

On the day Stayner was charged with Joie Ruth Armstrong's murder, Beverly and her husband Art Smith—devout Mennonites—celebrated their twenty-sixth wedding anniversary. What good feeling they may have salvaged from that celebration evaporated when they heard it reported that Cary had been dreaming of killing women for thirty years. Beverly stubbornly refused to believe that her daughter could be dead at the hands of Cary Stayner. "Vanessa is still alive out there somewhere, I strongly believe that," Beverly told reporters following Cary's confessions. "We have to find her and bring her home." In the beginning at least, the Merced County Sheriff's Department tended to agree with her.

"Nothing ties him to any of the cases," said Sgt. Rick Marshall, stressing that the Smith case "has always been open and continues to be open."

As the search for links between Stayner and other murders continued, the Smiths continued their efforts to locate Vanessa. They staged a fund-raising dinner, solicited donations from neighbors, and held Tupperware parties to raise money for a nationwide search for their daughter. With their savings and cash contributions, the Smiths bought large laminated posters at $650 apiece bearing a portrait of Vanessa— the only one that the Smiths had, because their religion prohibited photographs. Fortunately, she had a class photo taken of her at school shortly before she vanished, and the Smiths were able to blow it up for the posters.

In an arrangement with long-haul truckers, the posters were attached to big rigs that would carry the word of Vanessa's vanishing act from one side of the country to the other.

"We have 120 of them out on the interstates now," Beverly said. "We intend to have 500 more in the next few months. We'll do whatever we have to do to keep our search going."

The Smiths' nickel-and-dime operation to get the word out about their missing daughter got an unexpected boost from an unlikely source through an even more unlikely supporter in the weeks following Cary Stayner's arrest. Stayner's former sister-in-law—Steven's widow Jody—put in a call to the Carole Sund/Carrington Memorial Reward Fund which, in turn, made one of its first grants to Beverly and Art Smith: a $10,000 reward for information leading to Vanessa's return.

"What the Carringtons are doing is absolutely incredible," said Jody Stayner, who noted the terrible irony that Kay and Delbert Stayner might not have had to wait seven years for the return of Steven had such a foundation existed in the early 1970s.

Seriously handicapped by a lack of money, Jody's former in-laws could not offer money for Steven's return. All they could do was blanket the state's school districts with as many "missing child" flyers as possible and hope that some responsible teacher, parent, or student would recognize him. When the flyers arrived—as they did at the very schools in Santa Rosa and Mendocino County where Dennis Gregory Parnell was enrolled as a regular student—they were misplaced, ignored, or simply tossed in the trash. Nobody made the connection between Dennis and the lost little boy from a working-class family in Merced.

Adding to the irony was the $15,000 reward that Timmy White's grateful parents gave to Steven after returning their son who had only been missing two weeks.

"If someone had put up the money when Steven was first missing, I wonder if Parnell would have ever gotten away with it," mused Jody.

* * *

After the discovery of Juli's body ended all hope that any of the three women would be found alive, the Carringtons did not simply withdraw the $250,000 in reward money that they offered in February for information leading to their loved ones' return. After paying out $50,000 to Jim Powers for finding the wrecked Grand Prix that broke the case open, the Carringtons used the remaining $200,000 as seed money for the foundation, setting up permanent offices in Modesto—the city they adopted, and that adopted them, during the most awful season of their lives.

For until Valentine's Day 1999, the Carringtons had lived quite well, but anonymously. Though blessed with millions from a family real estate dynasty that bought and sold Northern California property profitably for a century, brusque but gentle Francis Carrington and his ruggedly regal wife Carole preferred genteel solitude to hobnobbing with other millionaires. They were content running their remote Butler Valley ranch in semiretirement while shepherding the family business out of a nameless building in downtown Eureka, where son-in-law Jens Sund oversaw day-to-day business.

"I have to keep my hand in the business, but my heart is in this reward fund," Francis Carrington said. "It's the only thing we can do. You'd like to turn the clock back, but you can't."

In the wake of the Yosemite murders, the Carringtons had taken time off from the family real estate business to devote their energies to launching the foundation they'd created in their daughter's name. Its primary purpose: to provide reward money to other less fortunate families who remained without resources or reward money to help resolve their own unsolved cases of lost children or senseless murder. Instead of crumbling in grief over the deaths of Carole, Juli, and Silvina, Francis and Carole Carrington refused to buckle under to depression and become just another couple of victims.

"We lost a daughter, a granddaughter, and a friend," Francis said. "If I wasn't careful, I could have lost our whole family. If we wanted to let this ruin our lives, it might have."

The same week Cary Stayner was being charged with killing Joie Armstrong, the foundation had already put up over $100,000 in reward money for more than a half dozen homicide or missing person cases, mostly in California. And there had already been positive results. A $10,000 reward offered by the foundation led to the arrest of a suspect in the March shotgun slaying of a young man in Grayson, about ten miles west of Modesto. Stanislaus County Sheriff Les Weidman publicly thanked the Carringtons for serving "a vital role."

But for all their philanthropy, the Carringtons were not content to leave police business strictly to the police. They had never been satisfied playing a waiting game, and were not going to start now that a solid suspect was finally in custody. Francis Carrington had FBI spokesman Nick Rossi's portable beeper number, and he used it often, demanding regular updates on the case. The Carringtons comported themselves in frequent television interviews with both dignity and grace, but they were nowhere near the pop psychology state of "closure" that has gained such currency among TV talk show hosts in the 1990s.

The odd regrets Stayner offered to them during his jailhouse interview with Ted Rowlands, when he said he wished "I could've controlled myself," only vexed the Carringtons. They refused to accept Cary's version of remorse, which Carole characterized as "a nonapology apology."

"Like it was *their* [the victims'] fault!" she said. "I think it was the poorest example of an apology I've ever heard."

While their son-in-law Jens never wavered from his vengeful announcement six months earlier that he would gladly pull the lever that would execute his wife and daughter's killer, Francis and Carole carefully worded their own feelings about the death penalty . . . particularly after Stayner's arrest.

"We don't want vengeance," Francis said during one televised interview. "We want justice."

More specifically, the couple demanded answers. They still harbored serious doubts that Stayner acted alone. Francis and Carole Carrington played out a variety of possible scenarios, trying to get to the bottom of what really happened to Carole, Juli, and Silvina. Despite Stayner's confession, there were a number of unanswered questions. For one thing,

Carole wanted to know if it was true that Rachel Lou Campbell got her daughter's checking account number within days of her disappearance, and if so, how she did it.

"How did that woman end up with my daughter's credit card numbers?" she asked. "We know she had the numbers. How did she get them?"

Another mystery remained unexplained in the pink blanket fibers from Room 509: How could they be so similar to the fibers found in Rufus Dykes's Wagoneer and Mick Larwick's Corvette that experts in the FBI lab had declared them a match?

The Carringtons also questioned how Cary could have gotten the drop on the three women without anyone at the motel hearing or seeing anything unusual. Both Carole and Juli Sund had taken self-defense classes, and Carole would have fought like a lioness to save Juli and Silvina.

Most perplexing of all was the mystery of Cary Stayner himself—a professed serial killer who seemed to bask in the spotlight in taking full credit for all four killings. Stayner boasted of how he persuaded someone else to lick the envelope in which he had mailed the letter directing the FBI to Juli's body. Yet that saliva donor never came forward to explain why or how he had submitted to such an odd request, even after the Bureau issued a press release confirming that the FBI lab had, indeed, discovered that the saliva on the envelope flap was not Cary Stayner's. In what some TourNap investigators dubbed an "all points spit bulletin," the FBI sought the mystery saliva donor, but got no one to come forward.

Cary seemed to revel in knowing the minutiae of the case, including all the details that only the killer would know, and yet there were discrepancies in his description of the state of Juli Sund's body. The Carringtons held on to the belief that many in law enforcement privately held: that Stayner's meticulous methods of cover-up in February followed by a shrewd five-month-long game of cat and mouse, would not suddenly give way in July to a reckless bloodbath that would get him arrested within forty-eight hours. In July, they conjectured, Cary probably acted alone. In February, he probably didn't.

"It's almost like someone else was directing everything in February and Stayner just did what he was told," said Francis Carrington. "With Joie Armstrong, it's like he decided to try it on his own and messed it up, royally."

After initial family denials, the truth of Cary Stayner's involvement in the murders began to sink in and one of his most outspoken supporters improbably found herself in partial agreement with the Carringtons.

"Cary may have been involved, but if he was, I don't think he did all of this by himself," said Kay Stayner. "I still believe this gang of methamphetamine users is involved in some way."

The week that Joie Armstrong's body was found, the Pelossos had returned to California to visit the Carringtons and to tape a TV news magazine about the case. When the news broke of Cary's arrest, they were bewildered at first, then disturbed.

"This surprises us a bit," said Paula Pelosso, Silvina's older sister. "It's given us a lot more questions. What happened to the people they were holding before?"

Stanislaus County Public Defender Tim Bazar, who represented Mick Larwick, had an answer—but it was not the one that either the FBI or the Pelosso family would have wanted to hear.

"They don't have, and never did have, any real evidence to connect [Larwick] or anyone else to the crime—even though they kept making the bold statement that they were confident they had the killer behind bars," said Bazar.

Fiber evidence from the pink motel blankets was commonplace, and dubious at best, he told an interviewer.

"You probably have some fibers on you right now from an acrylic blanket," he said.

The FBI probably focused on Larwick and Dykes because of public pressure and out of sheer desperation to solve the case, Bazar said. While both men were felons, their arrest and the detention of others like Billy Joe Strange and Darrell Stephens raised the specter of Richard Jewell, whom the FBI identified as its prime suspect in the still unsolved bombing of the 1996 Atlanta Olympics—only to have his name cleared completely and the government forced to pay restitution.

"I suppose the one thing they could have done is

announced publicly that they didn't have anything and still needed the public's help," he said. "But they didn't do that. They told everybody the killers were in custody."

Investigators had reason to believe they had the killers in custody, said Tuolumne County Sheriff Dick Rogers. Like Cary, one of them—Rufus Dykes—had even confessed.

"The question has been continually asked about why the case was so focused against the Modesto group of suspects," he said. "Three reasons: the leads which were received from the public obligated the task force to investigate in that direction; the actions and statements of some of those targeted individuals implicated them as suspects; and apparent physical evidence established a link to some of the suspects."

But others involved in local law enforcement were not nearly so quick to defend either the FBI or the TourNap task force that worked with them on the Sund-Pelosso case. Once the FBI moved into El Portal, as it did shortly after the kidnapping, agents should simply have put everyone who had worked at Cedar Lodge during the previous year on the lie detector, according to Merced County Sheriff's Commander Bill Blake.

"You can't use a polygraph to prove guilt, but you can use it to show innocence," reasoned the veteran homicide investigator. "I mean, you can rule the people who pass out of your equations. . . . If they would have used polygraphs on everybody that had any contact with the Cedar Lodge, everybody that was around at the time, Cary would have shown up like a spike on a polygraph and then they would have had something to poke at.

"The fact of the matter is they're not homicide investigators," Blake continued. "None of them are. . . . Their philosophy and our philosophy are different. It may be as simple as resources as opposed to theory. They send in tons of resources. They have them to throw away. They send in personnel from throughout the state, behavioral science in Washington, staff people from Quantico, forensic people . . ."

Local law enforcement, on the other hand, generally has little more than theory to work with, at least in the beginning of an investigation. A bounty of investigative resources, coupled with a process of "investigating by committee" (instead of depending upon two or three plain old plainclothes detectives), can muddle the kind of abstract reasoning that it takes to zero in on a suspect, according to Blake. Instead of keeping an open mind, the FBI married itself to a single theory that a gang of speed freaks murdered the three tourists and "once they married a theory, they stuck on it like a pit bull on an ankle," said Blake.

Although the FBI was pilloried for failing to nail Cary Stayner sooner, the Carringtons stood by the agents who had worked the case for months, running down thousands of leads.

"This was just something that none of us could have expected," Carole Carrington said sympathetically. "I can't fault them. Monday morning quarterbacking is a lot easier than when you're on the field."

In the closest that he would come to a mea culpa, a mildly contrite Sacramento Special Agent in Charge James Maddock told the media following Stayner's confession that he'd asked himself repeatedly if he could have "done anything to prevent the murder of Joie Armstrong." His answer, he said, was that the FBI did "everything that reasonably could have been done."

While even Commander Bill Blake remained sympathetic to the FBI's plight, he was critical of Maddock's stiff inability to admit a mistake.

"I think he could soften his approach and say, 'You know, maybe we need to eat a pile of shit on this one,'" said Blake.

XVII

On Thursday morning, August 5, the fourteen women and eight men of the Fresno federal grand jury took about fifty minutes to hand down Cary Stayner's first homicide indictment. He was charged with the decapitation murder of Joie Armstrong.

"This crime has horrified the community and the nation," proclaimed Paul L. Seave, the U.S. Attorney for the Eastern District of California. "There can be no real solace for the victim's family members, but there will be justice."

The following morning at 10 A.M., Cary Stayner stepped into Fresno federal court. The only notable difference between this appearance and that of the previous week in Sacramento was his innocent plea and the color of his jail jumpsuit—Fresno yellow instead of Sacramento orange.

Stayner, who turned 38 in jail in August, entered the routine "not guilty" plea on the advice of his attorney, Federal Public Defender Robert Rainwater. While Cary may have made a very public confession of guilt to a television reporter, an innocent plea in court gave Rainwater more bargaining power over the death penalty. A "not guilty" plea could be reversed, saving the cost, time, and trouble of a jury trial, if negotiations with the U.S. Attorney could lead to an agreement keeping Stayner in prison for life and out of the San Quentin death chamber.

"I didn't want to plead not guilty," Cary Stayner told a producer for the syndicated *Leeza* television show during a fifteen-minute call from his Fresno County Jail cell. "But then there is that survival instinct, and you do want to live. But I couldn't live forty years in jail."

Stayner also told the producer that he had only killed the four women—no one else—adding that he did it all by himself. He had no help in any of the slayings.

"There was only one person, to my knowledge there was only one person involved," Stayner said cryptically. "I baffled the FBI and I guess the information I gave them blew them out of the water. But I was the only one involved."

Pressed about why he had said essentially, "as far as I know," Stayner said it was only a figure of speech.

"There weren't more murderers," he said. "You know this will all come out at the trials. I think I should hold back until then."

But Cary could not hold back, despite a chiding

from his attorney to keep his mouth shut and quit calling the news media. Despite a televised lambasting he took from *Leeza* host Leeza Gibbons for seeking the spotlight when he should be cowering in contrition, Stayner also called a producer for ABC's *20/20*, who used their conversation as the centerpiece for the news magazine's fall season premiere.

"Probably all this happened," Cary said, because "I suffered from an obsessive-compulsive disorder."

Manifested as repetitive, uncontrollable pulling of the hair, Cary had suffered from the unusual mental disorder since he was three, according to Kay and Delbert. Ironically, Kay said she did not know the obsessive hair pulling had a name—trichotillomania—until she first learned about it on a different *20/20* report from an earlier TV season. Cary briefly took medication around the time of his brother's fatal motorcycle accident, but stopped because "I couldn't dream. I'm a big dreamer. I enjoy my dreams," he told *20/20*'s producer.

As with *Leeza*, Stayner refused to talk directly about the killings. He confined the conversation to his unhappy childhood and his brother Steven's kidnapping.

Cary continued to phone the media on a regular basis, much to the chagrin of his attorney. His guards literally brought a phone to him daily, mounted on a wheelchair, so that he could dial at will to the outside world from his isolation cell in the Fresno jail. While he was not especially happy about having to wear shackles every time he went to court or was moved from one part of the jail to another, on the whole he had quickly acclimated to incarceration.

In response to a letter that I sent to him the second week of August, he even called to let me know that he was considering letting me write his story. When asked how he was doing, he said he was "poking along day by day . . . starting to get used to the rhythm around here." Then he got down to business—essentially auditioning myself, Dennis McDougal, as his potential biographer.

"Basically, I've only had one actual author call me and ask that I read through their books," he told me. "I only got about halfway through it before they [the guards] confiscated it. . . . Her writing style isn't really—there's really no artistic flair to it. I was really kind of disappointed. It was a straightforward kind of writing of the facts and stuff, but there really wasn't . . ."

His voice trailed off, clearly implying that this particular writer had not met his high literary standards. Others had contacted him—mostly journalists or TV producers—but Cary had loftier aims for the telling of his tale. Based on my publishing track record, he said, I sounded "a little more substantial."

"Everybody seems to think I want a TV movie," he said. "And that's what they keep on saying in the newspaper and everything. But that's probably the last thing I want done."

Cary said he wanted no repeat of the "very hokey" presentation—both in print and on television— of his late brother Steven's story. Both Lorimar

Television, which produced NBC's *I Know My First Name Is Steven* miniseries, and the author of the book upon which it was based, "burned my family badly," he said. He was especially critical of author Mike Echols, who "leaves a bad taste in my mouth. Let's put it that way.

"If you say the name I want to spit, to tell you the truth," he said. "He kind of pissed off the whole family because he went behind all our backs. He went to Steve directly after he turned eighteen, after we'd been telling [Echols] basically 'Drop dead! Get away from us! You're weird!' And he befriended my brother who's a very trusting person with anybody, basically."

Naïveté was Steven's fatal flaw, according to Cary. He said that Mike Echols exploited that quality to the extreme. Echols's latest book, *Brother Tony's Boys,* was about a Pentecostal preacher named Tony Leyva, who portrayed himself as "SuperChristian" while buying sex and silence from the sons of his unsuspecting followers. The dust jacket described it as "the true story" of "the largest case of child prostitution in U.S. history." It was exactly the kind of sequel to *I Know My First Name Is Steven* that Cary thought Echols might write.

"I always thought, 'This guy's a little weird,'" said Cary. "Like he's so-o-o into the pedophile thing. And that's why . . . *before* he wrote the book, I didn't like the guy. He just gave me a bad feeling."

Cary was entitled to two visits per week, and could have up to three visitors, he told me. He would analyze my writing style, compare it to others and, if I made the grade, he would put my name on his visitation list, he said.

"Like I say, I won't know until I read some of your books," he told me. "But I'm sure your first book will let me know what you're all about, what your writing style is all about. And, hopefully, I will be impressed."

Apparently he wasn't. I never heard from Cary again.

Fresno resident J. L. Richards wrote a letter to the editor of the *Bee* that reflected much of the ambivalence felt up and down the San Joaquin Valley about the only remaining son of the beleaguered Stayner family. It was published on the *Bee*'s August 11 editorial page:

> Although I may sympathize with how his life was overlooked because of the tragedies in his family, you cannot convince me that he was justified in brutally murdering four innocent human beings. He gave in to the demonic seed and cultivated it.

Surprising everyone, including the *Bee*'s own staff, Cary Stayner wrote an answer to Mrs. Richards. A few days after the first letter was published, the *Bee* carried Cary's response, excerpted here:

> I have this to say "J.L. . . . You're right." Way too much attention has been placed on me. The

media's blitz to uncover the "How and Why?" someone like me could become a murderer is very unnerving. Any public sympathy should not be directed towards me but to my victims and their families.

My reason for wanting to sell the rights to my story was solely to pay as much restitution to my victims' families as possible. I realize that the money would be little consolation for the loss of their loved ones, but until the Jury, Judge and executioner fulfill their role in this matter, it's all I can offer. In conclusion I would like to say how deeply sorry I am for all the pain and sorrow I've brought upon so many people. Not only the Sunds, Pellossos [sic], Carringtons and the Armstrongs, but my fellow employees at Cedar Lodge, the community of El Portal, the people of Argentina, and all those across the nation who felt the sorrow of my victims' families.

Cary Stayner

When told of Stayner's response, Richards was a bit taken aback, but still somewhat pleased.

"Wow, I'm blown away!" she said. "I'm glad he has enough, to address his feelings toward the victims. I'll continue to pray for him. I hope he finds peace in all of this."

It was difficult to tell what Cary Stayner had found or would find, but it probably was not peace. He stopped courting the media after the *Leeza* and *20/20* broadcasts portrayed him as the very personification of evil. His parents' pleas with him to keep quiet along with Robert Rainwater's rebukes for failing to let his attorney speak for him, finally seemed to get through to Cary Stayner.

But while Cary lapsed into silence for a while, federal prosecutors began to speak up. They were out for his blood—literally. The government demanded two vials of blood, to be precise, as spelled out in court papers filed within a few weeks of his innocent plea in the Joie Armstrong case. Prosecutors also wanted twenty-five hairs from different areas of his head, twenty-five pubic hairs, and saliva swabs. In addition, they required two sets of inked prints of every ridged area on both of his hands, from his wrists to his fingertips.

In a telltale affidavit filed on August 30 by FBI Special Agent Mardee J. Robinson in support of the prosecution request, the FBI released some of the more grisly details of Stayner's confessions to law enforcement, and they painted quite a different picture of his crimes than the one he related to KNTV's Ted Rowlands. In direct contradiction to his jailhouse interview with Rowlands, for example, Cary had apparently described in lurid detail to the FBI how he sexually molested Juli and Silvina. While it was not a part of Robinson's affidavit, Modesto radio reporter Mary Jackson told me that she had seen an FBI bulletin that indicated Stayner may have shaved the pubic hair off of both girls. In a matter-of-fact recitation to the agents, he also discussed his other sexual violations of the two girls.

"It was as if he was describing drinking [a] bottle of water," said one TourNap task force member who heard the FBI's tape of Cary Stayner's cold confessional monologue. In addition to videotaping a reenactment of his murder of Joie Armstrong, Stayner told agents where to find two bloodstained knives that he said he'd used to slash the throats of Joie and Juli.

"Both knives appear to have dried blood on them and the Armstrong knife also appears to have some hairs on it," said Robinson's affidavit.

He got rid of most of the remaining evidence, but kept the camouflage pants and black athletic shorts he wore the night of the murder of Joie Armstrong. Stayner told agents the pants were in his International Scout, while he'd left the shorts back in his room at Cedar Lodge.

"Investigators have also recovered samples of the duct tape which Stayner claims to have used to bind his victims and the blanket he claims to have wrapped around Juli Sund," said Robinson's affidavit.

One mildly alarming revelation was an implication that the FBI almost let Stayner get away again at the nudist colony. After they confronted Stayner at Laguna del Sol two days after Joie's murder, agents told Stayner he was free to leave, but they added that they would seize his International Scout as part of their investigation. Hearing that, Stayner agreed to accompany them to the Sacramento field office, where he sat down with special agents Jeff Rinek and John Boles and spilled everything, first confessing to Joie's murder and then giving details about the killing of Carole, Juli, and Silvina that could not have been known outside of law enforcement, according to the affidavit.

Stayner described items taken from Room 509 at Cedar Lodge, for example, and also specifics about how he had left Juli's body near Don Pedro Lake. He also told the agents that "hair from his body was left on the bedspread in their motel room, but he returned later and changed the bed," according to the affidavit.

Despite Stayner's precautions, the FBI recovered trace evidence from Room 509, including hairs in vacuum sweepings and possible body fluid stains on a blanket. A palm print had also been left on a windowsill. The FBI also recovered two partial latent fingerprints on the notebook paper Cary said that he used to write the letter describing where to find Juli's body.

He told the FBI he learned cover-up tricks by watching true crime shows on television, prompting investigators to screen past episodes of *Cops* and *Investigative Reports*, among other shows, to learn whether Cary might have lifted any of his ideas from TV. He boasted that he got the idea of writing his anonymous letter by watching a documentary about the Unabomber, but improved on it by getting someone else to lick the stamp and seal the envelope. To throw the FBI off even further, he etched a few random names on the paper—as if it had been beneath another page in a pad—and referred to the Sund-Pelosso killers as *we*.

They had found fingerprints on Joie Armstrong's truck, which Stayner admitted touching, and there was trace evidence in her cabin, too.

"Vacuum sweepings taken from inside Armstrong's house, where Stayner claims to have bound her with duct tape, have yielded hair evidence," said Robinson's affidavit. "The FBI laboratory also has found possible body fluids on a bedsheet taken from Armstrong's residence."

The prosecution was able to match up the blood, hair and saliva that they got from Cary Stayner with various crime scene artifacts that agents swept, vacuumed, and examined under a microscope. As a result, Cary was slapped with three more charges on September 16. The new indictment accused him of "willfully and unlawfully [attempting] to cause another person and human being, Joie Ruth Armstrong, to engage in a sexual act, by threatening and placing her in fear that she would be subjected to death, serious bodily injury, and kidnapping."

A week later, Stayner again pled innocent on the additional charges, but still there were no charges at all filed against Stayner in the murders of the three sightseers—nor would there be for many weeks, if not months, according to FBI spokesman Nick Rossi. But there were good reasons for being slow and methodical.

For one thing, they wanted an airtight case that could not be discounted either on the evidence or on procedural grounds. For another, they wanted to be absolutely certain that Cary Stayner did, in fact, act alone.

By autumn, the Bureau had established a semipermanent command post in the tiny town of Mariposa dedicated exclusively to the continuing investigation of the Sund-Pelosso murders. Because the killings had taken place outside of Yosemite National Park, the FBI did not have the same jurisdiction as in Joie Armstrong's murder, and Stayner would have to be indicted by the state of California—most likely, by the Mariposa County District Attorney's office. If the case were actually tried in Mariposa, the trial would be conducted in the oldest courthouse still operating in the state: the 148-year-old two-story Mariposa County Courthouse, where legendary bad men from the Old West like Three-Finger Jack and Joaquin Murietta had once been held to answer for their crimes.

It was a foregone conclusion to most lawmen, however, that the biggest murder case in Yosemite history would be shifted to another jurisdiction, given the unprecedented publicity that Cary Stayner and his ill-fated family had generated in the region for nearly a generation. The impending fallout from the Joie Armstrong trial alone promised to sweep through the California Gold Country like a televised tidal wave.

That the Yosemite killer was apprehended at all was due in large part to the stubborn, angry courage of Joie Armstrong, according to the TourNap investigators. During Cary's initial interrogation in July, agents noticed a fresh cut on his hand and speculated then that he got the injury during his attack on the pretty but tough young naturalist. She had fought back, and even escaped from his truck despite the duct tape he'd bound her with. She was still fighting like a wolverine when he chased her down and sliced off her head with "a clean and forceful cut," authorities said. The murder scene mess that a panicky Cary Stayner left behind spelled his doom.

Not so with Carole Sund and the two teenagers who perished with her. They apparently believed that they could survive by going along, and died because of it. Based on court records, interviews, and newspaper articles, the latest and best scenario to date of what actually happened to the three women began at about 11 P.M. on the 15th of February, when Cary Stayner knocked on the door of Room 509.

Most of the Presidents' Day weekend guests had already left and the lodge was nearly empty. Every other room in the 500 building was vacant. Stayner told them he had to fix a leak and entered the room where Carole and the two teenagers were watching videos. He had a rope and a .22-caliber pistol, but they were hidden from view. Stayner disappeared into the bathroom for a moment, then came out flashing the gun. It was a robbery, he said, and ordered all three victims to lie facedown on the beds. They complied.

After binding their hands with duct tape and gag-

ging them, he ordered the two girls into the bathroom. All went smoothly, he explained later to the
FBI. They went like lambs to the slaughter. Then he
turned his attention to Carole.

He strangled the 42-year-old mother with his rope
and dumped her body in the trunk of the rented
Grand Prix parked just outside. Then he returned
to the girls. He ordered them to submit to sex, but
Silvina resisted. He looped a noose around her neck,
pulling the rope so tight, he said, that his knuckles
burned and his fingers grew numb. Stayner strangled
Silvina in the bathtub, out of Juli's sight, then forced
himself on the Eureka High cheerleader. Stayner
later boasted of having sex with her throughout the
rest of the night.

Hours later, he took Juli to an adjacent room and
began disposing of evidence. Again, without Juli
seeing, he loaded Silvina's body in the trunk next to
Carole, then tidied up the room. He got rid of hairs,
fingerprints, and any other incriminating human evidence he could think of. He wanted the room to appear to have been occupied, but abandoned by early
risers who did not want to have to drop the key off at
the front desk. He even left damp towels and a wet
tub to give the appearance that the three women had
showered in the morning before leaving.

Around 4 A.M., Stayner wrapped Juli, naked, in a
pink motel blanket and set her in the passenger seat.
Choosing back roads and lonely byways, he drove
north, through the big trees, canyons, and steep

mountains toward the rolling hills of western Tuolumne County.

About an hour later, with dawn already breaking, Stayner turned off at Lake Don Pedro and carried Juli up a worn dirt path to a small clearing overlooking the water. There, he cut her throat. With a mute dying gesture, she begged to be shot, pointing her forefinger and thumb at her temple. Cary told her that he couldn't oblige her. It seemed that there were no bullets in his gun. He finished her off with more slices to the throat, crossed the dead girl's arms over her chest, and left her wrapped in the blanket in a thicket above the parking lot.

Then he drove off into the morning with the remaining two bodies in the trunk.

XVIII

Yosemite's reputation suffered mightily as the millennium neared its end. Besides the murders, there was a rockslide off of Glacier Point in the spring which killed one hiker and injured several others. Higher gas prices and the Highway 140 road construction closures combined to cut park visitation even further. The same month that Cary Stayner was arrested, yet another blow sullied Yosemite when park officials revealed that Peeping Toms were lurking on the valley floor.

A visitor who was showering at Camp Curry discovered a palm-sized video camera hidden in an air freshener. Further investigation turned up another high-tech camera in a bathroom stall, and while a subsequent widespread search of showers and bathrooms throughout the park revealed no other cameras, rangers conceded that the two that had been found weren't part of any park security system.

With only 2.58 million tourists, hikers, and campers visiting the park from January through August of 1999, Yosemite had about 500,000 fewer guests than it did for the same period in 1998. By year's end, park officials estimated that that number could be off as much as 1 million from Yosemite's 1996 record year of 4.19 million visitors.

Boulder Beach, near the Two-Five bend in the Merced River along Highway 140, where Cary Stayner once liked to swim and sunbathe in the buff, had been rechristened Stayner Beach by some of the more sardonic local wags. Among those who lived in the area, the former favorite spot of Cedar Lodge's most notorious ex-employee remained an eerie curiosity. Most skinny-dippers now tended to avoid that beautiful bend in the river.

El Portal residents like Aaron Ludwig lapsed back into their relaxed routine with the end of the summer tourism season and what everyone hoped would be the last chapter of the Sund-Pelosso affair. Ludwig recalled a Cary Stayner who rarely spoke about his family or how his brother Steven had been missing for seven years.

"The only time was when foreigners would come in and he'd start telling them, 'Yeah, my brother's famous, he's been on television,'" Ludwig said. "But he never really told people who his brother was, that he was Steven Stayner. I found out through my mom."

Mostly, Ludwig remembered, Cary was quiet. His former friends and acquaintances at Yosemite still puzzled over how the tall, rugged, but seemingly benign handyman could have killed three women all by himself.

"The logistics of it say it had to involve more than one person," said Letty Caroleyn Barry, owner of Yosemite Redbud Lodge on Highway 120, near the sprawling mountain meadow where Joie Armstrong was hunted down and slaughtered. Investigators never suspected Cary Stayner, not when they first questioned him right after Carole Sund and the two girls vanished, and not three months later when the FBI returned to Cedar Lodge to flash pictures of the Modesto meth gang at employees. Cary Stayner, the affable handyman, was the menial lodge employee who unlocked the motel doors for the agents to collect blankets as potential evidence.

"He didn't set off any bells. He wasn't overly eager and he wasn't uncooperative," said one of the Tour-Nap investigators, trying to explain how Cary slipped through their fingers.

"The FBI says he's one of the smartest guys they've ever dealt with. And likeable too," said Delbert Stayner, who estimated that agents had visited him and Kay a dozen times since they arrested their son. "They said he's the most likeable guy. You spend ten minutes with him and you just like the guy. You can't help it. He's not a smart aleck. Never been a smart aleck all his life. Just been a good guy. He's never cursed. He's never used the Lord's name in vain. And I don't know why the Lord would put this on somebody if he's been so good to Him. I don't know."

Delbert said he wept for three straight days after the arrest. He is now on medication just to keep from breaking into tears.

"I guess I'm just a big old bawl baby. I don't know. Recently I'm just so tore up about this I can't hardly stand it," he said.

Kay, too, is taking medication. His wife "looks like she's probably aged ten years in the last couple of months," Delbert said.

The couple continued to be able to count upon the support of friends and family, even if that support was not necessarily extended to their son.

"We've known Cary since he was a little boy," said Sandy Cox. "And we have a hard time believing this. It just doesn't match up."

Jesslyn Stayner recalled how Cary and some of her other male cousins used to try to shock her by talking about skinning cats. She wondered now just how much of the talk was made up for shock value and how much of it might actually have been true.

"I'm going to have a hard time ever trusting anyone again," she said.

Her mother was equally incredulous. For the first time since her ex-husband's still unsolved 1990 murder, she was convinced Jerry Stayner died at the hands of his nephew—even though he was never charged and never even under suspicion.

"Now that we look back at it all, that was Cary's story," said Lori Stayner. "The police never gave us any information, basically, so everything we were relying on was what Cary was telling us."

"The joke's on us, because all this time, we didn't know," said Jesslyn.

"He should have gotten the Academy Award," echoed her mother.

On September 25, Merced High School held its twenty-year class reunion at a country club a few miles west of Merced. Once again, Cary Stayner was a no-show, but this time he was all that his former classmates could talk about.

"The talk was mostly disbelief," said reunion organizer Shawn Cline. "No one could believe he could do something like that."

Cline's assessment of the evening's dialogue echoed a by now familiar litany of most memories of Cary Stayner:

- There was nothing strange about him.
- He had a few friends he hung around with or else he was alone.
- He didn't run around with guys that were troublemakers.
- He never got in fights.
- He was quiet.

"He never looked for trouble, never caused trouble and never was in trouble," said Cline, summing up the feelings Cary's classmates had about the man who had become the most infamous graduate of the class of 1979.

"I don't think he did these killings to become more famous than his brother, but now that the opportunity arises, I think he's gonna take advantage of every bit of it," said Commander Bill Blake of the Merced County Sheriff's Department.

Like Sirhan Sirhan, Lee Harvey Oswald, or John Wilkes Booth, Cary Stayner would have gone to his grave a nobody if he hadn't murdered someone.

"The Sund-Pelosso case won't be something that will go in a history book, but it certainly will put him in the spotlight for a while," said Blake.

"My feeling is he's not worth talking about much," said Carole Carrington. "I really don't want to hear about this guy anymore. I think he's out for notoriety, and I don't want to give it to him."

Her granddaughter Juli's sixteenth birthday was supposed to have started with a party, followed by a trip to the Department of Motor Vehicles to witness her driving test. Carole and Francis Carrington went to the cemetery instead, marking her grave with flowers and balloons.

"Such a waste," said her grandfather, his voice cracking.

Juli's aunt, Vickie Caton, wrote a bittersweet letter to her niece on the occasion of her sixteenth birthday and asked the *Bee* to publish it. She ended the posthumous birthday greeting with:

"I pray that Juli is in a safer place now and that she's with her mother forever. Happy birthday, dear Juli, you're in our hearts forever."

In Argentina, Raquel Pelosso often visited her

own daughter's grave. Silvina, too, was to have celebrated a birthday in September. She would have been seventeen.

There was one more tragic anniversary to be observed during the first days of autumn, 1999. On the sixteenth of September, ten years earlier, Steven Stayner died. Kay Stayner stated at the time of his fatal motorcycle accident that she believed Steven had been in such pain for so long that, subconsciously, he brought on his own death. In one of the rare moments that she agreed with her former mother-in-law, Steven's widow Jody also looked back on her late husband's passing as a sad, and perhaps logical, result of his reckless, tortured life.

"It was national news when he returned home, it was national news when we were married, and it was national news when he passed away," said Jody Stayner. "And when he passed away, the public did so much for me and my kids. I got hundreds of thousands of letters . . . my father set up trust funds [with contributions contained in many of the letters] and both kids are now set when they're ready to go to college."

She continued, "In my eyes, I felt the public did so much for me; it would be basically criminal for me to make any more money on Steven Stayner from interviews with the media. That's why I wanted to give it back." Joining the Carringtons in their crusade for a national reward fund that would provide cash incentives to help solve kidnappings, sex crimes, and murders, Jody began by selling an exclusive interview to the syndicated newsmagazine *Inside Edition* in September and donating the money to the Carole Sund/Carrington Memorial Reward Fund.

With minimal remorse and utter consternation, Jody viewed both her former in-laws and especially her ex–brother-in-law with a mix of pity and contempt. In Jody's eyes, Cary represented the result of generations of questionable behavior on both the Stayner and Augustine sides of her late husband's family. While presenting a content and well-adjusted facade to the world, Delbert and Kay Stayner were dysfunctional parents who reigned over an equally dysfunctional family, according to Jody. With her daughter Ashley and Steven's own namesake, Steven Stayner Jr., Jody hoped to break what she viewed as a sick familial cycle.

Kenneth Parnell, the child predator who seemed to have launched the Stayners' many agonizing ordeals one December day in 1972, served only five years of an eight-year sentence for kidnapping. Then, in the mid '80s, he began drifting from job to job, attempting to change his identity as often as he changed his address. At one point, he was Gene Kent, working as a security guard at an Oakland rehab center for troubled teens. At another, he was just a genteel old man who sat on his front porch in Berkeley, eyeing the boys in the neighborhood who passed by his house.

Except for Mike Echols, Parnell did not speak to journalists.

Merced Police Chief Tony Dossetti, who began

his own law enforcement career as one of the detectives who worked from time to time during the 1970s on the Steven Stayner missing person case, felt a double-edged pang about the Stayner family. A few days after Cary's arrest, Delbert appeared in his second-floor office, overlooking the Merced Civic Center, and sat across from Dossetti in tears. Delbert Stayner called upon his long positive relationship with the Merced Police to make some sense of the incredible charges leveled against Cary and to help him and Kay handle the media onslaught.

"I told him, 'Del, if he did what they said that he did, Cary is an animal,'" Dossetti said bluntly.

Delbert and Kay handled this latest catastrophe in much the same way they handled the trauma of Steven's teen years, when he had to come to grips with the rape of his childhood: by not talking about it.

"When we go to visit Cary, we don't ask him anything. We don't ask him why he did this or that. We're there just the same and we love him and we tell him that. We don't ask him any questions," said Delbert. "I just hope and pray all the time that he didn't actually do it and that he's hiding somebody, [taking the fall] for somebody else."

It wasn't until after the arrest that Delbert learned that his son had visited a psychiatrist a few years ago. On September 28, 1998, the Merced County Mental Health Department sued Stayner in Merced Municipal Court's small claims division for payment, alleging that he owed them $230 for services rendered. During a jail visit, Cary told his father that he didn't go back to see the psychiatrist because the doctor wanted him to go into group therapy.

"Cary is so shy, he didn't want to talk about his problems in front of a group of strangers," his father said. "I said, 'I wish you had gone back.' He said, 'I wish I had, too, Poppa.'"

Calling his son "honey" as if he were once again the small boy who raced through the Stayners' Snelling almond orchard, Delbert reflected on how little he really did know about his son.

"We didn't know anything about him having problems or hearing voices," he said. "He's had bad dreams for quite a while, but he's never told us nothing. He never told anybody anything. He was awful quiet.

"I don't know if he didn't do it or did do it, but if he did do it, he did it because something just snapped."

Delbert and Kay have visited their son each Tuesday evening since he was jailed. He appears before them in shackles, behind a pane of glass, and they chitchat about friends, local news in Merced, his sisters and nieces and nephews, but never the case. Delbert is afraid that "if we hounded him about it like everybody else, I don't think he would want to see us."

Cary sobbed the first couple of times his parents visited. Then jail doctors gave him calming medication like the drugs that Kay and Delbert got prescribed for them, and there isn't as much crying as there had been in the beginning.

Because Cary reads the *Fresno Bee* every day, he's

better informed than both of his parents, said Delbert. He gets loads of mail, but Del took the liberty of ordering a book for Cary from the Mormon Church in hopes that it might help him through his crisis. It's called *Conquering Your Own Goliath*.

Cary fears the wrath of the Carringtons.

"The deal is, they want him dead, which I think— if I was in their shoes—I'd feel the same way," said Delbert.

But the Carringtons do not necessarily want Cary Stayner executed. That, said Carole Carrington, is a matter for the courts to decide. What she and her husband want is answers. As of November, they had none. Cary wasn't talking about his crimes, not even to his own parents.

"I know if he did it, he's ill," said Delbert. "He needs help. And I would never want him to get out of jail if he did do anything like that. I would like to just keep him from getting the death penalty."

"I had a conversation with Delbert a few days after the revelation about Cary and, boy, I felt sorry for the guy," said Commander Bill Blake. "His wife was going through huge agony. I mean, you can only imagine."

Blake remembered seeing a bumper sticker on a car a day or two after he spoke with the Stayners, and it stayed with him like an all-too-true message in a Chinese fortune cookie. It said: I COULDN'T GO TO WORK TODAY. THE VOICES TOLD ME TO STAY HOME AND CLEAN MY GUNS.

"Probably the same voices that were talking to Cary," he said wryly.

Upon Steven Stayner's return to Merced, then–District Attorney Frank Daugherty had studied the horrifying upbringing of Kenneth Parnell to try to get some idea as to how such a creature could come to inflict itself on humanity. Bill Blake never forgot Daugherty's conclusion.

"He said, 'For every monster, there has to be a monster maker,'" Blake recalled. "So when you look back at the Steven thing and how it begot celebrity, you've got to wonder if there was a need for this guy [Cary] to become a celebrity. I think that's pretty thin thinking, although he did compare himself to Steven. But nobody with any kind of normality would ever use multiple violent homicides just for the press!

"I mean, he's got to have the soul and the heart of a murderer, and you got to wonder: How do you *get* something like that? And I've got to believe—even though every contact I've had with them has been real nice, you know, that Kay and Delbert are the monster makers here."

Cary Stayner sometimes sketches in jail. His keepers have him do pictures for them, and then they take them away to study them for clues. Getting inside Cary's head is very nearly as impossible as getting inside of his heart. Both locations have been off-limits to mere mortals for many years, and Cary has learned innumerable tricks to keep anyone and anything from circumventing his defenses.

He felt free in the wild. He was off backpacking with Big Foot—perhaps real, perhaps imagined, but always there, in the wide-open backwoods, away from his cramped childhood inside 1655 Bette Street or his claustrophobic anonymity in the shadow of his little brother Steven, once he had returned to Merced.

Cary Stayner is a model prisoner. He's . . . quiet. He knows he will probably never see Yosemite again, but that's all right with him.

"That's just the way it goes," he said. "I have good memories. I can just lay back, close my eyes, and I can be there again."

Afterword

On October 20, 1999, Mariposa County District Attorney Christine Johnson filed a four-page complaint in Mariposa's 145-year-old county courthouse. The complaint charged Cary Anthony Stayner with counts of multiple murder, burglary, robbery, forcible oral copulation, and attempted rape in connection with the deaths of Carole Sund, Juli Sund, and Silvina Pelosso. While it was a Mariposa County case, it was to be prosecuted by the state Attorney General—just one measure of how deep and broad the public's call for justice ran in the Yosemite murders. The federal case, involving the murder of Joie Armstrong on the grounds of Yosemite National Park, takes precedence over the Mariposa County indictment and will be tried first, according to TourNap sources.

Less than 48 hours after Stayner was charged in the Sund-Pelosso murders, the Sunds joined the

Pelossos in announcing the filing of a wrongful death suit, aimed at Cary Stayner and his former employer, Cedar Lodge. While the families of the slain women asked for unspecified damages, Delbert Stayner maintained that they would get nothing from his son. Cary had no other asset than his International Scout, which remained in the hands of the prosecution, a part of the mountain of evidence that had been built up against Cary Stayner.

"We're going to use (the power of plaintiff's) discovery to get into the records," Jens explained to me during a visit I paid him in early November.

A placid though deeply wounded stalk of a man who has never allowed the public to see his grief mix with his anger, one true thing can be said of Jens Sund: He has the resolve of a sole surviving grizzly. He *will* have justice. He *will* have a full and detailed explanation. And, while he might be loath to call it that, he *will* have revenge for the wanton slaughter of his wife and daughter.

During the taping of the *20/20* hour that aired in September, Jens kept his composure on camera, delivering the kind of bland performance that he consistently gives on TV. When he was sure that ABC correspondent Elizabeth Vargas's camera crew was temporarily out of videotape, he told her he would personally eviscerate Cary Stayner if he could.

"I told her that I had guns and that I had knives and that I'd like to do to him what he did to my wife and daughter," Jens told me. But when Vargas asked him to repeat what he had told her on camera, Sund just smiled stoically and shook his head. No, he said, that was not his way. His rawest emotions were not for voyeuristic consumption.

Jens still speaks of his wife in the present tense, as if he expects her to storm through his office door at any moment. Carole was the more vocal, driving half of their marriage—a tough lady who could occasionally rub Jens the wrong way. But he has learned in the most unspeakable way how difficult life can be without her, now that he is the sole parent of their three surviving children, and even more jagged for him to swallow are the harsh reminders of Juli's absence. A round snapshot of their daughter in cheerleading regalia is mounted on the lamp over Sund's desk—a constant reminder of a life cut tragically short by egocentric bloodlust. He has two growing boys and another daughter, Gina, who help to fill his days, but a hollow will always remain in his heart for Juli and her mother.

While the man who suffered the worst losses from Cary Stayner's rampage has some empathy, if not sympathy, for the plight of the TourNap task force in sifting through the thousands of false leads and dead ends, he is not as forgiving as his in-laws, Francis and Carole Carrington. Throughout the investigation, the FBI dealt with the family in much the same way that it dealt with the media: with condescension and a refusal to share any of its findings, according to Jens. At one point, he said, Special Agent in Charge James Maddock seemed more concerned about scaring off park visitors during Yosemite's summer tourist season than he was with catching the killer of Juli, Carole, and Silvina. Jen's anger may be more directed now than it was during the early days of the investigation, but it has not dissipated one iota.

With no small irony, Jens now applauds the news media more than any other institution.

"It wasn't until the TV and newspapers picked up on it that anyone did anything," said Sund. "For the first few days, it was just me and my family handing out the flyers to people and asking questions at the lodge and in Yosemite."

And even the media didn't seem to fully grasp the import of the story until Sund and the Carringtons offered a $250,000 reward. Only then did the FBI swoop in to take charge and turn the story into an international *cause célèbre*. Sadly and with a small note of contempt, Jens Sund bitterly points out the obvious: Money talks.

That is why he and the Carringtons have put so much energy into the reward fund created in Carole's name. His mother-in-law, who has been a social activist since her eldest child was diagnosed with irreparable brain damage over 40 years ago, has "been in training all her life" to run such a foundation, said Jens. The cause of poor or indigent parents who have lost children and have no means of offering rewards for their return is tailor-made for the Carringtons, he said. And, while he remains supportive of his in-laws, Jens himself is narrowing his focus to the mystery that he believes the FBI did not, could not, or would not solve: Who killed his wife and daughter—and, of equal importance, why?

In the weeks leading up to his filing the lawsuit, Jens and his lawyer, Zachary Zwerdling, heard from a woman who spent the night at Cedar Lodge at around the same time that Carole, Juli, and Silvina were there. She told them that she and her husband had returned to their room late one evening, and she sprawled on the bed while her husband used the bathroom. At that moment, there was a scratching at the front door, the knob turned, and two men stepped into the room. The woman sat up and stared at them for a split second before her husband emerged from the bathroom.

"That's when one of them said, 'Oops! Wrong room,' and they left, closing the door behind them," said Jens.

The couple reported the incident to the front desk the following morning but gave it little thought until nearly six months later, when Cary Stayner's mug shot appeared in the newspaper. Cary was one of the two men who had a key to their room and stepped in briefly that winter evening at Cedar Lodge, startling the vacationers and prompting them to complain to the management.

Among other documents in the Cedar Lodge records, Sund and Zwerdling hope to find proof of such intrusive incidents as that reported by the vacationing couple. Client and attorney are equally eager to find out just how many Cedar Lodge employees have had criminal records like Billy Joe Strange's and Darrell Stephens's, and how many have mental health and/or drug histories comparable to Cary Stayner's.

Bottom line: Neither Sund nor Zwerdling believe Cary Stayner acted alone when he killed Carole, Juli, and Silvina. Regardless of the hollow pronouncements of the FBI's James Maddock and Nick Rossi, both Jens and his lawyer believe another killer or killers remain at large. And they are not alone.

"I think there may be a cult out there, around El Portal," said Cary's estranged sister-in-law, Jody. "I certainly don't think he [Cary] did it all by himself."

"There is a lot of talk in this community about someone here being involved in the murders," echoed Miles Menetrey, manager of the Indian Flat RV Park next door to the Cedar Lodge. Some of the names that figured into the early part of the investigation have been resurfacing in the form of rumors around El Portal, he said. The FBI completely missed Cary, after all. Who's to say that the elite federal investigators didn't miss a killer or two on their second sweep through the Yosemite Valley?

"It's hard because if you say something and you're wrong, you can completely ruin someone," said Menetrey, citing the FBI's overkill on violating just about anyone who was on parole during the first few weeks of the investigation—whether they truly deserved to be sent back to jail or not.

"But if you *don't* say something . . . ," Menetrey continued, "well, who knows what to do? I sure don't."

* * *

Following her appearance on the *Leeza* show, Leslie Armstrong withdrew from public view.

One of Joie's favorite quotations was from the 19th-century English essayist Thomas Carlisle:

"The tragedy of life is not what we suffer, but what we miss."

Joie actively strove not to miss a single moment.

Under the headline THE ONLY CONSTANT IN THE UNIVERSE IS CHANGE, the Yosemite National Institutes published her final article in the autumn issue of the Institutes' newsletter, *Panorama*. In it, she soberly discussed the natural forces at play in bringing about the deadly rock slides that have plagued Glacier Point for several years, killing a hiker in June. Death and danger are part of the price human beings must sometimes pay in order to dwell in a place like Yosemite, she suggested.

"Part of the wonder of Yosemite Valley . . . is that natural processes are allowed to prevail at the occasional expense of human concerns. This . . . is especially valuable as our lives are increasingly isolated from the 'real world' by our culture of built and virtual environments. . . . What a fortunate thing it is to be attentive observers of nature's lavishness."

—Dennis McDougal
November 1999

A contribution from author's royalties will be made to the Carole Sund/Carrington Memorial Reward Fund. For more information or to contribute, write:

> Carole Sund/Carrington
> Memorial Reward Fund
> 1508 Coffee Road, Suite H
> Modesto, CA 95350

A memorial fund in Joie Armstrong's name has also been established for youth education programs. Contributions can be sent to:

> Joie Armstrong Memorial Fund
> c/o Yosemite National Institutes
> GGNRA, Building 1055
> Sausalito, CA 94965

Acknowledgments

Corey Mitchell and Carolyn Tafoya, researchers nonpareil, get top billing. Under pressure and in record time, they performed like well-oiled information machines, running down everything from obscure studies on the psychotropic effect of prolonged methamphetamine use to author Mike Echols's disgusting Internet website featuring Day-Glo hype for his books and photos of little boys.

My longtime friends David Levinson, Dorothy Korber, and Brian Zucchini read and edited the manuscript and helped me limp to the finish line. Thanks, too, to Little Miss Goldner, the Good Witch of Gramercy Park, and Mrs. "Catfish" Broeske, the Okay Witch of Santa Ana. Ah, heck. She's a good witch too.

Leslie Lazar and Mercedes del Gaudio transcribed tapes until their fingers were numb. Elizabeth Zack picked up the Yosemite project after my first editor, Susan Randol, left Ballantine, and she quickly grasped the true worth of the Cary Stayner parable, giving me the encouragement, inspiration, and resources to turn the concept into a fully fleshed-out story.

I shamelessly confess here in print, for the first but not the last time, that I am in love with Alice Martell, my own personal agent provocateur. Sorry, Michael.

As always, my strength lies in family: my loving, loyal wife Sharon; the five wonderful children we share between us; my supportive parents, brothers, and sister, and all the children they begat; and last but not least, the next generation, which includes Mega Luna Tuna, Howlie boy, two dudes from Reno, and Miss Tweety of Salt Lake City.

And a word about the working press.

In recent years, the mass media have been targeted for unprecedented criticism—much of it warranted and long overdue. But the criticism neglects a basic fact of American life: that along with the bad reporting, intended to titillate, exploit, and sell more soap, there is an ennormous amount of very good and essential journalism being practiced by a better educated and better-informed generation of journalists than we have ever had serving our information needs before. It is no accident that journalists are often miles ahead of law enforcement in getting to the nitty-gritty of a case like the Sund-Pelosso murders. While a good many follow the pack, especially if they are sound-bite-oriented, stand-up television news performers intent on getting their dour, well-pancaked faces on the six o'clock news, there are still practitioners of the *craft* of reporting the news, both in print and broadcast, who care more about informing the public of the truth than taking the credit for doing so. I could not have written this book without their help.

While all the unsung First Amendment heroes are too numerous to mention here, a few of the shining lights include: Ted Rowlands, the young KNTV reporter who was resourceful, patient, and audacious enough to get the first jailhouse interview with Cary Stayner; Christine Hanley, the Associated Press reporter who easily wins the award as the most thorough, incisive, and tenacious journalist on the Sund-Pelosso story; Jill Ballinger, managing editor, chief photographer, chief staff writer, receptionist, dust buster, and occasional advertising salesperson for the *Mariposa Gazette*, California's oldest continuously published weekly newspaper; Amy Nilson of the *Sonora Union Democrat*; Mike De La Cruz, veteran cop reporter for the *Merced Sun Star*; Kimi Yoshino and Matt Kreamer of the *Fresno Bee*, as well as their boss, *Bee* Editor Charley Waters, who gave me my initiation into the Sund-Pelosso morass; and Modesto radio reporter Mary Jackson, who graciously shared insights and information gleaned from months of reporting the Yosemite murders saga.

And, of course, last but never least, I must thank Irv Letofsky, the best editor a boy ever had.

The shocking true story of a mother who murdered her two daughters with the help of her own sons. . . .

MOTHER'S DAY

by Dennis McDougal

For nearly nine years, Theresa Cross got away with murder—until her youngest daughter, Terry Knorr Groves, finally found a cop who believed the incredible story of Terry's two murdered sisters. That story is all here, the shocking life of a woman whose violence, jealousy, rage, and domination led to brutally heinous crimes of ruthless ferocity.

Published by Ballantine Books.
Available in bookstores everywhere.

of monster who could kidnap, rape, torture, murder, and burn three innocent women.

"That's not in Mike," said his cousin Patty Black. "That's not Mike. He's been in and out of jail for years. But like I said, those are things from his family. He wouldn't [cause harm] to a stranger and hurt anybody. He's more of a helpful person."

"He was good people," said Trudy Kay Northern, who had been acquainted with Larwick for several years. "I've seen him burn a lot of bridges, but that was because of the drugs."

The press was not appeased by the Thursday morning trickle of Dykes/Larwick news that occasionally dribbled from a Grand Jury witness. With the Carringtons guesting on a host of shows ranging from *Oprah* to *Good Morning America*, and *People* carrying the tragic disappearance of the three women as a cover story, the mystery had become a national obsession, and the appetite for tidbits about the FBI's progress became insatiable.

Three theories kept leaking from local law enforcement and finding their way into speculative stories that appeared in newspapers throughout the spring, from San Francisco to Los Angeles. All of them featured the Dykes/Larwick group in a central role, but each had them vanishing from a different place:

#1 – the three women had been kidnapped or carjacked in Modesto, where they had been scheduled to catch their plane to San Francisco;

#2 – they took a v
    Tuolumne Cour
    play and their bo
#3 – they were kidn
    El Portal, where t
    belongings in the
    come back or were

In pursuit of this last
the FBI returned yet a
starting point for all the
veloped to date: Cedar l
rived in February, agents h
skepticism about the regu
restaurant and drank at tl
regular employees like Bill
Stephens, who worked in th
tied hard and heavy elsewhe
tors began to understand wh
when they referred tongue-ii
as "Speeder Lodge."

"I'm sure the guy who own
any idea what some are doin
Portal resident told the *Modes*
wouldn't be working there any

The third week of May,
town, recanvassing, retracing ar
May 19, agents interviewed han
yet again, this time at his girlfrie
calmly laid out exactly where he
women disappeared. No one no

fifteen poun
sweating, or
underlie his

"He was
source later

Investiga
reinterview
and so on,

A week
Stayner to
opened ev
maintenan
searched f
ones foun
see if tho
Rufus Dy
Corvette

Stanis
Larry D
peared
TourNa
Larwicl
nesses
booked
napping
in the S

Dur
womer
$200 a
held h

home. Meanwhile, Utley and the rest of his crew went on a spending spree. Using the kidnapped man's ATM card, they tapped into his bank account, then used the money to buy drugs, clothing, food, and gasoline, and to gamble at a casino in the Gold Rush town of Jackson, according to arresting officers.

The victim, who had never been tied up by his captors during his ordeal, became friendly enough with the Utley gang that they offered him some of their methamphetamine. He took it voluntarily, according to police. When the kidnap victim asked them if he could go outside for some fresh air on Monday morning, the 15th of February, he had earned enough of their trust to be allowed to step outside, breathe deeply, and make his escape.

The kidnapping had eerie overtones to well-rehearsed scenarios about what might have happened to Carole Sund and the two teenagers who were kidnapped with her. But there were no apparent connections between the Utley crime and the awful fate of the three Yosemite tourists who disappeared that same Valentine's Day weekend. After several weeks in jail, Utley's bail was reduced to $10,000 and he was released. All that the FBI's Nick Rossi would say about the Utley incident was that "during the course of our investigation we may come upon evidence of other crimes. We're not going to ignore that information."

Indeed, one of the unforeseen and somewhat ironic benefits of the Sund-Pelosso investigation was a noticeable drop in crime throughout the Sierra foothills during the spring of 1999. From vehicle break-ins and burglaries to more violent felonies ranging from assault to rape, the FBI roundup of petty criminals, crank peddlers, and parole violators seemed to have made towns up and down Highway 49 safer and more secure overall.

Still, crank had become the drug of choice for ex-cons and members of their poverty-level families who inhabited many of the run-down trailer parks and ramshackle housing projects of communities large and tiny, from Bakersfield to Sacramento. An insidious drug whose use had been on the rise in the San Joaquin Valley since the early 1990s, methamphetamine delivered an adrenaline rush and a false sense of invincibility comparable to crack cocaine, but at a fraction of the cost. Meth could keep its users awake and alert for several days at a time before they crashed and slept, again for several days at a time.

"Crank is the poor man's cocaine," said former Tuolumne County Sheriff's Deputy Norm Morrison. "All a crankster cares about is crank and his own pleasure."

The state of California's spurt in opening new prisons up and down the Central Valley during the 1990s only aggravated the problem. When felons were paroled from Tehachapi or Corcoran, Mule Creek or the inappropriately named Pleasant Valley State Prison, they tended to drift to the nearest community to rebuild their lives . . . and all too fre-